School of American Research Advanced Seminar Series

DOUGLAS W. SCHWARTZ, GENERAL EDITOR

Turko-Persia in Historical Perspective

SCHOOL OF AMERICAN RESEARCH
ADVANCED SEMINAR STUDIES

Published by Cambridge University Press

TURKO-PERSIA IN
HISTORICAL PERSPECTIVE

EDITED
BY
ROBERT L. CANFIELD

Department of Anthropology
Washington University in St. Louis

A SCHOOL OF AMERICAN RESEARCH BOOK

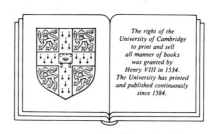

The right of the
University of Cambridge
to print and sell
all manner of books
was granted by
Henry VIII in 1534.
The University has printed
and published continuously
since 1584.

CAMBRIDGE UNIVERSITY PRESS

Cambridge
New York   Port Chester
Melbourne   Sydney

Published by the Press Syndicate of the University of Cambridge
The Pitt Building, Trumpington Street, Cambridge CB2 1RP
40 West 20th Street, New York, NY 10011, USA
10 Stamford Road, Oakleigh, Melbourne 3166, Australia

First published 1991

Printed in Great Britain at the University Press, Cambridge

British Library Cataloguing in publication data
Turko–Persia in historical perspective. – (School of
   American Research advanced seminar series) – (A School of
   American Research book).
   1. Central Asian civilization, history
   I. Canfield, Robert L.   II. Series   III. Series
   958

Library of Congress cataloguing in publication data
Turko–Persia in historical perspective / edited by Robert L. Canfield.
      p.   cm. – (School of American Research advanced seminar
   series)
      "The initial drafts of the chapters . . . were written as
   contributions to an advanced seminar . . . held at the School of
   American Research in Santa Fe, New Mexico, the week of April 15 to
   19, 1985"–Pref.
      "A School of American Research book."
      Includes bibliographical references.
      ISBN 0 521 39094 X
      1. Middle East–Civilization–Congresses.   2. Asia, Central–
   Civilization–Congresses.   I. Canfield, Robert L. (Robert Leroy)
   II. School of American Research (Sante Fe, N. M.)   III. Series.
   DS57.T83 1990
   958–dc20   89 -77394 CIP .

ISBN 0 521 39094 X

Contents

Contents

Maps

Contributors

YURI BREGEL
Professor
Department of Uralic and Altaic Studies
Indiana University
Bloomington, Indiana

ROBERT L. CANFIELD
Professor
Department of Anthropology
Washington University
St. Louis, Missouri

RICHARD N. FRYE
Aga Khan Professor of Iranian Studies
Department of Near Eastern
 Languages and Civilizations
Harvard University
Cambridge, Massachusetts

MILAN HAUNER
Director of East European Studies
Woodrow Wilson Center
Washington, DC

MICHEL M. MAZZAOUI
Associate Professor
Department of History
University of Utah
Salt Lake City, Utah

FRANCIS ROBINSON
Reader in History
Royal Holloway and Bedford New College
University of London
London, England

M. NAZIF SHAHRANI
Professor of Anthropology and Central Asian Studies
Indiana University
Bloomington, Indiana

Preface

The initial drafts of the chapters in this book were written as contributions to an Advanced Seminar on "Central Asia as a Culture Area" held at the School of American Research in Santa Fe, New Mexico, the week of April 15 to 19, 1985. The objective of the seminar was to produce a collection of essays that would enhance an understanding of the similar cultural patterns that for many generations have persisted in a region that I was then calling "Greater Central Asia." In the invitation for papers I identified Greater Central Asia as "the region from Turkey to Sinkiang (or Chinese Turkistan) and, on a more southerly latitude, from the Euphrates to North India," and I proposed that this region be examined as a discrete cultural region, on a par with the more commonly recognized neighboring cultural areas, the Middle East, Russian/Soviet Asia, and the Far East. I noted in the invitation for papers that, although the influence of Persianate Islam on this wide area has been widely recognized by historians, the region where it has profoundly affected social institutions in the Islamic period has not been generally considered a distinct culture area.

The seminar consisted of a group of scholars whose complementary skills would enable the long history of such a broad region to be surveyed. Karl Lamberg-Karlovsky came as an authority on the ecology, and the prehistoric as well as the early historic adaptations of human populations in this area. Richard Frye brought a broad historical grasp of the pre-Islamic and early Islamic period. Three historians considered the developments in the medieval and early modern period: Yuri Bregel, Turkic influences in inland Muslim Asia; Michel Mazzaoui, cultural developments in Iran and Central Asia; and Francis Robinson, the Islamicate culture of South Asia. Three anthropologists treated the traditional culture of key sectors of the region in the contemporary period: Lois Beck, Iran; Nazif Shahrani, Afghanistan and Muslim Central Asia; and Stephen Pastner, Muslim South Asia. Milan Hauner, a modern historian, represented the contemporary geopolitical issues in Greater Central Asia. I examined the historical continuities that linked societies in the region over a long period. Unfortunately, not all the papers could be included in this volume; those by Lamberg-Karlovsky, Beck, and Pastner will appear elsewhere.

The group consisted of five historians (Frye, Bregel, Mazzaoui, Robinson, and Hauner) and five anthropologists (Lamberg-Karlovsky, Beck, Shahrani, Pastner, and Canfield). Anthropologists and historians have for some time discussed the complementarity of their interests, but the seminar was for me a first experience in working with scholars from the two disciplines on a subject of mutual interest. In the discussions the participants were forced to deal with important differences in their research questions, approaches, and explanations, and the interchange affected the final versions of all the papers.

The seminar had a surprising impact on my own conceptual frame of reference. The papers and discussions enriched my understanding of the region, and helped me to rethink some of my presuppositions. I began to question some of the ways I had formulated the issues, and eventually a growing disquiet led me to adopt a different terminology.

To be specific, two conceptual problems bothered me, and both were implicit in the title I had chosen for the seminar. One was the term "Greater Central Asia." I had used this phrase because the cultural system to be examined in the seminar took form within the region that is often loosely called "Central Asia" and was from there carried to other territories, a process that of course not only expanded the influence of the original culture but also produced diverse variations within it. The term for the region, I thought, had to be broader than Central Asia but at the same time had to imply a close association with it, hence the juxtaposition of the word "Greater." I had hoped, by such usage, to ensure that Muslim South Asia could be included in the area as well as Persia and Turkey, for these areas were all, especially in the medieval period, influenced by this culture. There was, however, a well-known problem with the term "Central Asia," for scholars have never agreed on its exact parameters. Everyone in the seminar was aware of this problem, for the specific limits of the region have troubled scholars for years, and indeed the problem had only recently been a major issue at another conference. Mercifully, the ambiguities of the term were not further belabored in the seminar, but I believe the general ambiguity about what was meant by "Greater Central Asia" hampered our discussion of its cultural parameters.

The second disquieting conceptual difficulty of the seminar, also entailed in its title, was the term "culture area." I now realize that the underlying problem in the definition of "Central Asia" has been an imprecision in the notion of "culture area." One problem with "culture area," as I had used the term, was that it presumed an association between broad cultural systems and their environment. Originally introduced as a means of classifying the artifacts of different societies in museum displays, the concept owed major assumptions to zoogeography. As it came to be used, the term referred to territories where characteristic culture patterns could be related to certain ecologic conditions. However, the attempt to ground culture area definitions in geographic contexts distracts from the crucial definitional features; it is not the geography that defines but the cultural complex. My use of a geographic term for the culture that developed in Central Asia had masked the definitional importance of the cultural configuration itself.

Another problem with my use of the term was that it implied a static patterning of cultural traits. Actually, the geographic scope of the entity I was calling a "culture area" has changed over time; for the clusters of structured meaningful forms that mark "culture areas" not only change within themselves but also vary in their geographic scope in respect of the rise and fall of empires. The more appropriate term, I realized, was "ecumene," a term used often by historians but rarely by anthropologists. "Ecumene" suggests a historically perpetuated complex of meaningful forms – a "world" (Greek: *oekumené*) of shared understandings – in which the basic elements of public interaction are more or less well known.

My original terminology in the seminar does not, therefore, appear in this volume. I have avoided the term "culture area" and have instead spoken of an "ecumene." And I have replaced the term "Greater Central Asia" with the more precise "Turko-Persian ecumene," or, more compactly, "Turko-Persia." In the Introduction I have accordingly treated the object of study as a historically developing cultural complex. Probably the seminar would have been more effective had I described the problem and the issues in these terms; however, without the seminar I might never have seen the ambiguities in my own usage of the crucial terminology.

In working on this book I have incurred a number of debts which I here gratefully acknowledge, particularly the School of American Research for sponsoring the seminar, and especially Doug Schwartz, its president, Jonathan Haas, its director of programs and research, and Jane Kepp, its director of publications. I am, of course, much indebted to the participants in the seminar for their counsel and patience from the beginning. Also, I am obliged to the following people for particularly important services: Elisabeth Case, for the expert professional and editorial advice and assistance without which this volume might never have been published; Lois Beck, for advice in planning the seminar and many useful comments and criticisms on the project, especially during the period of its inception; Christopher Dingwell, for producing the maps; and Jennifer Day, Kathleen Laird, and Aimee Fishkind-Campbell for assistance in producing the text, each with extraordinary grace and patience.

1

Introduction: the Turko-Persian tradition

ROBERT L. CANFIELD

This book is about some developments in the history of a distinctive culture that arose, flourished for several hundred years, and then seemed to fade in early modern times as European influences were imposed upon it; however, recently it has been the culture to which contemporary Muslims of inland Asia have turned for inspiration and the expressive means to represent their interests.[1] Turko-Persian Islamicate culture, as it will be called here,[2] is an ecumenical mix of Arabic, Persian, and Turkic elements that melded in the ninth and tenth centuries in eastern Iran – that is, in Khurasan and Transoxiana. From there it was carried by conquering peoples to neighboring areas, so that it eventually became the predominant culture of the ruling and elite classes of West, Central and South Asia.[3] In this introduction I will trace the rise and florescence of this culture and point out the topics that receive particular attention in this book. For a detailed chronology of events, please see the chart, pp. 217–29.

ORIGINS

The underlying stratum from which Turko-Persian Islamicate culture sprang was Persian. Two Persian empires – the Achaemenids of the

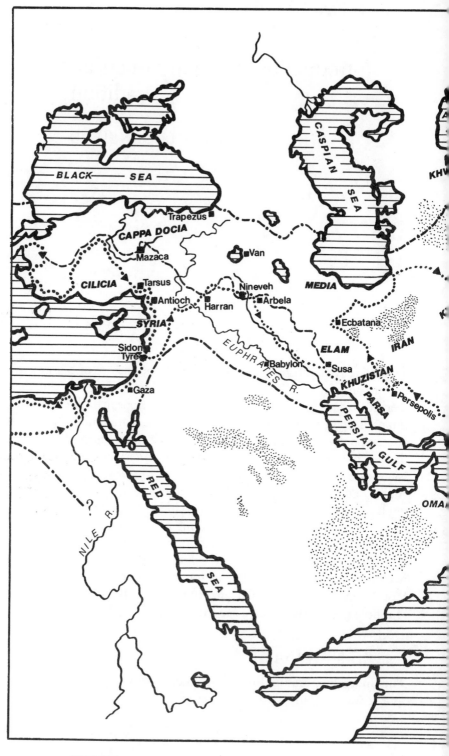

FIGURE 1 Domains of the Achaemenids (500–330 BC) and the path of Alexander (333–323 BC)

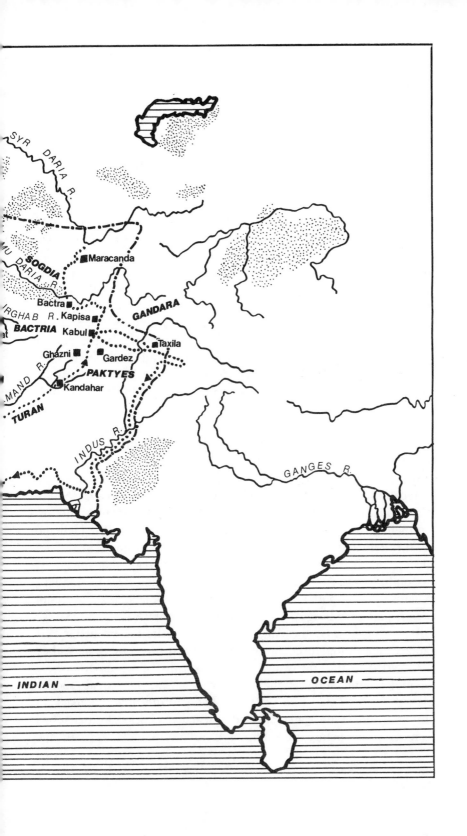

fourth and fifth centuries BC and the Sasanians of the third to seventh centuries AD, both centered in south-western Iran – disseminated Persian customs and ideas across most of the region between the Mediterranean Sea and the Indus River. These customs included the veneration of sacred shrines, reverence for the spirits of the dead, and the tying of rags to sacred trees for protection and blessing (Yarshater 1988:4). The ideas that were propagated included the recognition of social hierarchies and elaborate rules of deference towards rulers. The emperors, to emphasize their majesty, built lofty palaces, cultivated luxuriant gardens, presided from grand thrones, and wore huge crowns; they also patronized specialists of "high" culture: architects, artists, fine craftsmen, poets, and scholars. Claiming total power, Persian emperors ruled as warrior-chiefs, as protectors of the realm, builders of civilization, cultivators of wastelands, and paragons of equity (Yarshater 1988:5–12; Banani 1988; Hanaway 1988; Perry 1978:203). Subsequent generations celebrated in particular the glory of the Achaemenid emperors, Cyrus and Darius, and after the Hellenic invasion, Alexander. Persian legends about great heroes nourished hopes among the populace for great rulers who would arise to punish the wicked and fill the world with justice.

When the Iranian peoples of Persia (south-western Iran) and Khurasan and Transoxiana were overwhelmed by the Arab Muslim armies in the seventh and eighth centuries, they became part of an empire much larger than any previously under Persian rule. Under the Arab caliphs, especially in the "high" caliphal period (AD 692–945), a cosmopolitan culture was wrought from the strands of many traditions: commercial and tribal law from Arabia, philosophy from the Hellenic world, architecture from Syria and Persia, and astrology, medicine, music, and mathematics from India.[4] The language that integrated this culture was Arabic, and of it many Iranians became masters; Iranians made important contributions to the scholarship and works of fine art that were burgeoning in the Islamic empire.

At the same time the Arab conquerors of Iran were being Persianized, for although they were originally garrisoned as soldiers, they soon settled in the towns and cities, especially in Khurasan, where conquerors and subjects melded into a single Persianate society (Daniel 1979:19–22; Frye 1975a). The culture that emerged in Khurasan and Transoxiana reflected a great deal of the culture that had been in place before the coming of Islam. Middle Persian, the

4

language of Sasanian Persia (whose written form is called Pahlavi), continued in wide use. Well into the second Islamic century (the eighth century AD) it was the medium of administration in the eastern lands of the caliphate – that is, in the Iranian plateau and Transoxiana. When Arabic did become the language of official matters in this sector of the Islamic world, it was itself reshaped by Persian influences, as was Persian by Arabic (Clinton 1988:75–7; Ullah 1963:46). But despite the Arabicization of public affairs, the Iranian peoples retained much of their pre-Islamic outlook and way of life, adjusted to fit the demands of Islamic dogma. They still hoped for a savior who would bring justice, only they no longer called him the "Soshyant" but the "Mahdi"; they still believed the dead were tested at a bridge into eternal life on the Day of Judgment, only they called the bridge "Serat" instead of "Chinrat"; and their ancestral parents, whom they had known as "Mashay" and "Mashyana", they now called "Adam" and "Hawwa" (Yarshater 1988:4).

Towards the end of the first Islamic century, the Iranians began to resent the cost of sustaining the Arab caliphs, the Umayyads – who had become not only oppressive, but also blatantly profane – and in the second Islamic century (eighth century AD) some of the Iranian peoples rose up against the Umayyad caliphs, sparking a general uprising that eventually brought another family, the Abbasids, into the caliphal office. Under the Abbasids, Persianate customs became the style of the ruling elite. Affecting the demeanor of Sasanian Persian emperors, the Abbasids wore Persian clothing, instituted such Persian offices as vizier and executioner, established their new capital, Baghdad, near the site of the Sasanian capital, and like the Achaemenids and Sasanians erected grand palaces and supported artists and scholars who celebrated their rule. The Abbasid caliphate at its nadir was the climax of Persianate panopoly: they were "remote in a world of awesome luxury, walled off by an elaborate courtly etiquette, whose casual word was obeyed like divine law" (Hodgson 1974 I:283).

In the ninth and tenth centuries there were movements, political and cultural, among the Iranian peoples that indicated a growing frustration with the Abbasid caliphate and the Arabic hegemony. Although the Abbasid caliphs were brought to power with the support of the Iranian peoples, they soon lost their grip on Iranian territories. First, their governors in Khurasan, the Tahirids (822–73), became semi-independent; then a group of bandits from Sistan, the Saffarids

(867–908) overran the eastern lands. When the Samanids (819–1004) who were based in Transoxiana and Khurasan replaced them, they remained essentially autonomous (although they showed perfunctory deference to the caliph). Also, in the ninth and tenth centuries there were a number of radical popular movements among the Iranian peoples that were apparently inspired by pre-Islamic religious impulses (these would later be called "extremist" [ghālī] by Muslim heresiographers). And in the tenth century in Iraq itself the Abbasids were subjected to the rule of an Iranian tribe, the Buyids (932–1062).

EMERGENCE

The separation of the eastern lands from caliphal control and the rise of radical religious and social movements reflected the growing assertiveness of the Iranian peoples. It was finally to be expressed in a distinctive culture that would become the dominant culture of West, Central, and South Asia, and the source of innovations elsewhere in the Islamicate world. It would persist, at least in the form of the Ottoman Empire, into the present century. This new culture was marked by the use of the New Persian language as a medium of administration and literature, by the rise of Persianized Turks to administrative control, by a new political importance for the ʿulamā, and by the development of an ethnically composite Islamicate society.

New Persian

The New Persian language emerged as the idiom of administration and literature in the ninth century in Khurasan and Transoxiana. Middle Persian (called Pahlavi in its written form) had been the *lingua franca* of the region before the Arab invasion, but afterwards Arabic became the preferred medium of literary expression. The Iranian Tahirids continued to use Persian as an informal language (although for them Arabic was the "only proper language for recording anything worthwhile, from poetry to science" [Frye 1975a:1921]), as did the Saffarids (ibid.:188–200), but the Samanids made Persian a language of learning and formal discourse. The language that appeared under their patronage in the ninth and tenth centuries was a new form of Persian, based on the Middle Persian of pre-Islamic times but enriched by a copious Arabic vocabulary and written in the Arabic script. The

6

Samanids began to record their court affairs in this language as well as in Arabic, and they used it as the main idiom of public declaration. Under their patronage this Persian language became, along with Arabic, an idiom of learning and *belles-lettres* (the earliest great poetry in New Persian was written for the Samanid court). Besides using Persian for official purposes the Samanids encouraged the translation of religious works from Arabic into Persian. Even the learned authorities of Islam, the ʿulamā, began to use Persian to appeal to the public, although they still used Arabic as the medium of scholarship. One effect of the wide application of Persian in this society was that the marginal Iranian peoples were incorporated into the Islamic ecumene; Iranian speakers in the marches of Khurasan and Transoxiana began to imbibe and contribute to Islamic learned culture (Frye 1965; 1975a:200ff.).

The crowning literary achievement in the early New Persian language appeared as the Samanid dynasty was fading. The *Shāhnāma* of Firdowsi, presented to the court of Mahmud in Ghazni (r. 998–1030), was more than a literary achievement; it was a kind of Iranian nationalistic memoir. By the time Firdowsi wrote his great epic poem, the Iranian peoples were looking back to their Persian heritage, and Firdowsi galvanized Iranian nationalistic sentiments by invoking pre-Islamic Persian heroic imagery. "Perhaps no single man of letters, with the possible exception of Homer, has had such a profound and decisive effect on the language and life of his people" (Banani 1988:109). Firdowsi enshrined in literary form the most treasured stories of popular folk-memory – written, moreover, in a style largely free of Arabic forms.[5] It is perhaps because Firdowsi captured Persian nationalistic images in the cadences of poetry that poetry became "the art *par excellence* of Persia, and her salient cultural achievement" (Yarshater 1988:15; Mottahedeh 1985:161–2). In later generations poetry, including especially lines from Firdowsi, became a common source of sayings, even among Iranians who could not read. Illiterate peoples in the Persian-speaking world have for generations learned by heart the lines of Firdowsi and other great Persian poets and used them as sayings and proverbs. Poetry has often been a powerful idiom of popular protest.

Turkish supremacy

As New Persian appeared under the cultivation of the Samanid court other developments, social and structural, were taking place that the court did not foster. One of these was the ascension to power of Persianized Turks. These Turks would be the main patrons of Persianate culture, for they brought it with them from Transoxiana and Khurasan as they subjugated Western and Southern Asia. Turkish political ascendancy in the Samanid period was manifest in three tenth- and eleventh-century developments: in the decay of Samanid territories, which fell to Turks; in the fall of the Samanid ruling institution to its Turkish generals; and in the rise of Turkish pastoralists in the countryside.

An early dramatic indication of the rise of Turks in Samanid times was the loss of their southern territories to one of their Turkish slaves (*ghulāms*), who was supposed to be governing on their behalf. This Turk, with the help of a coterie of other Turkish slaves, set himself over the southeastern extremities of Samanid territories, ruling from the city of Ghazni. The empire he founded became the most powerful in the east since the Abbasid caliphs had been at their peak, and his capital at Ghazni became second only to Baghdad in cultural elegance (Bosworth 1963). It attracted not only Turkic warriors but also many learned authorities of Persian and Arabic culture – poets, historians, linguists, and mathematicians (Firdowsi's epic poem was presented at their court). The Ghaznavids (989–1149) were essentially Persianized Turks who in the manner of the pre-Islamic Persians encouraged the development of high culture.

Already before the Ghaznavid Turks broke away, however, the Samanid rulership was internally falling to its Turkish servants. The Samanids had their own guard of Turkish slaves, who were headed by a chamberlain, and a Persian- and Arabic-speaking bureaucracy, headed by a vizier. Besides these institutions there was an army, composed of mostly Turkish slaves, and a palace school, mainly populated by Turkish youths, where the servants of the court were prepared for service. By the latter part of the tenth century, as the Samanid rulers were themselves preoccupied with "high" culture, they gave the direction of their army to Turkish generals. These generals eventually had effective control over all Samanid affairs.

As these Turks were gaining control of the Samanid rulership from

8

within, other Turks, the Qarakhanids (999–1140), were gaining preeminence over the countryside. The Qarakhanids were pastoralists from noble backgrounds and they cherished their Turkish ways. As they gained strength they fostered the development of a new Turkish literature alongside the Persian and Arabic literatures that had arisen earlier.[6] As the tenth century ended, the Turkish generals of the Samanid regime gave way to the pastoralist Qarakhanids.

Social prominence of the *ʿulamā*

Another trend that began in Samanid times was the growth of the public influence of the *ʿulamā*, the learned scholars of Islam. In early Samanid times the *ʿulamā* were but one of three kinds of learned authorities, the other two being the scribes (who served in the bureaucracy), and the literati. Early in the Samanid period these were relatively equal in their influence, but the *ʿulamā* grew in prominence as the Samanids gave special support to Sunnism, possibly to emphasize their difference from their Shiʿite neighbors, the Buyids. In particular, the Samanids supported the Sunni *ʿulamā* of the Hanafi school of jurisprudence in opposition to the Shafiʿis. Hanafi jurists enjoyed a strong position in the city of Bukhara early in the Samanid period (ninth century), and their influence grew until, as the Samanids declined, they became increasingly involved in city affairs. (Hanafi jurists became particularly powerful under the Samanids' successors, the Qarakhanids, when Bukhara became a center of Hanafi learning, although other parts of Transoxiana and Khurasan remained strongly Shafiʿi.) It was, in fact, the decline of the Samanids in the tenth century and the rise of the Qarakhanids that established the dominance of the *ʿulamā* in the cities, for as societal stability weakened, the network of recognized Islamic authorities became the alternative social instrument for the maintenance of public order. By alliance with the Qarakhanids, who preferred to preside from outside the cities, the *ʿulamā* became the effective leaders of the cities. From their new positions of power they brought the bureaucratic class under their influence and eventually conjoined it with themselves (Frye 1965; 1975a:200ff.).

9

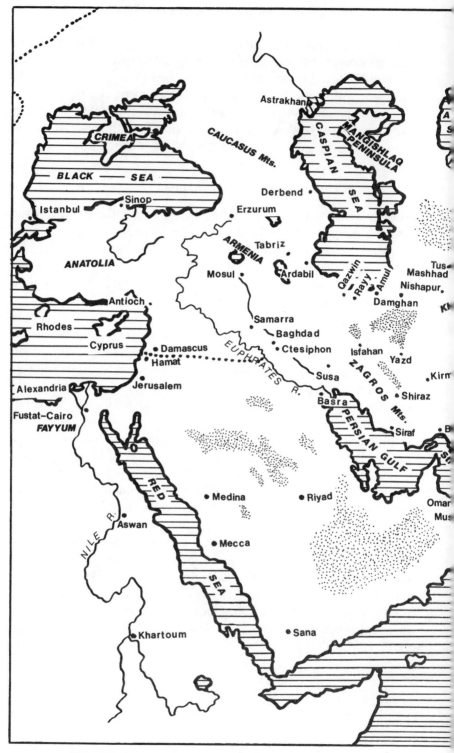

FIGURE 2 Territories of Turko-Persian culture and environs in medieval Islamic times

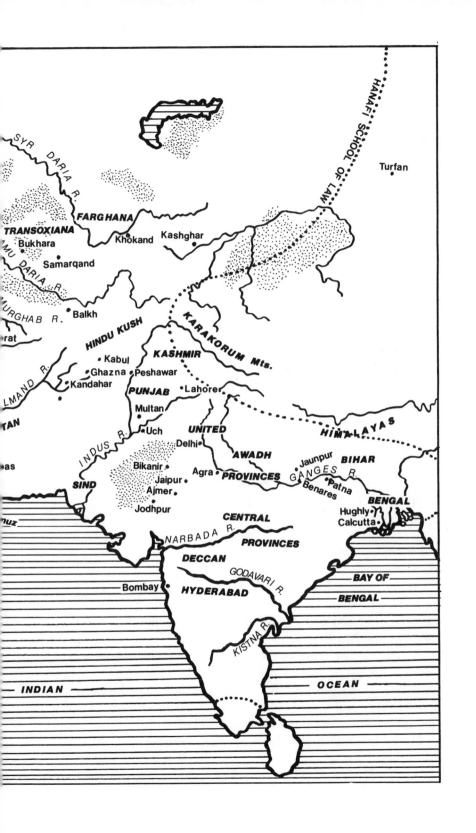

SYR DARIA R.

TRANSOXIANA

AMU DARIA R.

FARGHANA

Bukhara

Khokand

Kashghar

Samarqand

MURGHAB R.

Balkh

HINDU KUSH

KARAKORUM Mts.

HANAFI SCHOOL OF LAW

Turfan

rat

LMAND R.

Kabul

Ghazna

Peshawar

Kandahar

KASHMIR

PUNJAB

Lahore

Multan

HIMALAYAS

TAN

INDUS R.

Uch

UNITED

Delhi

as

Bikanir

Jaipur

Agra

PROVINCES

AWADH

Jaunpur

BIHAR

Benares

GANGES R.

Patna

SIND

Ajmer

BENGAL

Jodhpur

Hughly

Calcutta

CENTRAL

NARBADA R.

PROVINCES

nuz

DECCAN

GODAVARI R.

BAY OF

Bombay

HYDERABAD

BENGAL

KISTNA R.

INDIAN

OCEAN

Composite society

Another development was taking place in this society that would affect
the shape of Islamicate society, namely the formation of an ethnically
and dogmatically diverse society. The eastern lands of the caliphate
were ethnically and religiously still very diverse. Christians, Jews, and
Zoroastrians still existed in fair numbers, as did several minority
Islamic sects. As the Samanids declined, security decayed in the
countryside, and these diverse peoples withdrew in great numbers from
their farms and towns and took refuge in the cities. Bukhara and
Samarqand swelled and ethnic and sectarian neighborhoods formed,
most of them physically sequestered behind walls, each with its own
markets, caravansarais, and public squares. At the same time the
religious authorities of these non-Muslim credal communities became
their spokesmen, just as the ʿulamā were for the Muslim community;
they began also to oversee internal communal affairs. Thus, alongside
the rise of the ʿulamā there was a corresponding rise in the political
importance of the religious leaders of other doctrinal communities.

A composite urban society thus took form as the Samanid dynasty
gave way to the Qarakhanids in the eleventh century. The ruling
institution was dominated by Turks of various sorts, some highly
urbanized and Persianized, some rural and still very Turkish. It was
managed by bureaucrats and ʿulamā who used both Persian and
Arabic. And its literati participated in both the Arabic and the Persian
traditions of high culture extant in the wider Islamicate world. The
credal communities of the cities retained their local Iranian dialects.
This composite culture was the beginning of the Turko–Persian
variant of Islamicate culture. It was "Persianate" in that it was centered
on a lettered tradition of Iranian origin; it was Turkish in so far as it was
for many generations patronized by rulers of Turkic ancestry; and it
was "Islamicate" in that Islamic notions of virtue, permanence, and
excellence infused discourse about public issues as well as the religious
affairs of the Muslims, who were the presiding elite (Hodgson 1974
I:58). The agglutination of these elements into an Islamicate society
had a far-reaching impact on the religion of Islam. For Islam was
thereafter disengaged from the Arab background and bedouin mores
from which it had sprung, and it became a far richer, more adaptable,
and universal culture (Frye 1965:vii; 1975a:200–7).

The appearance of New Persian, the ascendancy of Turks to power in place of the Iranian Samanids, the rise of the ʿulamā in the cities, and the development of an ethnically and credally complex urban society thus marked the emergence of a new Islamicate culture. The transformation became increasingly evident as this Turko–Persian Islamicate culture was exported into the wider region of Western and Southern Asia.

EXTENSION AND FIRST FLOWERING

The Turko-Persian Islamicate culture that emerged under the Samanids and the Qarakhanids was carried by succeeding dynasties into Western and Southern Asia – in particular, by the Seljuqs (1040–1118) and their successor states who presided over Iran, Syria, and Anatolia until the thirteenth century; and by the Ghaznavids, who in the same period dominated Afghanistan and India. Because of their strength and prosperity these two dynasties together drew the center of gravity of the Islamicate world eastward. And under them trends that had been set in motion in the Samanid period were established as institutions that stabilized this Islamicate society into a form that would persist, at least in Western Asia, until the twentieth century.

The Ghaznavids, who first carried the Islamicate culture into the Indian subcontinent, were eventually drawn further into India by its wealth. They moved their capital from Ghazni to Lahore, which they turned into another center of Islamicate culture. We have noted how the early Ghaznavids by their patronage encouraged the production of literary and scholarly works. Under the later Ghaznavids poets and scholars from Kashgar, Bukhara, Samarqand, Baghdad, Nishapur, and Ghazni congregated in Lahore. Thus, the Turko–Persian Islamicate culture of Khurasan and Transoxiana was brought deep into India (Ikram 1964:36); it would be taken further in the thirteenth century.

The Seljuqs, who brought this culture westward into Iran, Iraq, and Syria, were the successors of the Qarakhanids in Transoxiana. Also pastoralists, although of more humble origin, the Seljuqs won a decisive battle with the Ghaznavids and then swept into Khurasan. Pressing westward they brought Turko-Persian Islamicate culture into western Iran and Iraq. Thereafter western Iran (Persia) and eastern Iran (Khurasan and Transoxiana) became the heartland of Persianate language and culture. As the Seljuqs came to dominate Iraq, Syria, and Anatolia, they carried this Turko–Persian Islamicate culture

13

beyond this heartland and made it the culture of their courts in the region to as far west as the Mediterranean Sea.

Several important institutional trends, already evident under the Samanids, gained strength under the Seljuqs and the Ghaznavids. The Islamic religious institutions became more organized and Sunni orthodoxy became more codified. In particular, the great jurist/theologian al-Ghazali proposed a synthesis of Sufism and the *sharīʿa* that became the basis of a richer Islamic theology. Moreover, formulating the Sunni concept of the division between temporal and religious authority, he provided the theological basis for the existence of the sultanate, a temporal office that existed alongside the caliphate, which was by that time merely a religious office. The main institutional means of establishing a consensus of the ʿulamā on these dogmatic issues were the *madrasas*, formal Islamic schools that granted licensure to teach. First established under the Seljuqs, these schools became means of uniting the Sunni ʿulamā who as a body legitimated the rulerships of the sultans (indeed al-Ghazali was a teacher in a *madrasa* founded by a Seljuq vizier). The bureaucracies were also staffed by graduates of the *madrasas* so that both the ʿulamā and the bureaucracies were under the influence of esteemed professors at the *madrasas* (Frye 1975a:224–30).

The period of the eleventh to the thirteenth centuries was a time of great cultural florescence in Western and Southern Asia. In spite of political fragmentation and much ethnic diversity in the region from the Mediterranean to the mouth of the Ganges there was, among the elite Muslim classes, a great deal of shared culture. In this time "Iran . . . truly asserted itself as the most lively component of the Islamic *oikoumenē* . . . [This was] a brilliant period of Persian literature and art, [when] . . . the Persian literature of the time was greater than the Arabic; [when] it was Persians who for the most part . . . served as intellectual and political advisers for the Turkish princes; [when] . . . so many themes and ideas of art and architecture were carried from east to west" (Grabar 1964:45).

DEVASTATIONS, RENEWALS, AND MATURITY

The predominant new impulses that shaped the culture of the Turko-Persian world in the thirteenth, fourteenth, and fifteenth centuries came out of inland Asia in the form of invading armies. Although the armies of the Mongols (1220–58) and of Timur (Tamerlane, *c.* 1336–1405) laid waste the urban societies of Central and West Asia, they also had the effect of stimulating the development of Persianate culture. One reason for this was the new concentrations of specialists of high culture that were created by the invasions, for many people were forced to seek refuge in a few safe havens; the most notable of those havens was India, where scholars, poets, musicians, and fine artisans intermingled and cross-fertilized. Another reason was the broad peace secured by the huge imperial systems that were established by the Mongols (in the thirteenth century) and the Timurids (in the fifteenth century); for in the quieter periods when travel was safe, scholars and artists, ideas and skills, and fine books and artifacts, circulated freely over a wide area. Also, importantly, the Mongols and Timurids deliberately patronized high culture. Under their countenance new styles of architecture developed, Persian literature was encouraged, and miniature painting and book production flourished. And under the Timurids Turkish poetry prospered, based on the vernacular known as Chaghatai (today called Uzbek).

In this period the Turko-Persian culture of India prospered. The Ghaznavids, however, were no longer in power, having lost their position in the twelfth century shortly before the first Mongol invasion of Transoxiana and Khurasan. Another Muslim dynasty, the Ghorids, had disgorged from the Hindu Kush mountains, possessed Ghazni (which they burned) and taken Lahore. Pressing further into the subcontinent, they made Delhi their capital. The Ghorids were themselves soon overtaken by their own slave guards, who were mainly Turks and Mongols (along with some Tajiks, Khaljis and Afghans), so that from the thirteenth to the fifteenth centuries India was dominated by "slave kings" who ruled as sultans in Delhi. It was their society that was enriched by the influx of Islamic scholars, historians, architects, musicians, and other specialists of high Persianate culture that fled the Mongol devastations of Transoxiana and Khurasan. After the sack of Baghdad by the Mongols in 1258, Delhi became the most important cultural center of the Muslim east (Ikram 1964:42, 112).

Like the Ghaznavids and Seljuqs, the Ghorids and the Delhi Sultans modeled their life-styles after the Turkish and Persian upper classes who now predominated in most of Western and Central Asia. They patronized literature and music but became especially notable for

15

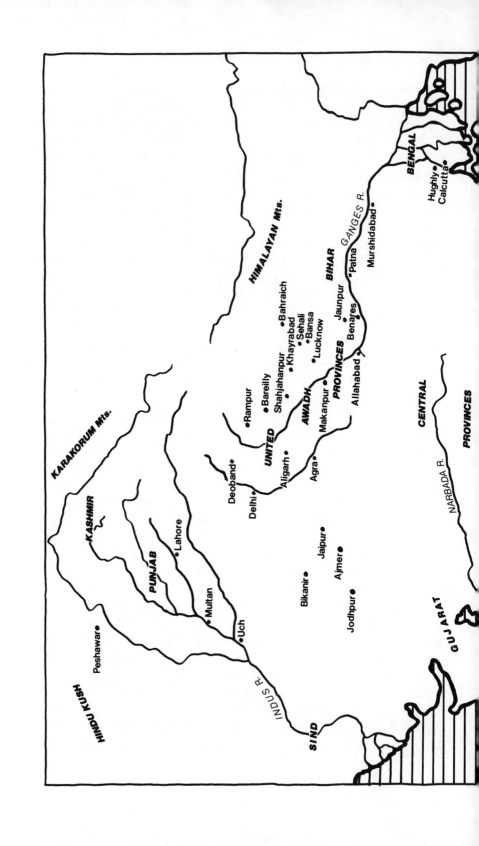

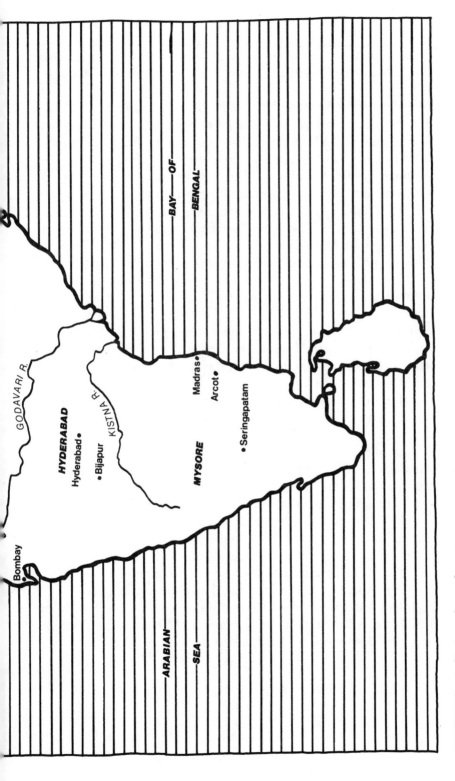

FIGURE 3 India in early modern times

for their architecture; for their builders drew from the architecture elsewhere in the Muslim world to produce "a profusion of mosques, palaces, and tombs unmatched in any other Islamic country" (Ikram 1964:120). The eminence of the Delhi sultanate persisted well into the fourteenth century, but it was fading when Timur's army invaded and sacked Delhi in 1398. Nevertheless, the regional Muslim kings that succeeded the Delhi sultans in the fifteenth century continued to patronize Persianate culture. They fostered the production of fine books and illustrations in the Persian (especially the Shirazi) style, and assembled large collections of books from many other parts of the Turko-Persian world, on Islamic, scientific, and philosophical subjects, written in Arabic as well as Persian (Titley 1983:161–73).

As the predominant influences on Turko-Persian Islamicate culture in Mongol and Timurid times were imposed from Central Asia this culture became in this period more sharply distinguishable from the Arabic Islamicate world to the west; the dividing zone between these two ecumenes fell along the catchment area of the Euphrates. Socially the Turko-Persian world was marked by a system of ethnologistically defined elite statuses: the rulers and their soldiery were Turkish; their administrative cadres and their literati were Persian. Cultural affairs were thus marked by characteristic pattern of language use: Persian was the language of state affairs and literature; Persian and Arabic the languages of scholarship; Arabic the language of adjudication; and Turkish the language of the military. The artistic traditions of Turko-Persia prospered as miniature painting withered among the Arabs, probably because of a shortage of wealthy patrons in the Arabic world, combined with the disapproval of painting by the ʿulamā (Titley 1983:16). Also, the Hanafi school became the prevailing standard of Islamic jurisprudence in contrast to the Maliki school that predominated in most of the area to the west (the Shafiʿi school being prominent in Arabia and still strong in some parts of Iraq and Iran; Robinson 1982:29). And further marking the Turko-Persian ecumene, some important Sufi orders originated and prospered in the eastern lands, notably the Naqshbandiya and Kubrawiya in Khurasan and Transoxiana, the Mawlawiya in Anatolia, and the Chistiya in India.

18

CLIMAX: THE GUNPOWDER EMPIRES

The Turko-Persian tradition reached a climax in the "gunpowder empires" that formed in the sixteenth century. These empires arose with the help of canonry, which contributed to a change in the balance of power between the settled and the nomadic populations of Turko-Persia. The pastoralist peoples had for centuries dominated Central and West Asia because of their better mobility and horseman-ship. But the development of canon gave the settled populations a new advantage. The empires that arose in Turko-Persia and carried Turko-Persian Islamicate culture into new territories were able to contain the strength of the pastoral-based armies and to establish secure centers of wealth and power. The empires that arose in the sixteenth century were the Ottomans in Asia Minor, the Safavids in Iran, and the Mughals in India; in Transoxiana another Turkic dynasty, the Shaybanids, presided, but with less strength and osten-tation than the rest. Thus, from the sixteenth to the eighteenth cen-turies the territories from Asia Minor to East Bengal were dominated by Turko-Persian dynasties.

The Turks from the house of Othman – the Ottomans – rose to predominance in Asia Minor at the beginning of the fourteenth cen-tury and developed an empire that subjugated most of the Arab Islami-cate world as well as south-eastern Europe. The Ottomans patronized Persian literature for five and a half centuries; and, as Asia Minor was more stable than the territories further east, they were able to attract writers and artists in great numbers, especially in the sixteenth century (Yarshater 1988:15). But because of the huge expanse of their empire and the importance of their Arab and European subjects the Ottomans developed distinctive styles of arts and letters. Unlike Iran they gradu-ally shed some of their Persianate qualities: they were the first of the gunpowder empires to give up Persian as the court language, using instead Turkish – that is, the vernacular of the western Turks – a decision that shocked the Mughals in India. And by the nineteenth century the Ottomans would lose interest in the illustration of manu-scripts in the Persianate manner (Titley 1983:159).

In the fifteenth century the Safavids were leaders of a Sufi order, venerated by Turkmen tribesmen in eastern Anatolia. As they ascended to predominance in Iran in the sixteenth century, they patronized Persian culture in the manner of their predecessors, to

19

enhance their image. They erected grand mosques and built elegant gardens. They also collected books (one Safavid ruler had a library of 3,000 volumes) and patronized whole academies of calligraphers, artists, gilders, and bookbinders (Titley 1983:105). The Safavids (originally Sunnis themselves) introduced Shi'ism into Iran to distinguish Iranian society from the Ottomans, their Sunni rivals to the west (Hodgson 1974 III:16ff.).

The Mughals – Persianized Turks who had invaded from Central Asia and claimed descent from both Timur and Genghis – strengthened the Persianate culture of Muslim India. They cultivated the arts (literary works, book production, artistic illustration, architecture) in the Persianate style, enticing to their courts Persian artists and architects from Bukhara, Tabriz, Shiraz, and other cities of the Iranian plateau (Titley 1983:186); the Taj Mahal, commissioned by the Mughal emperor, Shah Jahan, was indebted to the Persian style. The Mughals dominated India from 1526 until the eighteenth century when Muslim successor states and non-Muslim powers – Sikh, Maratha, and British – replaced them.

The Ottoman, Safavid, and Mughal empires fostered specific variants of a broadly similar Turko-Persian tradition. Across the territories of Western, Central and South Asia there was a remarkable similarity in culture, particularly among the elite classes. The wealthy and powerful of these empires affected similar manners and customs, wore similar styles of dress, and enjoyed much the same literature and graphic arts. In building their palaces, mosques, and mausoleums, rulers competed for the services of the same great artisans, artists, and scholars, whose eminence enhanced their reputations. The Persianate culture of these elite classes was absorbed into many of the local cultures. Although the populations across this vast region were rent by conflicting allegiances (to sect, locality, tribal coalition, and ethnic affiliation) and spoke many different languages (mostly either an Indo-Iranian language like Persian, Pushtu, Baluchi, or Kurdish, or a Turkic language like Azeri, Turkmen, Uzbek, or Kirghiz), people on many levels of the society had similar notions about the ground-rules of cooperation and dispute, and in other ways shared a number of common institutions, arts, knowledge, customs, and rituals. These similarities of cultural style were perpetuated by poets, artists, architects, artisans, jurists, and scholars, who maintained relations among their peers in the far-flung cities of the Turko-Persian

20

Islamicate ecumene, from Istanbul to Delhi (Hodgson 1974 III:80–6).

As this broad cultural region remained politically divided, the sharp antagonisms between the gunpowder empires nurtured the appearance of distinguishable variants of Turko-Persian culture. Probably the main reason for this was the introduction of Shi'ism by the Safavids into Iran, which they did in order to distinguish themselves from their Sunni neighbors, especially the Ottomans. Iranian culture, in any case, developed distinct features of its own after 1500, and the inter-position of a strong Shi'ite culture there hampered the flow of con-course between the Sunni peoples on Iran's western and eastern frontiers. The Sunni peoples of the eastern Mediterranean (Asia Minor, Syria, Iraq, Egypt) and the Sunnis of Central Asia and India developed somewhat independently. Ottoman Turkey grew more like its Arab Muslim neighbors in West Asia; India developed a virulent South Asian style of Turko-Persian culture; and Central Asia, gradu-ally more isolated, changed relatively little.

DECLINE AND DISMEMBERMENT

In the seventeenth and eighteenth centuries, two developments weakened the Turko-Persian empires. One of these was the Europeans' discovery of a sea route to India. The Iranian lands of the Turko-Persian world – that is, Iran, Khurasan, and Transoxiana – had prospered because of the flow of goods and travellers along the over-land routes between the more densely populated areas of Eurasia, that is, between India, the Fertile Crescent, Europe, and the Far East. But the Iranian lands began to lose their importance in the fourteenth century, when the Mongol rulers of Persia found the coastal sea routes to China to be safer. By the 1500s, a fair amount of traffic was moving along the coasts of India, Persia, Arabia, and Egypt, as well as through the Arabian Sea to Mogadishu and Zanzibar (Robinson 1982:88ff.). The Europeans' discovery of a sea route to the East completed the trend away from overland routes, and by the seventeenth century the bulk of long-distance traffic was being carried by European vessels on the high seas. The reduction in overland traffic affected the wealth of inland Asia and was probably a factor in the decline of the gunpowder empires.

The other factor in the decline of the gunpowder empires was the introduction of hand guns, which gave the horsemen of the pastoral

21

societies greater fighting capability. The nomadic populations of Iran, Khurasan, and Transoxiana became notably stronger than the settled populations, and in the eighteenth century the whole region was rent by tribal wars. At the same time, in India the Mughal Empire decayed into warring local states. Only Ottoman Turkey survived into the twentieth century.

In the meantime the European powers encroached into the Turko-Persian region. The British, Dutch, and Portuguese came from the south, the French and British from the west, the Russians from the north-west. Because the interests of the Europeans worked in contrary directions, they contributed to the political fragmentation of the region. By the nineteenth century, secular notions of social obligation and authority brought by the European industrializing nations, along with a superior technology, rivaled many established institutions among the nations of Turko-Persia. Under the influence of the European industrializing world, rulers began to emulate western models of governance, and the cultural similarities that had formerly been so apparent among the peoples of Turko-Persia were overlaid by western political idioms.

The Europeans, encroaching from the southern coastlands and from the north-western agricultural heartlands of Russia, saw the cultural complexes of Asia in terms that reflected their experience. By identifying the cultural regions of Asia as the Middle East, South Asia, Russian Asia, and East Asia, the Europeans in effect dismembered the Turko-Persian Islamic world that had culturally united a vast expanse of Asia for nearly a thousand years. This dismemberment was further manifested in the rise of local literatures in such languages as Chaghatai Turkish, Urdu, Pushtu, Sindhi, Punjabi, Kurdish, and Baluchi – each modeling itself after the Persian literary tradition that had flourished for the previous eight hundred years (Mottahedeh 1985:161–2).

But these regions of Asia were more than constructs in European minds. They were physically imposed on the Asiatic landscape in the form of roads, depots, ports of transit, railroads, and telegraph installations – technological means by which the Europeans exploited resources, administered populations, and protected strategic interests. These material installations were imposed from the margins of Asia inward, from the south by the Western Europeans, and from the north-west by the Russians. Along the coasts of India, Iran, and

22

Arabia, the Western Europeans built the infrastructures that connected the territories under their control to the shipping arteries of the high seas that nourished the rise of Europe. The northern sections of Turko-Persia were similarly subjected by the Russians, except that for the Russians it was railroads and riverboats that linked the central metropolis to the inland territories of Asia. Russian settlers became ensconced in the Caucasus and inland Asia in increasing numbers, especially after 1861 when serfdom was abolished. The Trans-Siberian Railway, the main east-west artery of Russian expansion, was authorized in 1891 and completed in Central Asia by 1904 (although not all the way to the Pacific until 1917). Also, by 1904 a railway had been laid southward from the main line to Kushka and Merv, to Orenburg and Tashkent, and, by 1916, to Termez on the Afghanistan border.

The construction of these transport infrastructures enabled the Europeans and their clients to carry their influences further inland, at each advance chipping away more of inland Asia. By the middle of the nineteenth century Europeans were claiming separate zones of influence. In the east, British gunboats prowled Chinese coasts; in the north-west Russia loomed over the Caucasus and Transoxiana; in South Asia the British were astride the "jewel" of their world empire, India; and in the Middle East Ottoman Turkey, the one gunpowder empire that survived, itself undergoing a transformation through its exposure to Europe, wrestled with Britain, France, Germany, and Russia for pre-eminence.

In between these zones of European influence, in the shrinking space in the inland interior, lay the territory of Central Asia that was outside the easy reach of the empires. A large part of this area would become the modern country of Afghanistan. By the latter part of the nineteenth century, the British and Russians were in contention. In 1907, weary of their "Great Game" in Central Asia (Russia having lost a war with Japan and British interests having been threatened by the Germans), they formally defined their respective spheres of interest in inland Asia. Iran was carved into pieces; Afghanistan and some other parts of inland Asia were left outside their control (although Britain claimed the right to represent Afghanistan's external affairs, a right that the Afghanistan government repudiated in 1919). A consequence of this agreement was that as the British and Russians developed the infrastructures for integrating their respective empires, the more inaccessible areas of inland Asia, and notably Afghanistan, were left relatively undeveloped. Together these areas formed a barrier, a zone of separation, between the two imperial systems of Asia.

This geopolitical configuration affected the relationship of the nations of the region to each other and to the outside world. Iran came to identify its interests largely with the nations of the Middle East, as its transport and communications infrastructures were more developed towards the west and south. Pakistan, which carved out a place for itself after 1948, was preoccupied with South Asian affairs, partly because the British-made infrastructure tied the interest of these nations so close together, but also because of its persistent tension with India. Gradually linked into the Russian/Soviet communications and transport network, the Muslim republics of the Soviet Union were drawn northward and westward in interests. Afghanistan lay at the margins of these North Asian and South Asian transport systems, and, because of its own limited means of transport and communications, remained relatively isolated.

The imposition of European influences on Asia affected social affairs throughout the region where Persianate culture had once been patronized by Turkic rulers, but the impact was not uniform throughout the society. The public sector of the society was most radically affected. The rulership and elite classes were much influenced by the new configuration of social and economic relations. European imperial policies undermined many established practices: in India, for example (as Robinson describes in this volume), aspiring young intellectuals began to write in English instead of Persian. But in other sectors of these societies there was less change; and particularly in informal relations a great deal of social life remained unaltered. Relations among family members, kinsmen, and neighbors were maintained much as they had been before. Also, popular customs and notions of virtue, sublimity, and permanence, ideas that were entailed in Islamic religious teaching, persisted relatively unchanged. These established institutions helped people retain and reproduce in their offspring similar ideas, similar feelings of continuity with the past, similar loyalties to their cultural heritage and similar notions of their place in the trajectory of history. Unlike the European images of them, they saw themselves as the heirs of an illustrious past, and still situated on a central stage of history.

THE NEW IMPORTANCE

The twentieth century has seen a crescendo of changes in inland Asia that have further exposed the contradictory cultural trends in the region. The technological development of inland Eurasia – that is, of eastern Iran, Soviet Central Asia, Chinese Sinkiang, and Afghanistan – is transforming the region. Paved roads, airfields, pipelines – and, in Iran and the Soviet Union, railroads – have been put into place, with the practical outcome that inland Asia has become much more accessible. Opportunities for social and economic interaction have consequently increased (Canfield 1985b). As these formerly inaccessible "buffer" territories of inland Asia have been brought into closer contact with each other and with the wider world they have become, as they were in medieval times, potential conduits for the flow of goods and corridors for the extension of power and political influence.

Alongside the technological improvements linking the inland areas of Eurasia into a massive, interconnected continental transport infrastructure, another kind of change has been taking place: Islamic ideals have become the predominant idiom for discussions about public affairs. This new rhetoric of public ideals has captured the interest of peoples of all sorts throughout the Islamicate world, including the area where Turko-Persian culture once had a more prominent place in public affairs. The Islamic moral imagery that persisted in informal relations has now emerged as the idiom of a new kind of ideology expressed in its most virile form in the Islamic revolution of Iran and in the Islamic idealism of the Afghanistan *mujahedīn* resistance movement.

A less noticed, parallel development has been the renewed interest in Islamic culture among the Muslims of the Soviet Union, that is, in the Central Asian republics of Turkmenistan, Uzbekistan, Tajikistan, Kirghizia, and Kazakhstan, and in the Caucasus.[7] Islamic art and calligraphy are enjoying a renaissance among Soviet Muslims, and fictional writings about the medieval period of Islamic florescence in Central Asia have become remarkably popular. Islamic rituals are also being more widely and faithfully observed by Soviet Muslims. Islamic specialists – mullahs and Sufi *pīrs* – have become more prominent in social affairs. Pilgrims to the shrines of the Sufi saints are said to number in the thousands. And young Soviet Muslims have taken a keen interest in Islamic revolutionary movements elsewhere: not only

25

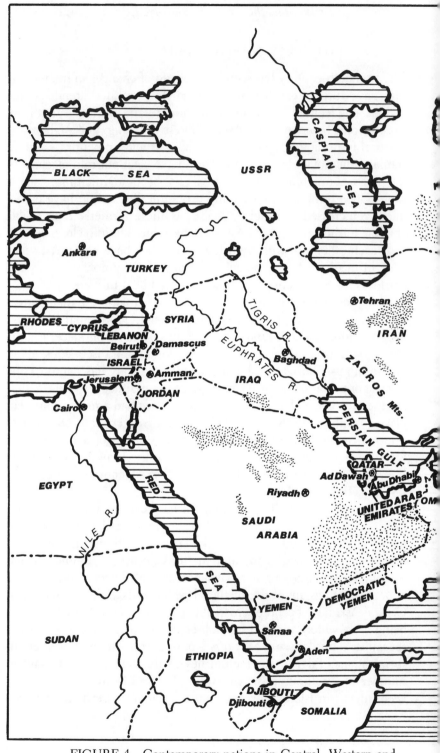

FIGURE 4 Contemporary nations in Central, Western and South Asia

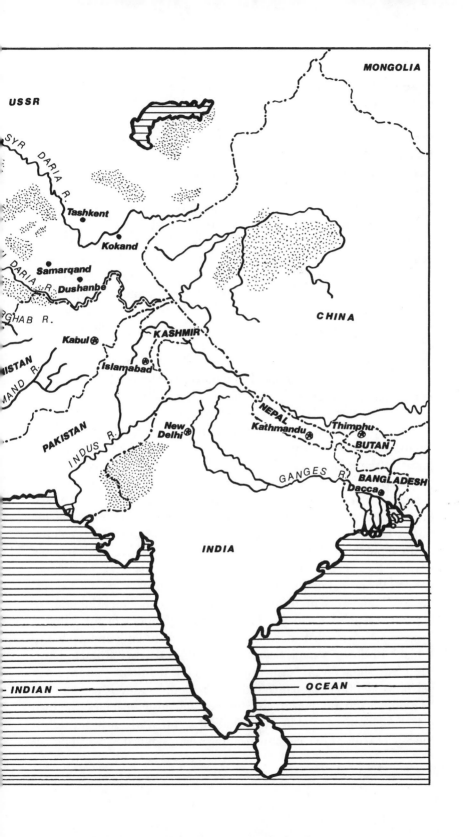

those in adjacent Afghanistan and Iran, whose populist qualities have attracted special notice, but also those in distant Algeria and Libya. The importance of such developments should not be overdrawn – there is little chance that an Islamic revolutionary movement of the Iranian or Afghan sort could spring up in the Soviet Union – but the fresh interest in Islamic customs and rituals and the increased respect enjoyed by Islamic specialists reflect a change in popular mood among Soviet Muslims that parallels the more fervid expressions of Islamic political zeal in the Muslim nations to the south.[8]

The so-called "Islamic resurgence" has been less a renewal of faith and dedication than a public resurfacing of perspectives and ideals that under the impact of European secular influences were previously relegated to less public, informal relations. They are not, of course, simply early and medieval Islamic perspectives and ideals, but selected notions and images from the past that have remained vital to many of these peoples and now are used to interpret the problems of contemporary times (Roy 1986; Ahmed 1987). In so far as the movements in Greater Central Asia in the 1970s and 1980s reflect an attempt by Muslims to find meaning in their past, the Turko-Persian Islamicate tradition has provided the elements they have used to express their shared concerns.

A striking example of this use of the past to interpret contemporary circumstances is a map of Central Asia published in 1987 by the Jamiat-i Islami Party of Afghanistan. The map represents Afghanistan, the Soviet Central Asian Republics (Kazakhstan, Turkmenistan, Uzbekistan, Tajikistan, Kirghizia), and Sinkiang China in colored tones, leaving the surrounding territories of Pakistan, Iran, and the Soviet Union untinted. The map does not indicate that the Central Asian republics fall within the Soviet Union ("USSR" appears only north of Kazakhstan), although Sinkiang is marked as a part of China. Around the border of this map are pictured some of the great personalities of Turko-Persian history: conquerors like Sultan Mahmud of Ghazni, Genghis Khan (!), Timur, Babur (founder of the Mughal dynasty), Ahmad Shah Baba (founder of Afghanistan); and poets like Rudaki, Firdowsi, Sana'i, Sayyed Jamalludin-i Balkhi ("Rumi"), Jami, Amir 'Ali Sher Nawai, Nasir-i Khusraw, and Abdullah-i Ansari. Each person is identified by name and time period. Produced in Peshawar by a *mujahed* party, presumably for the Afghanistan peoples, the map places Afghanistan, and by implication the *mujahedīn* struggle against the Soviet Union, in a certain "Central Asian" context. The peoples of

Afghanistan and the Turko-Persian Muslim peoples of Soviet Central Asia are put together not only geographically but culturally, as the heirs of a glorious past, when great conquerors and great scholars and poets created a magnificent culture.

CONTENTS AND THEMES OF THIS BOOK

This book is about the cultural tradition to which contemporary Muslims of inland Asia have turned for inspiration and for the symbolic means to represent their interests. The chapters are case studies about sectors of the Turko-Persian cultural tradition, from the early period before it gathered into a distinguishable Islamicate culture up to the present. No cultural tradition, however, whose geographic scope has expanded and contracted with the rise and fall of empires, and whose distinctive features have been stark in florescence and vague in decline, can be simply characterized. The chapters in this book, which discuss separate aspects of the Turko-Persian tradition, can be regarded as tableaux from an unfinished mural. They provide a selection of images of Turko-Persian culture, each in its specific context, but they do not display the whole picture, as large sectors of the mural remain uncompleted.

In the next Richard Frye describes the Iranian tradition as it existed prior to the Arab invasion. Then Yuri Bregel explains the impact of the many Turkish migrations into Central Asia, where Persianate culture was immediately accessible to steppe influences. Michel Mazzaoui's and Francis Robinson's essays examine different sectors of the Turko-Persian Islamicate world as they were undergoing significant changes in the later medieval and early modern period, Mazzaoui to explain the literary tradition of Iran and Central Asia, and Robinson the literary and scholastic traditions of India. Robert Canfield's and Nazif Shahrani's chapters examine certain continuities of thought and belief that persisted through medieval and modern times. Canfield focuses on "heretical" notions about leadership and authority that for generations captured the imaginations of some marginal populations; Shahrani focuses on the character of "orthodox" Islamic belief reflected in medieval works now used in mosque schools in Afghanistan. Milan Hauner in the final essay describes a less well-known case of the European confrontation with the Turko-Persian world, the Russian/Soviet intrusion into Central Asia.

29

The chapters focus on three themes in Turko-Persian culture. One of these is the importance of literature in this culture, addressed from different points of view by Mazzaoui, Robinson, and Shahrani. Mazzaoui and Robinson discuss poetry and scholarly literature as it was produced and appreciated among the elite and learned classes; Shahrani is interested in the content of widely read school books, to see the values inculcated in modern Afghan school children. Mazzaoui and Robinson examine the social context of literary and scholarly production in the period of transition from the late medieval into the early modern period; Shahrani examines the social reproduction of Islamic thought in contemporary children, through texts written in medieval times.

All three authors presume an importance for literature in this society that is not always appreciated by outside observers. Literature, oral and written, has long had a prominent place in Islamicate societies. We have noted the pivotal role of poetry in Turko-Persian culture after the eleventh century. Literary and scholastic works of the sort mentioned by Mazzaoui and Robinson were widely shared as a popular source of entertainment. Books, especially the stories and the poetry, were read to sovereigns and their courts, as well as to the ordinary people. Wherever people gathered, in caravansarais, tea shops, homes, or mosques, literary works were read or recited aloud, sometimes even from memory; favorite works, even entire epic poems, were learned by heart, even by people who could not themselves read. Literature, especially poetry, has continued to hold a prominent place among these peoples, despite the high rate of illiteracy, because the few individuals who could read have made it available to the rest.

Scholars have tended to examine this literature for its literary worth. The less elegant works have been neglected, including in fact some that have been widely appreciated. This is the importance of Shahrani's essay on two catechistical books used in Afghanistan mosque schools. His concern is not with the literary elegance of these books but with their content, the values and religious practices they inculcate. Books of this sort are used in mosque schools all over the region, not only in Afghanistan, but also in Iran, Central Asia, Pakistan, and elsewhere in the Islamicate world. They contain, if not the same works that Shahrani examines, then at least works of a similar sort. The ideas they teach are still widely received as authoritative. Written in the medieval past, such works preserve and perpetuate ideals and images that were vivid in previous generations.

A second theme that recurs in this book is the tension between central and peripheral institutions in Turko-Persian societies. Frye points out a contrast in the pre-Islamic society of the Iranian plateau between the processes that supported the consolidation of the Achaemenid imperial system *versus* the processes on the periphery, which worked against the empire's centralizing interests. He specifically stresses the tension between, on the one hand, the relatively dense, settled oasis societies where power was, and still is, centralized and stratified, and, on the other hand, the relatively dispersed, pastoral, nomadic societies of the steppes and desert. This tension has been played out variously in different parts of Central and West Asia. Bregel describes the specific consequence of this tension in Central Asia, where the oasis communities are easily accessible to the steppe peoples. He argues that in Central Asia Turkic nomads exerted a powerful influence on the oasis communities and over the long term weakened their "high" Persianate culture. A different manifestation of the tension between central and peripheral processes is the "extremist" movements described by Canfield. In those movements ideas defined in terms considered theologically out-of-bounds became the organizing themes around which certain marginal communities expressed their frustration with the predominant culture of the Turko-Persian Islamicate world and sought to break away from it, to create societies that more perfectly exemplified their ideals and hopes.

The third recurrent theme in these studies is the confrontation of the Turko-Persian Islamicate world with the European. Mazzaoui and Robinson point out that the impingement of European culture set in motion Islamic reactionary movements. Mazzaoui traces the reaction in Iran and Central Asia, while Robinson describes the final demise of Persianate Islamic culture in India, and explains how indigenous culture was asserted in the form of Muslim revivalism; he suggests that in recent times the Persianate traditions of South Asia provided some of the imaginative impetus for the formation of Pakistan.

Hauner looks at this cultural confrontation from a different angle: the Russian attitude toward Central Asia in the late nineteenth and early twentieth centuries, when the Russians were encroaching into Central Asia. He surveys their notions of the possibilities and strategic importance of this territory, and traces the developments that led them to commit themselves to it. His explanation of the impact of this

31

commitment on the British in India resonates with contemporary geopolitical circumstances in Asia.

The common ground that holds these studies together, Turko-Persian culture, has scarcely been recognized as an examinable cultural entity. Much more needs to be done to show the cultural developments that marked this tradition, to identify their geographic scope, and to follow their particular manifestations in the idioms of the present. It is hoped that these studies will stimulate other research that will fill the lacunae in the tableau of Turko-Persian Islamicate culture.

NOTES

1. I am indebted to several colleagues who have commented on various drafts of this introduction, none of whom has seen it in this form. These include the contributors to this volume, and also the following: Lois Beck, Carter Bentley, Elisabeth Case, David Edwards, Holly Edwards, Kathleen Laird, and Patty Jo Watson. I have been emboldened and helped, in this attempt to define this cultural tradition, by the recent work of Ira Lapidus on the Islamic ecumene. I have also benefited from personal communications with William McNeil and Beatrice Manz. None of these scholars is of course responsible for any part of this statement.

2. In using the word "Islamicate" I follow Hodgson (1974 1:58) who points out that "There has been . . . a *culture*, centered on a lettered tradition, which has been historically distinctive of Islamdom the *society*, and which has been naturally shared in by both Muslims and non-Muslims who participate . . . fully in the society of Islamdom. For this, I have used the adjective 'Islamicate'. I thus restrict the term 'Islam' to the *religion* of the Muslims, not using the term for the far more general phenomena, the society of Islamdom and its Islamicate cultural tradition."

3. An issue in this discussion is how an ecumene or culture area should be identified and defined. What has been said of European civilization may be said of this and all ecumenes: its "major characteristics of commonality" are only identifiable at a distance; when looked at close up, the differences among its various peoples obliterate their family resemblance (Wolters 1982:35). The difficulty of identifying the "family resemblances" in cultural pattern that identify ecumenes has intimidated scholars; in his seminal work on the Middle East Eickelman

(1981), for instance, refrained from identifying the cultural criteria by which he delimited his region; he merely provided a list of nations. The difficulty is discussed with great insight by Emmerson (1984) with respect to South-East Asia.

In my attempt to define this culture area I follow the usage of Hodgson (1974), who worked out a terminology for his monumental social-historical study of the Islamicate world. Hodgson carefully distinguished territorial regions (e.g., the Nile to Oxus region) from the cultural traditions that developed in them, such as the "Irano-Semitic" tradition or the "Islamicate" tradition (1974 i:109). He was interested in the culture of the agrarian-based citied societies in the region between the Nile and the Oxus, and in such elements of their culture as the "master-pieces of art, dynastic policies . . . religious geniuses, and scien-tific discoveries" (1974 i:190). Given this emphasis, he gave special attention to "the few privileged men [who] shared such masterpieces and discoveries," even though they lived in different places and came from different backgrounds (1974 i:90). Hodgson also freely used (although without definition) the term "cultural tradition," by which he meant identifiable complexes of cultural features that were shared among large sectors of people within a "great tradition" such as Islamicate culture (1974 i:61, 91 and ff.). I have deliberately avoided reference to the cultural currents in South-East Asia, where influences from both the Turko-Persian and the Arabic wings of the Islamicate world converged.

4. On the antecedents of Islamic law, see Schacht (1959) and discus-sions on *sunna* in Hodgson (1974); on the antecedents of Islamic philosophy see discussions of *faylasuf* in Hodgson (1974); on Hellenic influences in the high caliphal period see Hodgson (1974 i:235, 239ff.); on antecedents of Islamic architecture see Hoag (1975); on borrowing between Baghdad and India see Ikram (1964:14–19).

5. Once Persian became an acceptable written medium of com-munication it was quickly infused with a rich Arabic vocabulary. This development probably took place as the bureaucracy of the Samanids and the ʿulamā began to use it. The bureaucracies of the Samanids and their successors of course directly descended from those of the Persian period – only now they were mostly Muslims and were profoundly influenced by the cosmopolitan Arabic culture burgeoning throughout the Islamicate world.

6. The impact of the Turks on Turko-Persian culture is imperfectly defined. Bosworth (1963:205–6) says that the Turks and Iranians were culturally similar, or at least intermixed. The main dif-ference between them may have been their livelihoods: pastoral (for the Turks) and sedentary (for the Iranians). The rise of Turks to power probably mainly entailed a greater prominence of

pastoralist culture (Frye 1965; 1975a:200ff.; and Bregel, this volume).

7. The Soviets do not normally include Kazakhstan as part of "Central Asia." There are problems in naming this region generally. See Bregel 1980b; Frye 1965; Nalle 1983; Sinor 1969, 1970.

8. I am indebted to Sherrill Okyal for bringing my attention to the outstanding miniature art, copied in the medieval Mughal style, now being produced in Soviet Central Asia. According to H. B. Paksoy (personal communication) a renaissance of Islamic art and calligraphy has been going on in Soviet Muslim Asia since the 1960s. On the strength of Islam in the Soviet Union see Bennigsen (1984) and Bennigsen and Broxup (1983) and sources cited therein, and Paksoy (1984, 1986, 1987a, 1987b). For different opinions see letters to the editor by Atkin (1985) and Olcott (1985) and Bennigsen's reply (1985). For a measured treatment of the evidence on Tajikistan see Atkin (1989).

2

Pre-Islamic and early Islamic cultures in Central Asia

RICHARD N. FRYE

The spatial and temporal limits of the contents of this essay are arbitrary according to my studies of Central Asia, but they are based on historical and cultural factors. Naturally in covering such a large area many generalizations must be made which may require qualifications and exceptions; but on the whole I believe they are valid.

GENERAL OBSERVATIONS

Spatial dimensions

For centuries the vast area from the plains of Hungary to the western edge of the Great Wall of China and from the Siberian tundra in the north to the Indian Ocean in the south has had an overall cultural unity built upon similar geographical features and similar ways of life. The Iranian plateau, comprising the modern states of Iran and Afghanistan, is usually not included in any concept of Central Asia, but it always has been connected with Central Asia in a more intimate symbiosis than has either China proper or woodland Russia. One reason for this was the spread over and domination of the steppes by Iranian-speaking peoples for almost two millennia of human history.

35

The geography of the area was conducive to this spread and domination.

If one travels over this vast area the salient features of the landscape are steppes and deserts, mountain ranges bounding the area, and relatively little rainfall. One striking feature of the entire area is the existence of oases wherever water is found. Of course the steppes of Mongolia or Kazakhstan are different in many respects – climate, vegetation, etc. – from the well-known oases to the south of them, but throughout time there has existed a symbiosis between the steppe and oasis societies, and both steppes and oases are different from the great settled areas such as Egypt and Jordan. But in those cases the line of demarcation is a long but distinct line between settled, cultivated lands and the steppe or desert. The desert may advance or retreat but the lengthy strip separating the two areas always exists. In Central Asia, on the contrary, settled areas are almost invariably oases *surrounded* by steppes or deserts. The oases may be quite large, such as Bukhara, Khotan, Isfahan, or Tashkent, but they are still oases surrounded by deserts and steppes. Throughout history walls have been built around many oases of Central Asia to protect the cultivated, watered land from desert sands or from roving nomads: walls such as those around the oasis of Merv, the *kampīr duvāl* of the oasis of Bukhara, and elsewhere. In more recent times the Iranian people inside the oases were different in language, culture, and customs from those outside who, in most general terms, might be called Turkic-speaking nomads. Here, however, we are concerned with early periods.

Many students of Central Asian history have characterized the steppes as a sea over which tribes or whole peoples moved to islands: settled, fertile areas, which they conquered or penetrated. The analogy of the ocean and islands comparable to the steppes and the oases and mountains in them need not be pushed too far, however, for mountain areas have always been places of refuge for defeated ethnic or religious groups that have retreated to the heights to escape domination or persecution, whereas the oases either absorbed invaders or were overwhelmed by them. The geographical unity of a large area with diverse features, such as steppes, mountains, and oases, is best characterized by the peoples living in that area; and both the mountains and the plains, as well as the oases, of Central Asia were predominantly occupied by Iranian-speaking peoples in antiquity. So we may turn from geography to the peoples who inhabited the vast area which may be called "Greater Central Asia."

Pre-Islamic and early Islamic cultures

In the ancient Near East, Mesopotamia, with its Babylonian culture and cuneiform writing, was a center or heartland from which influences radiated to the Iranian plateau, to Anatolia, to Syria and beyond. A similar role was played in Central Asia by the Iranian-speaking peoples of the oases of the region between the Oxus or Amu Darya and the Jaxartes or Syr Darya, a Central Asian "Mesopotomia." The inhabitants along the lower course of the Amu Darya, before it emptied into the Aral Sea, were the Khwarazmians, who are mentioned in Classical sources and in the Old Persian inscriptions of the Achaemenid kings. The Khwarazmians were great traders or middlemen between the northern lands and Iran and India. In the first millennium AD Khwarazmian traders seeking furs, amber, and honey travelled on the Volga and other rivers of Russia bringing silver plates, textiles, and other manufactured objects in exchange. In the tenth and eleventh centuries the Khwarazmians brought Islam to the people of the upper Volga, later Kazan. To the east of the Khwarazmians, with centers in the oases of Bukhara and Samarqand, lived the Sogdians, who spoke an Iranian language related to Khwarazmian and were counterparts of the Khwarazmians in the east. Sogdian merchants reached China and Mongolia bringing cultural influences as well as wares. Among the cultural influences may be counted styles of music and painting as well as musical instruments; and the Sogdian alphabet was the source of Turkish forms of writing. The nomads of the steppes consequently received continuous influences from the settled Iranian-speaking peoples of what was formerly called Western Turkistan.

Temporal dimensions

Although the expansion of the Iranians over this vast area began in the second millennium BC, we really have little definite archaeological evidence to pinpoint clearly this spread. Our information is very sparse until the foundation of the Achaemenid Empire in the sixth century BC, and even then the scanty information is mainly based on fragmentary writings of the Greeks about the area of Central Asia. The domination of the Iranians, culturally and ethnically rather than politically, lasted down to the close of the first millennium AD when Turks replaced the Iranians, first as political masters of Central Asia and then as the dominant linguistic group.

37

The inhabitants of the steppes extending from south Russia to the Altai Mountains in the east, and probably beyond, were Iranian-speaking Sakas or Scythians, as the Greeks called them. This is not to deny the existence of Finno-Ugrian-speaking peoples in the western part of this vast area and Turko-Mongolian speakers in the east; but both of these peoples in the pre-Christian era were forest dwellers in Russia and Siberia, while the Sakas dominated the steppes, and their material culture, to judge from remains in excavated tombs such as Pazyryk in Siberia, had clear connections with the culture of their sedentary cousins in Iran of the Achaemenid period. One may conjecture that the Sakas of various tribes and groups had extended from the borders of China to the Balkans in the Achaemenid period of the sixth through the fourth centuries BC.

Obviously Iranian culture, as well as the penetration of the Sakas, in the Altai Mountains, for example, was weaker than in the Kazakh steppes or in Sinkiang; but one may conjecture that horse-riding Iranian-speaking tribes continued to be dominant all over Central Asia in pre-Achaemenid times, and that Altaic-speaking peoples began their expansion only at the beginning of our era. They gradually replaced Iranians – first in the east and then in the land between the Amu and Syr Darya by the end of the first millennium. Refugee areas in the mountains, such as the Pamirs, retained much of their character and past languages and cultures even after the expansion of the Turks in the tenth and eleventh centuries AD.

The ancient Iranians moved southward from Central Asia about 1000 BC and spread over the Iranian plateau. They were closely related to the Indians who had moved into the subcontinent earlier, and both peoples called themselves "Aryan." Whatever the meaning or etymology of the word ("manlike" or "noble," related to Eire or Ireland), the Indian Aryans who settled in the subcontinent mixed with the aborigines and adopted many local customs and traits, and only kept memories of their northern origin as their religion developed into Hinduism, which we know today. The Aryans in Central Asia and eastern Iran, however, seem to have been less influenced by a small aboriginal population, and in all probability they maintained more of the original Aryan beliefs and culture.

Through the centuries the movement of peoples was consistently from north to south, even from the forest regions of the farther north. The hardy nomadic folk of the steppes were probably lured to the south by the milder weather and by the wealth and easier livelihood of the rich lowlands of India, China, and the "Fertile Crescent." We know of no similar movements of people from settled lands of the south to the steppes of the north. Only merchants or missionaries from the south braved the rigors of mountains and deserts to trade southern wares for forest or steppe products. The migration of people from east to west was mainly the result of the expansion of Chinese political domination, but Chinese culture gradually reached further onto the steppes and greatly influenced the inhabitants.

Another region of political and cultural expansion was the Iranian plateau, especially after the formation of the Achaemenid Empire in the sixth century BC; and, although those Sakas who presumably lived in Siberia were never under Achaemenid rule, Achaemenid art objects, or local products strongly influenced by Achaemenid art, have been found in graves at Pazyryk, Siberia, dating probably from the fifth century BC (Rudenko 1960:336–7). The history, as opposed to the archaeology, of Central Asia begins with the Achaemenids.

THE ACHAEMENID EMPIRE

Foundations

The Iranian tribes moving from the north onto the plateau which bears their name undoubtedly borrowed many concepts and practices from the long-settled peoples of the western part of the plateau: Elamites, Kassites, Manneans, Urarteans, and others. The process whereby the Iranian tribes settled must have resembled the movement of Turkish-speaking tribes who would invade the plateau much later. But once settled, this conglomeration of tribes was transformed into a new social and political entity, an empire, first of the Medes in the north and then of the Persians in the south of the plateau. The disparate peoples of the region became subject to an instituted rulership. The effects of the formation of this rulership of the Achaemenid Empire, amply recorded in the written sources, can be seen in two important social changes. There was a decline in importance of the clan and a corresponding rise in importance of the extended family. There was also the change from a tribal army, in which all able-bodied men participated, to a professional or primarily mercenary army. Let us examine each in turn.

From clan to family.   Herodotus (i.125) tells us that the Persians were divided into ten tribes (or clans), one of which was the Pasargadai, from which the family of the Achaemenids came. We do not need to discuss the interpretation of the Greek words for "tribe" (*genea*) and "family" (*frētrē*), for the meaning of the Ionian historian is clear: we have the universal designation of "Aryan" for the Iranian race or peoples, while the "tribe" or "people" of the Persians (Old Persian: *Pārsa*) was divided into clans and the clans into extended families. This was the situation when Cyrus began his revolt in the middle of the sixth century BC. Half a century later, under Darius (522–486 BC), the clans had lost their importance, and in his inscriptions and those of his successors references to clans do not appear. Thus Darius says (Kent 1953:DNa, 13–15), "I am . . . the son of Viştāspa, an Achaemenid, a Persian, son of a Persian, an Aryan, having Aryan lineage." The vanishing of the clan is not unusual; and soon too the identification of a person as a Persian was to diminish in importance while his membership in a larger unity of "Iranians" or as an inhabitant of an empire, or later as a follower of a certain ruler, gained in importance. This process took place in the Achaemenid heartland, the Iranian plateau. It happened more slowly in Central Asia, where Achaemenid rule was never firm and where the large tribal designations – Sogdians, Khwarazmians, Bactrians, and Sakas (or Scythians to the Greeks) – remained paramount. These peoples continued to use their native Iranian tongues and, as might be presumed, preserved their native customs.

From tribal to professional army.   Darius uses the word *kāra*, which is cognate with German *Heer*, Lithuanian *kāras* and others, to designate the armies against which he fought to secure the throne. But he also uses the same word to mean "people," or at least the male population who worked on building projects for the ruler. By Sasanian times (the third to seventh centuries AD) the word had lost its meaning of "army" and had come to mean "other people" or "foreigners," usually in the plural form (M.P. *kārān*). Although the O.P. word *spāda* (N.P. *sipāh*) for "professional army" is not found alone in Old Persian, but only in names, a form of it does occur in its cognate language, Avestan. From this usage and from Greek sources we may say that by the end of the Achaemenid Empire an army primarily of mercenaries had replaced the old tribal levies. This change, I suggest,

40

represents one of the differences between a "nomadic" state and a settled state or empire, the general differences between which we shall now examine.

The settled state and the nomadic confederacy

In order to discuss the differences between two modes of rule in Achaemenid times, reference will have to be made to later examples, but there is consistency throughout history in these differences.

The first contrast is in the structure of the rulership. In the nomadic or steppe empire the ruling group is usually a "charismatic" or "imperial" clan, sometimes part of a larger group such as the "Royal Scythians" (Herodotus IV.6) among the Scythians. Although ability and personal characteristics played a part in the selection of a leader, membership in a charismatic clan was a prerequisite for rule.

I do not use the word "charismatic" in its modern sense of one who by personal ability or charm wins a standing or position in the eyes of followers or admirers which greatly influences those followers. Rather, the original sense of charisma is intended here, of a divine or supernatural grace or power given to someone: in this case to a clan or family, one member of which was chosen, or even destined to rule by signs or portents. Just how or when charismatic clans or families of tribes came into being is unknown, but once accepted or acknowledged by other clans, the basis of rulership and continuity in rulership was established. Legitimacy or the right to rule others is then maintained and even developed into an ideology by the ruling clan or family. This concept of legitimacy and the right to rule is well expressed by Darius in his Behistun inscription (Kent 1953:DB 1, 6): "For this reason we are called Achaemenids. From long ago we have been noble [or powerful]. From long ago our family had been king." Darius proclaims that his collateral branch of the Achaemenid family had just as much right to rule as did the branch of Cyrus and Cambyses. This "charisma," perhaps better expressed as "royal glory," is found in writings throughout Iranian history as Avestan *xvar∂nah*, Old Persian (and Median) *farnah*, Middle Persian *xwarrah*, and New Persian *farn* or *farr*. Presumably the "royal glory" had once been the prerogative of a clan of the Persians until the Achaemenids limited it to a family and then institutionalized it as a sacral kingship, not however as a sacred or divinized king. Much has been written about the concept of *farn*,

41

including a book (Bailey 1971), and related concepts – in China *tien ming* "the mandate of heaven," or in Central Asian Turkic societies *tangri yarliqi* or *qut*.

By "imperial" I mean that clan of a tribe which, possessing the charisma of rule at times is able to become the spearhead in forming a steppe empire. It is impossible here to discuss these concepts in detail; I merely note that the Achaemenid Empire was formed in all probability by the transformation of the acceptance of a charismatic clan of the Persian people into allegiance to a royal family, the Achaemenids, who combined Iranian tribal concepts of rule with ancient Near Eastern beliefs in the sacral nature of kingship, a divine right to rule. The settled state or empire, however, was much more complex than a tribal society. While anthropologists would explain the change from a nomadic society to a settled society as a transformation of mode of life, here we are concerned with the change in loyalty and allegiance of a people from a clan or extended family of a tribe to a much smaller royal family whose power and position is based on institutions of settled folk administered by a bureaucracy.

The Achaemenid Empire was the first truly world empire: unlike the Assyrian and preceding empires, it permitted conquered peoples to maintain their own local laws, religions, and customs; and over the whole empire a secular, universal set of laws regulated trade relations, taxation and other matters common to all peoples of the empire. The ruling institution of the Achaemenid Empire was founded on the legitimacy of the Achaemenid family with a divine mandate to rule (the charisma), supported by a well-organized, hierarchical bureaucracy, with scribes from all peoples in the empire all using Aramaic as the imperial written language.

In the settled state, contrary to a nomadic empire, the bureaucracy, following certain old traditions deemed sacred, became the prime instrument of rule. True, this bureaucracy was frequently, and even at times primarily, a patrimonial rather than a professional bureaucracy, especially when the tribesmen who conquered settled areas moved into the bureaucracy. In the Achaemenid Empire, however, writing was vital for preserving records and the scribes held important posts. Much later in the history of Central Asia, the change from a charismatic family with a leader, such as Genghis Khan or Timur, to an empire with a well-established bureaucracy in the settled areas is apparent. The sacred traditions which guided the bureaucracy should be mentioned next in order to contrast the attitudes of the nomadic and the settled empires towards religion.

The deference and commitment of the settled state to the religious establishment is reflected in a statement of Darius at the end of his inscription at Behistum in Persia. Here he says (Kent 1953:*DB* V, 31–2), "Those Saka were faithless and Ahuramazda was not worshipped by them." For this reason Darius punished them. Why, however, should he be concerned whether the Sakas were or were not worshippers of Ahuramazda? There is no evidence that the Achaemenids tried to impose their religion on the Egyptians, Babylonians, Jews, and others whom they ruled; why then were Sakas (and the Elamites) punished, with the remark that they did not worship Ahuramazda presumably as the Achaemenid royal house did? I suggest that it was because other peoples of the ancient Near East, such as the Egyptians, Babylonians, or Jews, had their national or state religions; and the Achaemenids, in emulation of them, sought to impose a similar unity of worship among the Iranians. This imposition of obligatory beliefs on all Iranians who were under Achaemenid rule, as well as on peoples such as the Elamites, who lived in land now occupied by Iranians, was probably an early attempt at joining church and state, which under the Sasanians in the third century AD became a reality. A state religion of this sort did not exist under the Achaemenids. The Sakas may well have considered themselves the heirs of the traditional beliefs of the Aryan tribes with the nomadic choice of beliefs, or at least tolerance in matters of faith, and consequently not subject to settled Achaemenid attitudes.

We have mentioned already the change among the Achaemenids from a people's army to a professional army, which is an important feature of the change from a nomadic to a settled society. In the later Achaemenid Empire Greek mercenaries became the backbone of the army of the great king. In Central Asia, however, a new form of army was created, which was different from the mercenary armies of the Near East. This was the institution of slave guards, much later called the mamluk as in Egypt or the janissary corps of the Ottoman Empire. How early this institution developed in Central Asia is unknown; but it was certainly pre-Islamic since the Arabs found this system in use by the oasis states of Transoxiana, for example, when they raided the oases of Bukhara and Samarqand in the middle of the seventh century. The Arabs called the slave soldiers **or guards** of the Sogdian merchants *šākariyya* (N.P. *čākir*), the Sogdian word for which is unattested (Bartol'd 1963a:238; 1963b:209). These troops guarded the homes of the Sogdians who were engaged in far-flung trade with China. Later, under the Samanids (ruled *c.* 875–1000) Turkish slaves became the backbone of the army and eventually took over leading posts in the bureaucracy as well (Frye 1965:120–1). I believe, without conclusive proof, that this institution of slave guards or soldiers was a Sogdian creation (Frye 1975b:148–51).

There was also a difference in how the two systems incorporated outside groups. The Central Asian nomads created empires by con-federation; that is, conquests in the steppes usually resulted in the integration of various tribes into a tribal confederation. The formation of the Kushan Empire in the first century BC is a good example of the confederation of five tribes under the aegis of one of them – the Kushans (Zürcher 1967:367). Examples of the conquest of the apparatus of state in a settled empire are numerous and self-explanatory.

The economic base of a nomadic empire was primarily the exploi-tation of other nomadic peoples' pasture lands, according to Omeljan Pritsak (1975), while the economic base of a settled state was the exploitation and expansion of one's own land and production. When a nomadic empire made conquests over settled peoples, the same principle of exploitation of the land of the settled folk for the benefit of the nomads applied. The question of a surplus of animals in a nomadic society or surplus of grain in a settled society is another question. We see no examples of confederation in the history of settled empires, and only in the oasis states of Central Asia do we find examples of tribal union against outside invaders, although even here no empire or larger state by confederation was created. In a sense one might characterize the nomadic state, at least in its initial formation, as anti-production whereas the settled state fostered production.

The heritage of the Achaemenids

The influence which the world state of the Achaemenids had on its neighbors, both in the west and in the east, was enormous. Unfortunately, we have so few sources for the post-Achaemenid history of Central Asia that it is impossible to reconstruct these influences. We do have records from India, however, and it seems that

44

the Achaemenids' influence on the Mauryas, who followed Alexander the Great in establishing a large North Indian empire, especially under the emperor Asoka, can be discerned in the imperial spy or information service and the road system, as well as in art and architecture. Also, the imperial Achaemenid writing system using Aramaic provided a model for the Mauryas. Inasmuch as Indian influences on Central Asia were strong in later times, especially with the spread of Buddhism in the first centuries AD, it is possible that many originally Achaemenid features of administration, art, etc., came to Central Asia through India. Also one should not forget that Asoka ruled parts of present-day Afghanistan, and this area may have provided a road to other parts of Central Asia for Indian influences.

The Seleucids were the successors of the Achaemenids in ruling Western Turkistan, but their rule in Central Asia was relatively short lived and the heritage of the Achaemenids should be sought in the local states and local cultures which came into being in both Western and Eastern Turkistan. One aspect which may be mentioned is the development in writing in Central Asia. The Achaemenid bureaucracy which relied on the Aramaic language as its lingua franca, as is well known, had a paramount influence on the various systems of writing among the Iranian peoples of Central Asia. The Sogdians were the teachers of the Uighurs, who in turn influenced the Mongols, who influenced the Manchus. Various aspects of Achaemenid bureaucracy and rule undoubtedly had much influence in the subsequent world, but unfortunately our sources are so few and fragmentary that one may only speculate about them. The fact that the imperial or "king's" law (biblical: *dāta d'malka*) extended all over the empire is reflected by the borrowings of the Iranian word for law (*dāta*) in Armenian, Aramaic, Hebrew, and other languages, and in a real sense Achaemenid law was the precursor of Roman law. The eastern Iranians such as the Sogdians and Sakas, of course, have the same word in their language as well as related words derived from the Achaemenids.

We have archaeological remains of the Achaemenids at Pasargad, Persepolis, and elsewhere, which have impressed tourists; but more important hydraulic works such as canals, dams, cisterns, and the famous *qanat* (Central Asian: *karez*) underground canals have received insufficient attention. The centralized government of the Achaemenids was able to organize large numbers of workers to engage

45

in irrigation projects on a large scale. Concomitant with large irrigation and other water projects went a great expansion of trade, which undoubtedly influenced Central Asia as it did other parts of the empire. The system of taxation, even though we have little detailed information about it, seems to have been highly organized and multifaceted under the Achaemenids. The Achaemenid period of history was a time of the formation of marriage alliances and the prestige of the Achaemenid family, and the desire of later rulers to trace their pedigrees back to the Achaemenids was found not only among later Iranian princes but also in places as distant as Commagene, in southern Anatolia, where a local ruler Antiochus (69–34 BC) built a tomb with statues of his ancestors, including Darius (Ghirshman 1962:57). The prestige of the Achaemenids lived long after their passing from the scene, and Alexander the Great in later popular traditions was merely a continuation of the Achaemenids in the eyes of many Iranians (Frye 1985).

THE NOMADIC AGE AND THE KUSHAN EMPIRE

The breakdown of centralization

The Greeks or really the Macedonian successors of Alexander were unable to continue the unification under one rule of Iranian peoples which the Achaemenids had achieved, at least nominally. Seleucid rule was weak in the east and Greek traditions of the *polis* and the city state helped to promote the rise of small political entities everywhere in the east Iranian cultural area. The centralized Achaemenid bureaucracy collapsed and was not replaced by a Greek one in Central Asia. Although sources are very few and fragmentary, stray indications suggest that the following geographical and cultural regions gradually became independent of any central control.

In western Iran we know of small kingdoms which existed in Persis (Fars), Azerbaijan, and in the mountains of Luristan and the Caspian area. Further, we may say that Seleucid control was strong and effective only along the silk route from Mesopotamia to Bactria, through the modern cities of Hamadan, Tehran (Rayy), Herat, Merv, etc. The local kingdoms, as far as we can determine, seem to have maintained minor courts modeled after the Achaemenid court and maintaining, or at least attempting to maintain, many of the Achaemenid institutions. There is no evidence of any change to nomadic institutions or even nomadic domination, or any great movement of tribal peoples into western Iran at this time.

In eastern Iran and Central Asia we may postulate the emergence of a number of oasis states after the decline of Seleucid rule by the middle of the third century BC. If we are to believe much later Arabic sources, such as al-Biruni (Sachau 1876:35), and indications from archaeology, Khwarazm, not surprisingly, was an independent kingdom from very early times after the break-up of the Achaemenid Empire. The oases of Western Turkistan, however, could support only a small population, and the oases of Eastern Turkistan or Sinkiang were even smaller. All of the oasis states were obliged to seek their fortunes in trade and the production of handicrafts rather than in agriculture, save perhaps the Ferghana valley which was better watered than most other areas of Central Asia. In any case, each oasis state presumably went its own way in developing its own traditions and its own writing system and culture during the Seleucid period of history.

The nomadic interlude

In western Iran the collapse of Seleucid rule, dating from the middle of the second century BC, was followed by Parthian sway over the plateau. The Parthians were probably a mixture of a Central Asian nomadic tribe, called the Parni in Classical sources, with the settled people of Khurasan; the language of the settled people was adopted as the official tongue of the Parthian state. There was no restoration of the centralization of the Achaemenids, however, and one is probably not off the mark to call the Parthian state a feudal kingdom in which chivalric or heroic traditions of rule were honored even though the minor courts maintained as best they could the forms of the old Achaemenid bureaucracy. Greek culture, of course, had a strong influence on both Iran and Central Asia as witnessed by the art, the coinage and the use of the Greek language in documents; but basically it was the heritage of the Achaemenids, especially outside the main cities on trade routes, which continued to exert its influence in western Iran.

Central Asia and eastern Iran underwent successive invasions by nomads from the north, and we learn about the migration of tribes from both Chinese and Classical sources. For almost a century and a half beginning about 150 BC various tribes established their hegemony over most of Central Asia and present-day Afghanistan. Even though they were Iranians in speech, there was no unity of rule, and we only learn of their wealth and culture from archaeology, from sites stretching from Issyk Kurgan in present Kazakhstan to Tilla Tepe in northern Afghanistan, both sites revealing the surprising opulence and tastes of nomadic chiefs (Akishev 1978:53 and Sarianidi 1984). Although we have no sources other than coins and archaeology, it seems obvious that Greek culture was much stronger in the east, even after the fall of the Greco-Bactrians, than in the west, and that Achaemenid institutions in the east did not have the same honored position they held in the west. This was to change, however, with the creation of the Kushan Empire.

The Kushans

The Kushan Empire was founded by one of the nomadic tribes that moved into Bactria from the north; and by the nomadic process of confederation the Kushans united other tribes to become the heirs of the Greco-Bactrians in the east. Whatever the date of the best known of the Kushan rulers, Kanishka, he is the one who changed the language on his gold and copper coins from Greek to Bactrian, written in modified Greek letters (Zürcher 1967:356). He was probably an active patron of Buddhism although on his coins we find the names of many Greek, Indian, and Iranian deities, showing a surprising religious diversity. The Kushans tried to establish a settled, centralized empire, and we may suppose that many features of settled rule were initiated by the Kushans. They were successful in establishing a legitimacy such that succeeding monarchs claimed legitimacy and justified their rule by claims to be descended from the great Kushan kings (Pandit 1968:xxxiv). The Kushan Empire was the only attempt in pre-Islamic times by the local inhabitants to establish a settled, centralized state in Central Asia and Afghanistan.[1]

THE TRIUMPH OF NOMADIC IDEALS

The fourth and fifth centuries AD can be characterized as a revival of Achaemenid centralization by the Sasanians in the west and the triumph of feudal traditions in the east. This dichotomy, in my opinion, persisted throughout the Islamic period almost down to our own time. One cannot go into details here about that dark period of Central Asian history from the time of the Kushans down to the coming of the Arabs; but one may suggest that the beginning of this period saw the last waves of Iranian-speaking nomads moving to the south, to be replaced by the Turkic-speaking nomads beginning in the late fourth century.

The coming of the Turks

The Huns who invaded Europe had relatives who similarly invaded the Near East and India; but our information about them, known in Classical and Islamic sources as the Chionites and Hephthalites, is so meager that much confusion has reigned regarding their origins and nature. Just as later nomadic empires were confederations of many peoples, we may tentatively propose that the ruling groups of these invaders were, or at least included, Turkic-speaking tribesmen from the east and north, although most probably the bulk of the people in the confederation of Chionites and then Hephthalites spoke an Iranian language. In this case, as normal, the nomads adopted the written language, institutions, and culture of the settled folk. To call them "Iranian Huns" as Göbl has done is not infelicitous, for surely the bulk of the population ruled by the Chionites and Hephthalites was Iranian (Göbl 1967:ix). But this was the last time in the history of Central Asia that Iranian-speaking nomads played any role; hereafter all nomads would speak Turkic languages and the millennium-old division between settled Tajik and nomadic Turk would obtain. The Turks of the Orkhon River in Mongolia (or the Gök Turks) established a ruling clan and henceforth, after the sixth century, the steppes of Central Asia were dominated by Turks; in the seventh century they moved southwards into the Near East.

The city states of Central Asia

Over several centuries after this most of the people of Central Asia gradually became Turkish in speech. Similarly, in Sinkiang both the Sakas in the southern rim of the Tarim Basin and the "Tokharian" speakers of the northern oases of Kucha, Karashahr and elsewhere were gradually Turkified, not without leaving Iranian and "Tokharian" influences on the Uighurs and other Turkic peoples of the region. In Western Turkistan the process was slower, for the city states had developed strong, literate cultures of their own, and the Sogdians of Bukhara and Samarqand had been the teachers of the Turks in many ways. As noted, the Sogdians were the merchants to China as the Khwarazmians were middlemen, bringing furs, amber, honey, and other articles from the Volga and Baltic regions in exchange for silver (the currency of the steppes), textiles and luxury products. The Sogdians had their own written language, alphabet, and religion – a local form of Zoroastrianism – while the Khwarazmians were different in language, and perhaps in other matters, from their Sogdian cousins. But both were predominantly traders.

The other great center in the east was Bactria, unified in language, written in a modified Greek alphabet; in religion, a form of east Iranian or Central Asian Buddhism; and also in art, more the heir of the earlier Gandharan art than either the Sogdians or Khwarazmians. Bactria was not unified politically, however, and at the time of the Arab invasion in the middle of the seventh century, many small principalities existed both north and south of the Oxus River.

The influence of Buddhism on east Iranian culture must have been great although we have few sources which give information about the spread of Buddhism in this part of the world. It is now clear, however, that Buddhist monasteries and reliquaries (*vihāras, stupas*) existed as far west as the Merv oasis and late into Sasanian times (Koshelenko 1966:175). Some of the cultural differences between Persia and eastern Iran/Central Asia may be traced to Buddhist influences, such as the seemingly greater tolerance for religious diversity in Central Asia than in the west at the time of the Arab conquests. Buddhism was a religion of deeds rather than creeds, which probably fostered the attitude of tolerance. Much more research is needed on the extent of Buddhism in the east before we can reach more than tentative proposals.

To the south, over the Hindu Kush Mountains, Indian influences were paramount. Even Buddhism had given ground to a resurgent Hinduism, as witnessed by finds dating from this period of statues of Siva, Ganesh, and other Hindu deities in the Kabul region. The Kabul–Ghazna line was the real border between Indian and Iranian cultures, but with the expansion of Islam under the Ghaznavids in the eleventh century the frontier would move down from the mountains onto the plains of the subcontinent.

In the west, oases such as Merv and Herat were Sasanian in culture and language, and both were usually the limits of Sasanian rule in the east. Although the political frontiers shifted from time to time the cultural frontiers remained relatively stable until the expansion of the Turkic-speaking peoples.

The Sasanians (AD 224–651) came to power in Fars province as did the Achaemenids, although the latter had been forgotten except for the vague conception of a great Iranian empire in the past. Nonetheless, the Sasanians developed a centralized monarchy with a bureaucracy and a new factor in history: a religion recognized and supported by the state – Zoroastrianism. The Sasanians had a distinctive art, coinage, and culture as reflected in Middle Persian or Pahlavi writings. The traditions of church and state as twins supporting each other became a veritable dogma in later Islamic Persian writings about political philosophy. Sasanian ideas about this duality of rule (church and state) with the "king of kings" as defender of the faith came to the fore again in the ninth century and later when we see the rise of local Iranian dynasties in the eastern part of the Islamic world. Also, practices of the Sasanian bureaucracy were continued into Islamic times with only a change in language from Pahlavi to Arabic under the caliph Abd al-Malik about 699. But the new religion, Islam, was the faith of the Arabs.

The Arabs and Islam

Although in spirit the bedouin Arabs were similar in many respects to the nomads of Central Asia, by the eleventh century, after orthodoxy had been established, the Islamic states became as intolerant as the Zoroastrian state religion of the Sasanians. Although the bedouin tribes followed the principle of confederation as did the Central Asian nomads in their expansion, this practice gave way to support for the settled, bureaucratic institutions of the Sasanian Empire already under the Umayyads, but more clearly under the Abbasid caliphate. At the same time the Arabs must have felt more at home in Central Asia than they did in Persia. Muhammad after all was a merchant and so were the Sogdians and Khwarazmians. I suggest that one reason for the rapid spread of both Islam and the Persian language in Central Asia after the Arab conquests was the frontier nature of Transoxiana. No state religion like that in Sasanian Iran existed in this region. Instead, there were many religions – Christianity, Buddhism, Manichaeism, Zoroastrianism, Judaism, and others – and at least a semblance of tolerance was a necessity. Such an atmosphere of tolerance allowed divergent opinions, free thought, even heresy, as the centers of Islamic power and control were far to the west, in Baghdad and elsewhere. So the peoples in Central Asia carried their religious orthodoxy rather more lightly. In Bukhara newly converted Muslims even had to be paid to come to the mosque to pray in the period after the Arab conquest (Frye 1954:49). The Central Asians in fact found kindred spirits, especially the members of the Azd tribe from Oman who were, like the people of the Bukharan oasis, renowned for their textiles. Bukhara and Samarqand became cosmopolitan centers and produced many Islamic scholars in the early centuries of Islam. Henceforth Central Asia was changed as it began to face westward and Mecca became the direction not only of prayer but of inspiration for culture, social institutions, and indeed every facet of life. Islam not only brought a profound change of direction but it also unified the peoples of Central Asia as never before, indeed perhaps as they never would be again. The ancient traditions of Central Asia nonetheless assert their influences from time to time. One may infer this, for example, in the feeling between Uzbeks and Tajiks today, both of whom refer to the past in asserting their distinctiveness. Some Tajiks still feel more akin to fellow Persian speakers in Kabul than to the Uzbeks of Tashkent. Indeed, continuity in culture and the yearning to seek one's roots are more important today than the general Islamic heritage, but both may yet play an important role in the affairs of those peoples.

NOTE

1. It is no wonder that the present government in Afghanistan has sought to exalt the Kushans as their ancient, glorious ancestors, much as the late Shah of Iran turned to the Achaemenids as the ancient prototype of his rule. The present International Center for Kushan Studies in Kabul is a symbol of the search for prominent roots in the past.

3
Turko-Mongol influences in Central Asia

YURI BREGEL

Central Asia in this essay[1] is defined as the western part of the inner Asian heartland. It stretches in the west to the Caspian Sea and the Ural basin; in the north, to the west Siberian taiga; in the east, to the Tarim basin; and in the south, to the Gorgan valley, the Kopet Dagh mountains, the Band-i Turkistan range, and the Hindu Kush. Central Asia thus defined coincides with Turkistan as it was understood in the nineteenth and early twentieth century (see Bartol'd 1934:895). The term Turkistan would still be appropriate; but since it originated in Iran, it tends to overemphasize one particular feature of the area as distinct from Iran and makes one forget the role of the Iranian ethnic element and Iranian culture in the region. Therefore, the neutral term "Central Asia" is preferable. On the basis of the major ecological division of Central Asia, the area is subdivided into two zones, northern steppe and southern, "sedentary" part. The term sedentary is used here for brevity and as a matter of convenience: it means only that this zone was dominated by sedentary civilization, although it includes also large areas of deserts and steppes, and nomads were present there sometimes in large numbers. The dividing line between the two parts of Central Asia goes roughly from the Aral Sea along the northern limits of the Syr Darya basin and the Tien Shan.[2]

53

The two zones together form a frontier area between two Eurasian civilizations: Islamic–Iranian sedentary and inner Asian nomadic; culturally, Central Asia belongs to both of them. In their political history, nomadic and sedentary zones of Central Asia had one common feature, a lack of political centralization, which also made them different from Iran on the one hand and the eastern steppes of inner Asia on the other. The sedentary zone of Central Asia did not belong to the imperial tradition of Iran, and the nomads of Dasht-i Qipchaq did not share the imperial tradition of the nomads of East Asia. Both zones tended to remain politically fragmented, and the temporary centralization which they from time to time experienced was brought by the conquerors from the outside: Persians and Arabs from the south, eastern Turks and Mongols from the east, and finally Russians and Chinese. This land has been indeed "le milieu des empires," as two French authors have aptly called it (Cagnat and Jan 1981).

To evaluate the role of Turks and Mongols in Central Asia, we have to try to consider two main issues: how these two peoples penetrated Central Asia; and how this process affected the history of the region.

THE PENETRATION OF TURKS AND MONGOLS

The indigenous population of the whole of Central Asia, both sedentary and nomadic, was Iranian, and it still inhabited the region at the beginning of our era. By the sixth century, the steppe belt seemed to be completely Turkified and a similar process was about to begin in the sedentary zone.

The penetration of Turks and Mongols into the sedentary part of Central Asia was accompanied by Turkification[3] in a narrow, linguistic sense. That is, the Turkic-speaking population grew at the expense of the Iranian speakers owing to an influx of Turks from the steppe belt (as well as, probably, their higher rate of growth) and to the use of Turkic languages by increasing numbers of the indigenous population. The result of this process can be seen now, when about 89 per cent of the total indigenous population of Central Asia are registered as speakers of various Turkic languages and only 11 per cent as Tajik speakers.[4] But the rate and the stages of this Turkification are not so obvious and not always understood properly.

At the beginning of the Islamic period (eighth century), Central Asia was still roughly divided into two well-defined linguistic zones: Turkic, which included all of the northern steppe regions, and Iranian, which included the regions of sedentary culture. In border areas (mainly the Syr Darya basin, including the eastern part of the Ferghana valley) some linguistically mixed groups probably existed. The main exceptions to this general division were these: (1) some Turkic-speaking groups were in Afghan Turkistan (Tokharistan) and to the north of the Gorgan (Dehistan) by the end of the sixth or the seventh century, and in Eastern Turkistan at least by the sixth century; (2) on the other hand, Sogdian colonies were dispersed far into the inner Asian steppes, reaching northern China. Turks (or various peoples speaking Turkic languages) were among the principal adversaries of the Arabs in Transoxiana and Khurasan in the seventh and eighth centuries. However, it is uncertain how numerous and important the Turks in the sedentary regions of Central Asia were before they began their major migrations to the south-west.

Bartol'd (1963b:113; cf. 1963a:317ff., 1968:59) seemed to have connected the first penetration of Turks into Transoxiana and Khurasan with the expansion of the first Turk qaghanate and the partition of the Hephthalite state of Central Asia between that qaghanate and the Sasanid Empire between AD 563 and 567. But he did not discuss the possible ethnic and cultural consequences of this event, apparently seeing only political significance in the comparatively short episode of the Turkic domination. Frye and Sayili (1943) argued that the Turks were already in "fairly large numbers" in Khurasan and Transoxiana at the time of the Arab conquest, and not so much as nomads, but rather as town and village dwellers. Bosworth (1973) made an attempt at a general evaluation of the scale and effects of the incursion of the Turks into the Islamic lands during the first centuries of Islam. He disagreed with Frye and Sayili, noting that their assertion was hard to prove and that it would still be safer to regard the Turks in the service of Sogdian princes at the time of the Arab conquest as largely mercenary soldiers from the steppes rather than a part of the indigenous population of Transoxiana.

As Bosworth admitted, in the first three centuries of Islam there was some settlement of Turks in the border region of Islamic lands in Transoxiana and Khurasan. Bosworth also mentioned that Soviet archaeology had shown that there had existed Turkic rural settlements in some parts of Semirechye and on the lower Syr Darya. Archaeological evidence, however, is not conclusive, since the methods of attributing various archaeological "cultures" to specific ethnic groups are still much disputed and often arbitrary. At least in the case of the Syr Darya region, the ethnic attribution of the archaeological material does not necessarily follow from the material itself.[5]

One exception to the conclusion that the Turkification of Central Asia during the first three centuries of Islam was insignificant has to do with the situation in Eastern Turkistan. According to a generally accepted view, Turkic sedentary groups were found in the city oases of Eastern Turkistan already in the eighth (second Islamic) century (Gabain 1973:18), and a complete, or almost complete, Turkification of this region took place in the second half of the ninth (third) century, after the destruction of the Uighur qaghanate by the Kirghiz and the mass migration of the Uighurs from the Mongolian steppes to the south. Apart from this political event the early and rapid Turkification of Eastern Turkistan was facilitated by certain ecological and demographic peculiarities of the region. First, owing to the extreme aridity of climate, the oases of Eastern Turkistan were small and isolated, not surrounded by pasture lands that could accommodate any significant nomadic population (as distinct from Western Turkistan); big groups of nomads who migrated to this region therefore had to sedentarize. Second, the sedentary Iranian population appears to have been smaller in the isolated city oases of Eastern Turkistan than in the western part of Central Asia, while the regions of major concentration of nomads were closer to them. Thus, Eastern Turkistan became the first region of Central Asia where the two basic elements of its culture – sedentary Iranian and nomadic Turkic – came together.

The next stage of the Turkification of Central Asia is believed to have been connected with the development of the Mamluk system after the middle of the ninth century. As is well known, the steppe zone of Central Asia was the principal source of supply of Turkic *ghulāms* (slaves)[6] for the armies of Muslim rulers (Ayalon 1976:202–4). The Samanids, who had the best access to this region, profited the most from the slave trade: first, because the transit trade in slaves was an important source of their revenue, and, secondly, because they never lacked new *ghulāms* for themselves. In the Samanid state, earlier than anywhere else in the Islamic world (except the capital of the caliphate), the role of the Turks as Mamluks became extremely important, and the culmination of this peaceful Turkic infiltration of the Islamic lands came with the establishment of the Ghaznavid rule (Bosworth 1973:9), which inherited the Khurasan part of the Samanid possessions.

The question is, however, whether the increasing military and political importance of Turks in the sedentary areas of Central Asia (to which I will return below) was accompanied by a parallel increase in the Turkic population of the region until Turks became a majority. Unfortunately, we do not have the necessary data to resolve this question. We have very little information even about the number of Turkic *ghulāms* in the armies of the Samanids and their successors in the eastern part of the Islamic world. Ayalon in his article on the importance of the Mamluks repeatedly refers to their quantity, but almost always he uses such general expressions as "immense numbers," "innumerable" prisoners of war, "very great numbers," "great force," etc. (Ayalon 1976:204, 207, 210; cf. also Frye 1975a:214). It is not difficult to notice that "these terms imply numbers, and numbers need counting" (Fischer 1970:124), but the data are usually not provided by the sources.[7] Lambton (1975:229–30) made an attempt to evaluate the size of the standing army of the Seljuqs. The highest figure she could find for the time of Malik-Shah (i.e., when the Seljuqs were at the peak of their might) was 40,000 "horses";[8] in the later period, according to her, the standing army of the sultan numbered only 10–15,000. These figures are quite comparable with those given for the Ghaznavid army, which must have been at least no smaller than that of the Seljuqs. The highest available figure (given by Gardizi) for their numbers in 1023, in the time of Sultan Mahmud, is 54,000 (excluding the troops in the provinces and garrisons); for 1036, 40,000 (given by Bayhaqi). Figures for individual expeditions are much lower (Bosworth 1963:127–8). These were the figures for the whole Ghaznavid army, of which the *ghulāms* formed only a nucleus, and not all these *ghulāms* were Turks. We have some figures also for the Samanids and the Qarakhanids: the total number of *ghulāms* of Nasr b. Ahmad (914–43) is said to be 10,000 (Bosworth 1963:100); the Samanid governor of Khurasan, Alp-Tegin, had 2,700 Turkic *ghulāms* (Bosworth 1963:100); the Qarakhanid Arslan Khan Muhammad (1102–30) allegedly had 12,000 *ghulāms* (Barthold 1913:462; Bartol'd 1963a:382n . 5).

When we consider the number of Turkic *ghulāms*, it should be remembered that they were brought to the sedentary regions of Central

Asia (as well as to the other Islamic countries further south) as individuals, without families; when later they could marry, wives apparently often came from the local population. We do not know the size of the population of Central Asia in the ninth and tenth centuries but we may assume that it was hardly less than two million. Even if, to be on the safe side, we take only half of this number, one million,[9] the existence of Turkic Mamluks could not have had a noticeable demographic effect.

Why, then, do the Turks seem to be "lurking everywhere" in Central Asia as early as under the Samanids, especially in the tenth century? Evidently because their military and political role was out of all proportion to their demographic importance, and, being involved in major political events, they were the subject of special interest in all the contemporary chronicles. In the main administrative centers, especially in the capital, Bukhara, where these *ghulāms* were quartered in peacetime, their presence must have been particularly visible.

The Turkification of many areas of the Islamic East (including Central Asia) is usually associated with the conquests and migrations of the Seljuq Turkmens, which started in the early eleventh century. These events for the first time brought to the sedentary countries of the Middle East entire tribal groups of nomadic Turks – not just male warriors, but also their families and livestock. This movement, however, impressive as it was in its far-reaching political consequences, apparently did not involve large numbers of people. The available information about the size of the Turkmen groups that came to Iran with the Seljuqs is, as usual, scarce; but the numbers given on certain occasions in the sources are quite modest, the highest being, probably, 16,000 Turkmen warriors in the battle of Dandanqan in 1040 (Lambton 1973:113). Assuming the commonly accepted ratio of 1:5, the total number of Turkmen tribesmen represented by these warriors would be 80,000.[10] The fact pointed out by Lambton (1973:113), that the Seljuq invasion "seems to have caused remarkably little dislocation, and certainly no more than that brought about by the movement of government troops in the late Ghaznavid period," apparently indicates that the relative number of Turkmens who came with the Seljuqs (together with those who preceded and immediately followed them) was small.

These considerations, however, concern Iran and the lands farther to the west more than Central Asia. In Central Asia the Turkmen migration affected only its south-western corner – roughly, the part which now forms the Turkmen Soviet Republic. Some Turkmen groups (part of almost each of the twenty-four Oghuz tribes) did not penetrate Iran with the Seljuqs but remained in the region which became Turkmenia, being dispersed from the Mangishlaq peninsula to the Amu Darya. There are no data allowing us to make even an approximate estimate of their number and, consequently, of the effect of their migration upon the ethnic composition of that region. Some of them were in close proximity to the small oases along the northern rim of Khurasan, and there are indications (although circumstantial and vague) that sedentary or sedentarizing groups may have appeared among them by the early thirteenth century.

For the Turkification of the major sedentary regions of Central Asia – Transoxiana, Ferghana, and Khwarazm – of far greater importance than the Seljuq movement must have been the Qarakhanid conquest of Transoxiana in AD 999 and the rise of the Khwarazmshahs in the twelfth century. The Qarakhanid conquest, like that of the Seljuq, was apparently accompanied by a migration of entire Turkic tribes, mainly of the Qarluq group, to Transoxiana and Ferghana. Unfortunately, there is no information about their number or their places of habitation and way of life after the migration (we do not know whether they remained nomadic, which is most probable, or began to sedentarize). But it is possible that the proportion of the Qarakhanid Turks in the total population of the western Qarakhanid qaghanate was greater than the proportion of Turkmens in the total population of the Seljuq Empire. It is usually assumed that the period of Qarakhanid rule was an important stage of the Turkification of Central Asia. However, the distinction is not always made between the land of the eastern qaghanate (which had already been Turkified – with the probable exception of Ferghana[11] – before the rise of the Qarakhanids) and the western qaghanate. It is clear at least that in the western qaghanate Persian remained the language of "high culture." It would be pure guesswork to try to figure out to what extent an ethnic intermixture of Turks and Iranians took place under the western Qarakhanids.

The rise of the Anushteginid dynasty of Khwarazmshahs in the twelfth century was accompanied by the arrival in Khwarazm of the Qipchaqs. Nomadic Qipchaqs were the northern steppe neighbors of Khwarazm from the middle of the eleventh century on, but their penetration into the country is related mainly to the reign of

Khwarazmshah Tekesh (1172–1200), who invited them to serve in the Khwarazmian army (apparently in 1182; Bartol'd 1963a:404–5, 413; Bosworth 1975:191). It seems that the Qipchaqs served the Khwarazm-shahs as mercenaries, but were organized in tribal units (although the sources give no direct indication of this). It is not clear whether they were accompanied by their families. The number of Qipchaqs in Khwarazmian service must have been large enough, since it was primarily due to them that Tekesh and his son Muhammad achieved supremacy in Central Asia; but, again, no exact numbers are available. Only a part (and, most probably, a smaller part) of them could have stayed in Khwarazm proper, because they were employed in other regions, especially in Iran. As in the case of the Qarakhanid Turks, it is a matter of conjecture whether a substantial ethnic intermixing between them and the indigenous Khwarazmian population took place. Barthold (1927:909; Bartol'd 1968:119) thought that the country had already been Turkified by the beginning of the thirteenth century, but he did not give convincing evidence to support this opinion, except for the existence of Turkic place-names. But from the evidence of a complete, or almost complete, Turkification of Khwarazm in the fourteenth century one may conclude that this process must have begun before the arrival of the Mongols.

The Mongol invasion brought to Central Asia much greater numbers of inner Asian nomads than ever before. Most of them were Turks, not Mongols; the latter formed only a social and military elite and were very rapidly linguistically assimilated by the Turks. It is with the Mongol invasion that some quantitative estimates of the numbers of inner Asian nomads (Smith 1975; Morgan 1979; Munkuev 1977:393–401) can be made instead of the use of impressionistic terms like "many," "very many," "large proportion," etc. However, these attempts show how precarious such calculations can be, being based on unreliable and incomplete figures that also allow different interpretations. Still, it seems that useful results can be obtained from a cautious and systematic comparison of the available contemporary sources with modern data on population and natural resources (especially pasture lands) in various regions of the Mongol Empire.[12] As long as this systematic work has not been done, the use of impressionistic terms is unavoidable.

Thus, returning to the Mongol conquest, we may only suppose that new and certainly large groups of inner Asian nomads, mainly Turks but some also Mongols, moved into the southern part of Central Asia, their numbers totalling probably more than all the nomads that had penetrated the country previously. A result must have been an increased linguistic Turkification, a process which went faster in the regions that were closest to the areas of major concentration of nomads or were depopulated in the course of the conquest. More or less certain indication of this exists only for Khwarazm. We can doubt that during the thirteenth century there was a substantial intermixture of the sedentary Iranians with the newly arrived Turkic nomads; but such an intermixture could have begun with the earlier arrivals – Qarluqs, Qipchaqs, etc. There is no direct information about this process in the thirteenth century, but this was the pattern which is more or less attested for the Uzbek period, and we may assume that a similar process, under similar circumstances, happened in the Mongol period.

There was no influx of Turkic nomads from the steppes to the sedentary areas of Central Asia during the Timurid time (*c.* 1370– *c.* 1520), which was a period of relative political stability. This stability and the cessation of the wars of conquest were apparently favorable for a gradual sedentarization of the Chaghatai tribes, and were accompanied by the final Islamization of Central Asian nomads and by a growing assimilation of the Chaghatai Turks by the Islamic-Iranian culture. The most visible manifestation of this process was the development of Chaghatai literature and literary language common to all Central Asian Turks. This growing assimilation of the Chaghatai Turks must have facilitated their ethnic intermixing with the Iranians and the spread of Turkic language.

A new stage of the Turkification of Central Asia came with the Uzbek conquest of Transoxiana, Ferghana, and Khwarazm in the early sixteenth century. The question of the number of the nomadic Uzbeks who took part in the conquests of Shaybani Khan has been a subject of concern for modern Uzbek historians. Mukminova (1954:70–81) tried to prove that this number was not large and there-fore the conquest did not substantially change the ethnic composition of the regions affected by it. Mukminova's purpose was clearly to prove that the Uzbek people had a respectable ancient origin and that it was the same old sedentary population of Central Asia, which only adopted the name Uzbek after the Shaybani's conquest. However, both the data on which this conclusion was based and the methods

61

of their analysis were inadequate and could hardly prove the thesis.[13]

The Uzbek conquest was certainly a smaller-scale nomadic movement than the Mongol invasion. However, it brought to the sedentary zone of Central Asia a new wave of Turkic nomads *in addition* to all those who had already been there; and it was followed during the next two centuries by migrations of several other Turkic groups from the steppe, most of whom joined the Uzbeks.[14] Additionally, all nomads brought by the Uzbek conquest to the sedentary part of Central Asia remained there, while only a part of those who had invaded these regions under the Mongols had remained in the *ulus* of Chaghatai. During the same period the nomadic Turkmen population in the south-western part of Central Asia probably grew faster than their sedentary neighbors (cf. Smith 1975:293), and the demographic pressure as well as ecological changes in this area made the Turkmen tribes gradually migrate into the agricultural oases of the northern rim of Khurasan (where they completely replaced the Iranians), into the area of the middle Amu Darya, and into Khwarazm (Bregel 1981:29–30).

The nomadic Uzbeks, having occupied some of the best pasture lands in Transoxiana and Ferghana, either absorbed their Turkic predecessors, the Chaghatais and the pre-Mongol Turks, or (probably more often) pushed them out of the plains towards the western extensions of the Pamirs and into mountain valleys, together with a part of the Tajiks of the plains. As a result of all these migrations accompanied by the gradual sedentarization of the nomads that took place in the sixteenth through the early eighteenth centuries, very complex patterns of settlement emerged in most cultivated areas of Central Asia. Only seldom did there remain regions inhabited by homogeneous ethnic groups, Turkic or Iranian. Much more often they lived interspersed, creating a veritable ethnic patchwork, and thus facilitating cultural and linguistic assimilation.

The linguistic changes, however, did not always have the same form. Turkification took place, probably, in the regions where the Turks had become a majority of the sedentary population in the course of their sedentarization and especially where the Turkic tribal units settled in strong compact groups. In the regions where Turkic (especially pre-Uzbek) groups were surrounded by a numerically larger Tajik population, the Turks were sometimes Iranized. A very common case was also the emergence of bilingual groups, a process that in the opinion of Karmysheva was not a result of a simple influence of Turks upon the Tajiks but a result of their complete amalgamation, a physical merging. The spread of Turko-Tajik bilingualism (still insufficiently studied) was probably the most striking cultural feature of Transoxiana and Ferghana. A similar process had earlier taken place in Khwarazm.

Owing to the linguistic and cultural merging of sedentary Iranian and nomadic, seminomadic and sedentary Turkic groups, which began in the pre-Mongol time but intensified in the Timurid and Uzbek periods,[15] a truly mixed cultural type appeared in most major sedentary areas of Central Asia – Transoxiana, Khwarazm, Ferghana, and Tashkent (Shash). It was basically the same old Iranian population of the region, but strongly influenced by and partly intermixed with the Turks (those who came before the Uzbeks). The degree of this influence and intermixture varied from region to region and, accordingly, this population could be Iranian- or Turkic-speaking or bilingual; but both the physical type and the culture, apart from local variations, were very much the same. In Khwarazm, Ferghana, and Tashkent they were called Sarts, and they were more often Turkic-speaking, but sometimes bilingual; in Transoxiana they were called Tajiks or Chaghatais, and they were more often Tajik-speaking, or bilingual, but some (both among Chaghatais and Tajiks) were also Turkic-speaking. Both basic terms, Sart and Tajik,[16] designated one cultural type rather than an ethnic group, but in some regions they could assume an ethnic meaning.[17] This Sart/Tajik population of the plains remained by and large distinct from both the tribal Uzbeks on the one hand and the "true" Tajiks of the mountainous regions on the other; the latter were very little (if at all) influenced by and mixed with the Turks, and they were known under the names of their local groups (Kuhistani, Kulabi, etc.) rather than under the common name Tajik.[18]

Despite the intensified Turkification of Central Asia, the spread of bilingualism and the emergence of the mixed Sart/Tajik cultural type during the Uzbek period, the "ethnic resistance" of the indigenous Iranian population was rather strong; not only Tajik language, but also Tajik self-identification persisted much longer than is usually assumed. Work done by some Soviet ethnographers since the 1960s clearly shows that until the early twentieth century the percentage of the Tajik population in the Khanate of Bukhara (including the part of it annexed by Russia in 1868) was higher than official and unofficial estimates tended to give. In some rural regions Uzbek replaced Tajik as the spoken language only in the early twentieth century (Karmysheva 1976:141); in the major cities, such as Bukhara and Samarqand, the population has remained predominantly Tajik-speaking until the present time (Sukhareva 1966:123–8, 1982:11). The most recent surge in the Turkification of Central Asia began with the so-called "national delimitation" of 1924, when many Tajik-speaking people in the territory of the Uzbek republic preferred to declare themselves Uzbeks, to belong to the ruling nation of the republic;[19] this tendency increased with the rise of nationalism in the Central Asian Soviet republics.

THE CONSEQUENCES OF TURKO-MONGOL PENETRATION

For almost a century scholars have been occupied with the questions of what the Turks and Mongols brought to Central Asia and the Islamic world in general, and how they affected the subsequent development of the sedentary civilization.

The fundamental feature of the steppe Turks and Mongols that determined the ways in which they influenced the course of history in Central Asia was that they were representatives of inner Asian nomadic civilization. This fact had certainly been more important (until their final sedentarization) than the languages they spoke. Therefore, probably, the whole problem under discussion should be reformulated as "the impact of inner Asian nomads on Central Asian history." The penetration of Turks and Mongols into Central Asia meant, first and foremost, the penetration of nomads. We can consider several spheres – economic, military, political, and cultural – in which the inner Asian nomads may have influenced the course of history in Central Asia and sometimes, from or through Central Asia, influenced the Islamic world in general.[20]

The economic consequences of the penetration of inner Asian nomads into sedentary Muslim countries, of which Central Asia was the first, were for a long time described by modern historians as purely negative. Destructions accompanying nomadic conquests were quite obvious. In one instance, during the Mongol conquests, they reached catastrophic proportions. In other cases their scale was incomparably smaller and, probably, they were not greater than some devastations caused by the armies of sedentary states in the wars between them or by internal disturbances.[21] Still, nomadic conquests and migrations did cause destruction and economic decline, both directly and indirectly. Cities were usually subject to plunder, although intentional destruction, except for the Mongol conquest, was rare. Perhaps more damage was caused to the countryside than to the cities – and in different ways: crops were trampled down and orchards were cut for fuel; some arable lands, abandoned by farmers fleeing from the invaders, remained uncultivated for a long time; the irrigation system was sometimes intentionally destroyed, but probably more often deteriorated because of neglect. As a result of all this, some previously cultivated lands would become waste and fall out of cultivation. When nomads replaced the old sedentary population in the oases, they would first tend to use the irrigated lands as pastures; and if they began to sedentarize, it would take years, even decades, for them to acquire the necessary agricultural skills.

Despite all this, the economic consequences of the penetration of inner Asian nomads into the sedentary regions of Central Asia were probably not entirely negative. It is well known that there existed a symbiotic relationship between nomadic and sedentary societies; the nomads utilized regions which, for ecological reasons, would otherwise remain unused, and economic specialization was favorable for the development of exchange and commerce. Lambton (1973:124) concluded that the Seljuq invasion did not have a negative effect on the economy of Iran; on the contrary, it may well have contributed to the prosperity of the country. Similar situations may have existed in certain regions of Central Asia during the Seljuq–Qarakhanid period. Later, however, with the sharp increase in the number of nomads penetrating the sedentary regions, the situation changed.

Generally, as long as there was enough pasture land around or between the sedentary oases for the arriving nomads, this arrival could be beneficial to the development of commerce and industry and to the growth of cities, which we actually see in Central Asia and Iran during the eleventh and twelfth centuries.[22] When a saturation point was reached, the situation could deteriorate. Political stability was easily upset by the fight for pasture lands between various nomadic groups; the nomads would encroach upon the cultivated lands; this would lead to a decay not only of agriculture but ultimately also of city life, because cities were dependent on their rural surroundings. In Central Asia this critical point appears to have been reached gradually, after the Mongol invasion.

There is a theory, put forth by Barthold and often repeated in modern scholarly works, that the devastating effect of the Mongol invasion on Central Asia and Iran was offset by the establishment of the Mongol world empire, which facilitated international trade and contributed to the rebirth of destroyed cities. This theory has a grain of truth, but is much disputed, and it is difficult to reach an exact balance. Barthold also noticed that when strong central power was absent, a prolonged stay of large groups of nomads in the vicinity of cultivated regions had consequences more disastrous than the invasion itself (Bartol'd 1963b:258; 1966:227). The Mongol invasion, in addition to earlier penetration and invasions of Turks and together with the later Uzbek invasion and Turkic migrations, had a decisive cumulative effect,[23] bringing about a much greater "nomadization" of the sedentary regions of Central Asia; sedentary culture and city life completely disappeared in certain areas.[24] It was only in the nineteenth century, when large-scale sedentarization of these nomads took place, that the economic life of the sedentary areas of Central Asia (with the exception of Eastern Turkistan) could begin to recover from the damaging results of the previous intensive nomadic penetration.

Another sphere of life of Central Asia in which the impact of Turks and Mongols was especially strong was warfare. There is no need to dwell upon the superior military prowess of inner Asian nomads and their inherent military advantages over the sedentary people as this is well known and has been the subject of a number of studies and essays. More interesting questions to me are the changes in the military organization of inner Asian warriors in Central Asia and the changes in their warlike qualities.

Before the Arab conquest Turks were employed in military service in Central Asia as mercenaries in Sogdian principalities. We do not know whether they came as individuals or as members of some tribal or kinship groups, or both.[25] Armies of Turkic qaghanates, mainly western, but sometimes also eastern, also appeared in Sogdiana as Sogdian allies and adversaries of the Arabs. These were apparently organized as tribal troops. But it was a comparatively short episode, and, in any case, the penetration of Turks into the sedentary zone of Central Asia as military force was blocked during the first century of Islamic rule. They reappeared in the middle of the ninth century as slave soldiers: Mamluks, or *ghulāms*.

The Mamluk system was studied especially by Ayalon (1976),[26] who

stressed the great importance of Turks for the emergence and development of this institution in the Islamic world and the importance of
Central Asia as the main supplier of Turkic slaves. According to him,
the Turkic Mamluks were of crucial importance for the whole history
of Islamic civilization. He ascribes this to "the superiority and relative
reliability of the Mamluk system on the one hand, and the far better
military qualities of the human material from which the Mamluk
recruits had been selected on the other" (1976:206). It is not clear,
however, whether Turkic slaves brought with them the fighting
methods they had used in the steppes. Ayalon describes at some length
the evidence of Turkic archery, showing the effectiveness of Turkic
ways of war and Turkic weapons. But the inner Asian nomads, besides
a superior archery, especially from horseback,[27] which was common to
all of them, knew two different (although related) means of battle. One
was based on light cavalry tactics; the other on the use of heavy
armored cavalry, *cataphracti.* These two seemed not to be combined
and were particular to different Turkic groups. The Turks of the
eastern qaghanate had a heavy armored cavalry, like some Iranian
nomads of Central Asia in the first centuries of our era; a similar type
of cavalry existed in Sogdian principalities of pre-Islamic Central Asia.
As distinct from this, the cavalry of the western Turks – those who
supplied slaves for the Mamluk troops – was light and unarmored. But
the Mamluk troops seemed to be heavily armored,[28] and their tactics
apparently were distinguishable very much from those of their Turkic
tribal adversaries (as well as auxiliaries), who are always described as
light cavalry. Therefore we may conclude that the training which the
Turkic Mamluks received was in the Iranian tradition rather than in
that of the western Turkic steppe warriors[29] and their contribution to
the strength of Islamic armies was mainly their military prowess, not
their methods of fighting.

More genuine steppe warfare was introduced in sedentary Central
Asia, as well as elsewhere in the Islamic world, by tribal groups of
Turks – those who came from the steppes in the course of conquests
and migrations. Three times, in three different periods, Turkic and
Turko-Mongol armies, which were organized on a tribal basis, proved
their superiority over the Mamluks: during the Seljuq conquest, during the Mongol invasion,[30] and during the wars of Timur. The Seljuqs
and the Qarakhanids returned to the Mamluk system (but also retaining tribal Turkic troops as auxiliaries) not because the Mamluks were

better warriors than the Turkmen or Qarluq tribesmen, but because the latter became less reliable. After the Mongol invasion the tribal army was the only type of military organization in Central Asia until the nineteenth century.[31] The disappearance of the Mamluks as the elite group of Central Asian armies was a result of at least two circumstances: the conversion of Turks of the Central Asian steppe to Islam, which made impossible their use as slaves, and the saturation of Central Asia by tribal elements as a result of "nomadization." During a fairly long period, the tribal character of Central Asian armies did not affect their military quality, which was well attested in the wars of Timur, and this tribal character was only reinforced by the Uzbek conquest of the sixteenth century.

The military prowess of Turkic and Mongol warriors was due to their supreme horsemanship, archery, and physical fitness produced by training that usually began in early childhood and formed one of the basic conditions of the nomadic way of life, but also by a sense of solidarity and cohesion, based on their social system, that surpassed that of the armies of the sedentary population. Thus, the military importance of Turko-Mongol peoples of Central Asia was inseparable from their nomadic way of life and social organization. When both began to be eroded in the course of sedentarization, military prowess inevitably declined. We see it repeatedly in the history of Central Asia, the best examples being the Chaghatais in Timurid times and the Uzbeks in modern times.

The political role of Turks and Mongols has been a matter of controversy. I have discussed elsewhere (Bregel 1980b:7–8) the effects of the strengthening of nomadic elements, Turks, and Mongols, on the political life of Central Asia. The conclusion I reached there should remain unchanged: although the inner Asian nomads (most notably the Mongols and to a lesser extent some of their Turkic predecessors and successors) were able, in the course of their conquests of sedentary countries, to establish powerful empires, they could not contribute to the stability of political order. Just the opposite: wherever the nomadic political concepts were put into practice more or less consistently, the central power rapidly declined and political disintegration and even anarchy followed. The negative political effects of the "nomadization" of Central Asia, like its negative economic effects, could be overcome only through the suppression of tribal separatism, and this became possible as the nomads sedentarized.

The cultural role of the inner Asian nomads in the history of Central Asia is also rather ambivalent. One aspect of it, their role as intermediaries between the great sedentary civilizations of Eurasia, is well known and examined in scholarly literature (Sinor 1970:104–5; Dörfer 1966). This was their role, however, as long as they remained in the steppe, outside the sedentary regions of Central Asia.[32] It is often assumed that the formation of nomadic empires (which partially included areas of ancient sedentary civilizations) was even more favorable for promoting cultural exchange (Sinor 1970:106) and, therefore, for the general development of culture. It was one of Barthold's favorite ideas that the emergence of the Mongol Empire, which for the first and only time in history included countries of both East Asian and West Asian civilizations, allowed an exchange of goods and ideas on a scale unheard of before and therefore contributed to the expansion of cultural horizons and the flourishing of culture (see Bregel 1980a:388). This assumption, however, is open to doubt. It is difficult to prove that commercial and cultural exchange between east and west would develop more slowly without the Mongol conquest and the establishment of the so-called "pax mongolica." Unless convincing proof to the contrary is provided, one can claim that sometimes political fragmentation can be no less, if not more, conducive to cultural intercourse and expansion than can political centralization. An example of it is provided in the history of Central Asia by the Sogdians, who expanded their activity, which had very important cultural consequences, from China to Sasanid Iran despite (or perhaps owing to) a total lack of political unification in their land.

As to the cultural impact of the Turko-Mongol penetration on the sedentary areas of Central Asia itself, there can hardly be any doubt that it contributed to a general cultural decline, not because of some special ethnic properties of Turks and Mongols,[33] but simply because they penetrated the civilized regions as nomads and "barbarians." The same aspects of their penetration that negatively affected the economy and political life of the region also adversely affected its "high" culture. Not only direct nomadic depredations, but also the lack of political stability and the decline of city life (in the post-Mongol period) had detrimental results for its cultural life.[34] Down to the nineteenth century, the great majority of Turks in Central Asia remained a military estate *par excellence*, socially clearly distinct from the sedentary Iranian population despite all the processes of cultural and linguistic assimila-

69

tion and amalgamation that had taken place. Civil administration and learning remained in the hands of Iranians;[35] these occupations were considered inferior to military service, and Turkic aristocracy as a rule had no incentive to engage in any activity other than the military one (and, of course, ruling, which was in a sense another aspect of military activity). This was one important reason (if not *the* reason) that an interest in science, scholarship, and Iranian literature, even among those nomadic and seminomadic Turks who lived within the borders of Dar al-Islam and in sedentary surroundings for centuries, remained relatively low.[36] The characteristic indifference of the new Turkic rulers toward the "high" cultural forms[37] was coupled with a weakening of the old Iranian urban aristocracy, which had been the principal bearer and transmitter of cultural tradition.

The cultural decline of Central Asia that resulted from the political ascendancy of the Turks and the gradual "nomadization" of Islamic society is evident as early as the first massive Turkic penetration of the sedentary part of Central Asia.[38] In the post-Mongol period the cultural decline of Central Asia is already quite clear. The interlude of the brilliant Timurid culture does not contradict this, because the main centers of this culture were outside Central Asia proper; the flourishing of such a city as Samarqand was due primarily to the people who were brought to Central Asia and left after a short while, though the original political center of the empire was in Central Asia.[39] A connection between nomadization and cultural decline becomes clear enough in the post-Timurid period, when cultural life in the regions of the old sedentary civilization that became most Turkified and at the same time most nomadized reached its lowest level, as in Khwarazm and Ferghana. Of course, it was not the only cause of the decline of Central Asia since the sixteenth century. Other reasons can be pointed out as well, such as the shift in the direction of major international trade routes followed by the rise of European East India companies, whose competition was detrimental for the traditional overland caravan trade (see Steensgaard 1974). Along with other, political, events, this shift resulted in the economic and cultural isolation of Central Asia not only from the rest of the Islamic world[40] and China, but especially from Western Europe – a development that had grave consequences for the region. Central Asia lost its main former advantage as an intermediary and connecting link between the great civilizations of Eurasia. But, besides this global situation, the most important negative factor in Central Asia's *internal* situation was its continuing (through the seventeenth century) nomadization, which came on top of devastations caused by several nomadic invasions.

All this does not mean that the Central Asian Turks did not contribute to the cultural life of the region. But their contribution was in direct proportion to the degree of their sedentarization and integration into the sedentary Islamic-Iranian culture of Central Asia.[41] This process began in Eastern Turkistan in pre-Mongol times, but in Western Turkistan it first became apparent only in the Timurid period. It was interrupted and reversed by the Uzbek conquest; and although it resumed soon after this, it was only in the nineteenth century that the Central Asian Turks became culturally more or less comparable to the Iranians.[42]

There was, however, one sphere of culture in which the Central Asian Turks played a greater role even before their mass penetration into the sedentary areas: Islamic religion. Central Asia almost from the time of its Islamization became a bastion of Sunni orthodoxy and remained that way until modern times. One possible reason for this was the position of Central Asia as a frontier area of Islam, where it had constantly to fight the infidel nomads and therefore could have assumed an especially militant character. The Turkic nomads embraced Islam in the form in which they either encountered it in the neighboring sedentary regions or received it from the missionaries in the steppe. In both cases, apparently, it appeared to be a militant orthodox Sunni Islam (cf. Cahen 1975:323). And when the Turks of Central Asia established their political hegemony throughout the Islamic world, they became a political instrument of reinforcing orthodoxy outside Central Asia. Paradoxically, the Turkic tribesmen themselves (quite similar to the Arab bedouins) have often been considered bad Muslims by the sedentary people, and they have kept many of their heathen beliefs and customs until modern times. It did not prevent them from being, or considering themselves, zealous Muslims, however, be they Sunnis or (as was a part of the Turkmen tribes of Iran and Anatolia in the post-Mongol period) Shi'is. It was the "intensity of faith" (Lewis 1973:190) that mattered, and not the details of religious practice and customary law.

The eleventh and twelfth centuries were the period during which Central Asia became one of the main centers of religious teaching and orthodox Sunni theology in the Islamic world. It was during this period that most of the classical works of Central Asian authors in Sunni *fiqh* and theology were written (Bregel 1980b:6). Religious leaders in Central Asia also acquired great political power in the cities. It is not quite clear what connection, if any, existed between this rise of the influence of Islamic establishment in Central Asia and the political hegemony of the Turks. Frye (1975a:222) supposed that the Qarakhanids in Transoxiana mistrusted the cities and ruled the country from their nomadic encampments, while the vacuum of power in the cities was filled by religious leaders. This remains to be proved. An argument against it may be that apparently the latest evidence of the nomadic way of life of the Qarakhanid khans of Transoxiana refers to the third quarter of the eleventh century (Bartol'd 1963a:378), while the rise of political power of the ʿulamā (the authorities of Islamic learning) of Transoxiana took place only in the twelfth century.

More evident is a connection between the nomadization of Central Asia and another phenomenon in the religious life of this region: the spread of Sufism. That the Sufis exercised much greater influence upon the Turkic nomads of the steppe than the representatives of the official Islamic establishment did, and played a major role in their conversion to Islam, is well known; the reasons have been pointed out (Bartol'd 1968:68; Levtzion 1979:17; Hambly 1969:13–14), though the whole process requires a more thorough study. Only one mass conversion of the Turks of the steppe is ascribed to a historically attested personality: the Golden Horde under Uzbek Khan converted under Sayid Ata, of the Yasaviya order.[43] Yasaviya was also later considered a primarily Turkic Sufi order, although its influence seems to have diminished and been limited mainly to Khwarazm. The Naqshbandiya was predominant in most parts of Central Asia, and, though it first emerged probably among the urban population, it very soon spread to the nomads. If we draw a map of the spread of the two orders in Central Asia in the eighteenth and nineteenth centuries, we will see that, besides the steppes, the sedentary regions where they attained the greatest influence and sometimes even political power (as in Eastern Turkistan and Ferghana) were the regions of complete Turkification.

In Barthold's opinion, the rise of Central Asian dervishism with roots in popular Islam and a hostility to refined urban culture was decisive for the subsequent cultural decline of Central Asia (Bartol'd

1964:121–2, 167). Although this subject deserves a detailed study, the claim seems justified that the spread of Sufism and especially the rise of the power of the dervish orders contributed to the decline of the secular culture.[44]

To sum up what has been said about the consequences of the Turko-Mongol penetration into Central Asia, I would conclude that this process gradually contributed *inter alia* to the political, economic, and cultural decline of the country. The most important advantage of the penetration of these inner Asian nomads into Central Asia, as well as into the Islamic world in general, was an increase in its military strength. With the progressive sedentarization of the Central Asian nomads in the eighteenth and nineteenth centuries, this advantage was lost, while the disadvantages of the whole process of nomadization were still very much in evidence.

NOTES

1. The general character of this essay precludes an extensive documentation. It is not a piece of original research based directly on primary sources, but rather a summary of research done partly by the author but mainly by others. The references are given mostly in cases of polemics, or when facts are mentioned which, in the opinion of the author, have not received proper attention.
2. The Turkmen steppes (mainly, the Karakum desert) can be considered as a south-western extension of the inner Asian steppe belt, but in some important respects this area is similar to other, "enclosed" steppe regions of the sedentary zone.
3. The appearance of the Mongols had the same result, see below.
4. Calculated on the basis of the table in Bruk (1981:207–12), which gives the figures for 1979. On the possible reliability of the official data see below.
5. Tolstov (1947:70) rejected the assumption of Barthold that the settlements along the lower Syr Darya were founded by sedentary people who came to the Oghuz territory, but his archaeological material does not give sufficient basis for an ethnic attribution.
6. The definition of *ghulāms*/Mamluks as slaves was questioned recently (Beckwith 1984).
7. Beckwith (1984:29 n. 2) referred to the notions of great numbers of Turkic nomads – the main suppliers of the Mamluks – as "extremely dubious ideas about the fecundity of Inner Asian peoples."
8. Cahen (1968:38) gives for the cavalry of Malik Shah a figure of 70,000, including tribal troops.

9. This would be, of course, an underestimation. At the end of the nineteenth century, the population of only two khanates, Bukhara and Khiva, was estimated at about three million.

10. The calculation based on the ratio of the number of tribal warriors to the total tribal population as 1:5 is probably exaggerated: in reality the able-bodied males (in the age range of 16 to 60) would form about 30–35 per cent of the total population, which will give the ratio of 1:2.85–3.3. Even if we assume that not all able-bodied males participated in any given military campaign (although they most probably did in important campaigns affecting the whole nomadic group, as in the battle of Dandanqan), the ratio of the number of warriors to the total population should not be higher than 1:4.

11. Most of Ferghana seems to have been included in the eastern qaghanate. It is significant that Babur, writing 500 years later, in his description of Ferghana could tell only about Andijan that its population was completely Turkic.

12. Cf. Morgan's remarks (1979:86–8). J.M. Smith (1975:288, 291, 293) tried to compare the evidence on the Mongols with some modern demographic data.

13. Mukminova claims that "we have a more or less correct idea about the total number of the troops of the so-called nomadic Uzbeks" (1954:75) on the basis of three pieces of evidence: 50–60,000 for 1500 (according to Muhammad Haydar); 100,000 for the whole army of Shaybani Khan (according to Muhammad Salih); 50,000 for 1501 (according to *Tawārīkh-i guzīda-i nusrat-nāma*). Mukminova does not say which of these figures she accepts, but she argues that Shaybani's army included not only Uzbeks and therefore the number of the latter must have been much smaller. She did not take into consideration, however, the subsequent migrations of other Uzbek groups; but even the figures which she mentions are quite substantial (they would make between 200,000 and 400,000 of the total number of Uzbeks, all of whom remained only in Transoxiana and Ferghana).

14. Among them were such numerous groups as the tribes of Manghit *ulus*, many of whom migrated to Khwarazm and Transoxiana in the seventeenth century (Bregel 1982:389), the Qipchaqs, who migrated to Ferghana in the late seventeenth or the early eighteenth century (Shaniiazov 1974:103–4), and the Qaraqalpaqs, who came to Khwarazm and partly to Transoxiana and Ferghana in the eighteenth century.

15. It was probably the pressure of the nomadic Uzbek newcomers that accelerated the fusion of the pre-Uzbek Turks with the Iranians (cf. Karmysheva 1976:145). But the Turkic groups which had remained nomadic until the time of the Uzbek conquest

rather tended to preserve their separate identity or to become assimilated by the Uzbeks.

16. The term Chaghatai in the meaning similar to that of Sart and Tajik was apparently used only in the eastern part of Transoxiana.

17. Thus, the Sarts in Khwarazm were clearly distinct both from all tribal Turks (including the Uzbeks) as sedentary and non-tribal people, and from the Tajiks of Bukhara as Turkic speakers (see Bregel 1978).

18. An excellent study of a very complex ethnic history of the eastern part of Transoxiana during the last centuries was done by Karmysheva (1976:123–61, 258–65); a good summary of data for Transoxiana and Afghan Turkistan is provided in Slobin (1976:66–88).

19. On a great deal of confusion that was caused in Bukhara by the need to decide about national identification see Sukhareva (1966:121–3). The importance of the Iranian ethnic element in Central Asia in the nineteenth and twentieth centuries shown by the works of Sukhareva and Karmysheva (based on solid ethnographic fieldwork) is mostly not mentioned in other Soviet ethnographic literature, or in Western works based on it.

20. I will limit my task to the effects of Turkic/Turko-Mongol penetration into the sedentary areas of Central Asia. Some of these subjects have already been discussed in my lecture on the historical role of Central Asia (Bregel 1980b).

21. Cf., for instance, the self-destruction of some cities of Khurasan in the course of violent factional conflicts of the eleventh and twelfth centuries.

22. It should be noted, however, that the growth of cities could be a result not only of the development of commerce and industry, but also of the influx of population from the countryside, who fled from the depredations of the nomads, as well as the increasing pressure of taxes.

23. See Bosworth (1973:11) on the cumulative effect of the penetration of Turks in pre-Mongol times on the ethnic complexion of the "northern tier of the Middle East." The cumulative effect of such a process on the economy must have been even greater.

24. This was the fate of the regions to the east of the Syr Darya basin already in the late Mongol period. Later the same happened to some regions in the middle and lower course of the Syr Darya and to the area of northern Khurasan (modern southern Turkmenistan). In Khwarazm sedentary culture was in a very deep decay until the end of the eighteenth century and "this ancient home of civilization had become a brigand state" (Barthold 1927:910). The expression "nomadization" used here and further on does not mean a transformation of a sedentary society into a nomadic one, but only the growing share of nomads in the total

population, their political pre-eminence, and their "penetration
. . . into the structure of urban life and civilization" (Lewis
1973:190).

25. They could have been mercenaries or adventurers organized
under temporary leaders, like later Turkmen raiding parties led by
sardārs. See Beckwith (1984) about inner Asian guard corps of
comitatus type.

26. Ayalon (1976) and a number of his other works; see also Bosworth
et al. (1956–).

27. Archery in itself did not distinguish the inner Asian nomads. The
bow was a weapon of both Turkic and Iranian military tradition
(Bosworth 1963:120). Bosworth mentions that the bow came to
the "ancient Iranians" from the north, but in ancient times the
north (i.e., the Central Asian steppes) was inhabited also by
Iranian nomads. "Parthian shot" had become famous long before
the Turks came into contact with Iran.

28. Probably without horse armor (Ayalon 1976:119), although the
information is perhaps insufficient.

29. Cf. the well-known passage in Nizam al-Mulk's *Siyāsat-nāma*
containing a suggestion how to get the young Turkmens enrolled
as *ghulāms* so that they "learn the use of arms and become trained
in service" and will be "organized and equipped like *ghulāms*"
(Nizam al-Mulk 1960:105; cf. Ayalon 1976:215). Apparently, not
only the organization, but also the use of arms and training of the
ghulāms, was seen as different from those of the Turkmens. It
seems that this meaning of Nizam al-Mulk's words has remained
unnoticed.

30. The battle of 'Ayn Jalut of 1260 did not prove the superiority of
the Mamluks, since the forces engaged were too unequal in number, and also for other reasons (see Lewis 1960; Saunders 1977).

31. It was supplemented by local levies and by palace guards consist-
ing of slaves, mainly Qalmaqs and Russians.

32. Nomads also played an important role in the trade within the
sedentary zone of Central Asia, not so much as merchants but as
suppliers of beasts of burden. Most of Central Asian internal
transportation was based on nomadic and seminomadic
stock-breeding.

33. As individuals, Turks and Mongols could be successfully assimilated by the sedentary culture and contribute to its development,
producing outstanding scholars, writers, and artists; but things were
different with the Turko-Mongol nomadic society as a whole.

34. We may probably compare the "barbarization" following the
Turko-Mongol penetration of Central Asia with the barbarization
of the provinces of the late Roman empire.

35. These Iranians could be either Tajik- or Turkic-speaking: it was
social and cultural tradition that was important, not the language.

36. It does not refer to the Ottoman Turks, whose situation was different.
37. There were, of course, exceptions, and some Turkic rulers were both great patrons of literature and art and themselves writers and poets; my remark refers mainly to many Turkic rulers newly established following nomadic conquests.
38. On the beginning of the downward cultural trend in Central Asia in the pre-Mongol period, see Bregel 1980b:5–7.
39. The difference between Transoxiana and Khurasan can be seen already after the death of Timur.
40. The effect of the relative isolation of Central Asia from the rest of the Islamic world should not be overestimated, because the whole Islamic world (especially the immediate neighbor of Central Asia, Iran) was in a state of stagnation and decay.
41. Referring to the contribution of Turks to cultural life, I exclude their "popular culture" (folklore, music, beliefs, etc.), which greatly influenced the indigenous Iranian population of Central Asia. This subject deserves a special study; probably the only existing example of such a study is Slobin 1976.
42. As an indication of this may serve the fact that only in the first half of the nineteenth century two main sedentary areas with Turkic-speaking populations, Khwarazm and Ferghana, produced significant literature in Turkic, and a revival of architecture in these regions took place at the same time.
43. A certain Kalimati, who may have been credited with the conversion of the Qarakhanids, is sometimes mentioned as a Sufi (Pritsak 1951:291). But the only source that mentions him, Sam'ani, speaks of him as a theologian (cf. Bartol'd 1968:74).
44. Cf. the evaluation of the effects of Sufism on culture by Rypka (1968:232–3; unfortunately, some not quite beneficial influence of Soviet writings can be seen here, esp. 233).

4
Islamic culture and literature in Iran and Central Asia in the early modern period

MICHEL M. MAZZAOUI

INTRODUCTORY REMARKS

There is ample justification to treat the subject of Islamic culture and literature in the two regions of Iran and Central Asia in early modern times as one entity. Indeed, there is less justification not to do so. A few remarks will attempt to explain these assertions, and will serve as a general introduction to the subject.

At no time in history has there been a clear demarcation line between Iran and the Central Asian steppes. There are no particular physical features – a range of mountains, a deep river valley, or a large body of water – that divide these two areas or separate them one from the other. There is, however, a well-defined Iranian plateau that ends somewhere in Khurasan, and a flat open country beyond. In one area the Iranians, whose language is predominantly Persian, have lived; and in the other the Turks, who speak Turkish – and beyond them the Mongols. But throughout the centuries, the mixture of peoples and languages was such as to make any clear-cut geographical delineations almost pointless. On the other hand, however, a general distinction between "Iran" and "Turan" has been preserved in the heroic literature and is seemingly engraved permanently on the collective subconscious of the people living on either side of the imaginary border.

There is no reason to belabor the point, or even to discuss where Iran ends in the west (is the Euphrates a recognized historic border?), or where the border line is between the Irano-Turks and their Slavic neighbors to the north, or where Central Asia ends and China begins in the east. It is more significant by far to stress the fact that geographically, ethnically, linguistically, and historically, the two regions of Iran and Central Asia constituted, and continue to constitute, a "culture area" with enduring characteristics, some of which will be touched upon in this essay. The border lines drawn on modern political maps are the artificial inventions of international boundary commissions constituted during the nineteenth and twentieth centuries to serve the imperial interests of colonial powers, with little regard for the local interests of the various communities living in these areas.

The terms "culture" and "literature" have such wide connotations as to defy any limited and meaningful definitions. Within the present context, "Islamic" is the crucial word. Islamic culture is the end result of a centuries-old tradition that goes back to the time, in the seventh century, when Arab-led armies brought to Iran and Central Asia a new religion and a new civilization based on a strongly monotheistic dispensation grounded in the Quran, Hadith, and Sharīʿa. To a considerable extent, this culture was the creation of Iranian Muslim scholars, many of whom hailed from Khurasan in the intermediate region where Iran ends and Central Asia begins. This region played such an important role in the formation, growth, and development of medieval Islamic culture that one may be justified in assuming the existence of a "Khurasan factor" as a basic foundation in the efflorescence of Islamic civilization – a topic which remains substantially unexplored.

The term "Islamic literature", unlike "Islamic culture", is clearly a misnomer; for literature as such can only be expressed in linguistic form; and so we can only talk of literature in Arabic, Persian, or Turkish (or in other Islamic languages). However, Islam as a culture could always be an underlying theme in any of these. In any case, culture and literature will be treated in their wider connotations. In the case of culture, both High Islam and Folk Islam will receive equal attention; in the case of literature, the discussion will not be limited to literary pursuits in poetry and prose but will also cover literature in the

79

humanities, such as historical writings (*tārīkh*), *belles-lettres* (*adab*), and diplomatic correspondence (*inshā'*).

No one seems to know for sure when "early modern times" begin or end. It is suspected that historians use this term to avoid the pitfalls of committing themselves to a specific period, especially when their generalizations do not seem to apply. The "later Middle Ages" is another such undefined time period. "Early modern times" presumably begin when the "later Middle Ages" end.

The conventional division of history into ancient, medieval, and modern (with the thousand years between AD 500 – 1500 constituting the middle period, leaving open-ended the time when it all began and the time when it will all come to a close), does not exactly serve our purposes. And, in any case, the whole concept is Eurocentric, based on the "fall of Rome" in AD 467 and the expansion of the world during the "age of discoveries" with AD 1492 as a major dating point.

Looking at it from the Islamic point of view is more helpful, with the much-maligned date of AD 1258 as a convenient milestone, marking the end of the myth of the Arab Caliphate system, but more importantly, ushering the Mongols into the Muslim ecumene. With this momentous event the history of Iran and Central Asia comes more sharply into focus, and the historian begins to discern what may be referred to as the phenomenon of the gradual rise of dynastic state systems in the Muslim heartlands: i.e., the post-Mongol successor state of the Ilkhanids on the Iranian plateau, the rulership of the Golden Horde lying to the north of the Caucasus range and the Caspian Sea, and the Chaghatai state in Central Asia. This rise incidentally corresponds to that of similar state systems in Europe at about the same time, and is also seen in two other regions of the Islamic world: that of the Ottomans in Anatolia and soon across the Bosphorus; and of the Mamluks, rounding up the major part of the Arab patrimony in Egypt, Syria, and the Holy Cities of the Peninsula.

A conqueror from the east, Timur Gurgan (d. 1405), tries to upset the developing state systems by an attempt at unification from a capital center at Samarqand. His attempt to "settle the Middle East question", however, fails – indicating the strength of the already established political and social orders. The Ottomans recover from his onslaught and re-establish their power and authority in eastern Anatolia and go on, under Mehmed II in 1453, to seize Constantinople, the last vestige of a long-dying empire. The Mamluks consolidate their hold on their possessions in Syria, lost temporarily to Timur, and persist until the Ottomans join them to their empire in 1517.

During the fifteenth century the Timurids (successors to the great conqueror) fail to hold on to their provinces on the Iranian plateau, and the experiment in "state building" continues, hesitantly perhaps but inexorably, under the two Turkmen federations of the Qara-qoyunlu and the Aq-qoyunlu, paving the way for the rise of the Safavids in 1501.

In Transoxiana, Timur's successors (Shah-rukh, Ulugh-bek, Sultan Husayn Mirza Bayqara, and others) maintain their authority in Bukhara, Samarqand, Herat, and elsewhere, and towards the end of the century and the beginning of the next spawn two new power structures: the Uzbeks of Central Asia, and the new dynasty of the Mughals in India.

Thus the confused and sometimes utterly confusing period from, say, AD 1250 to 1500 begins to appear more orderly and directional when considered, as we have tried to do, as the gestation period for the rise of Muslim "state systems." The fog begins to lift about AD 1500 when five discernible "entities" may be counted: the Ottomans, the Mamluks, the Safavids, the Uzbeks, and the Mughals. This historic state of affairs in the Islamic world may be taken to mark the beginning of "early modern times" – a term that will need further qualification later.

Several assertions have already been offered to the effect that, culturally speaking, the entire area from the Euphrates to the Syr Darya, or from Baghdad to Kashgar, enjoyed more or less uniform traditions, at least in Islamic times. It was in the earlier, purely Iranian period of a thousand years or so before Islam that three ancient empires flourished on the plateau (the Achaemenids, the Parthians, and the Sasanids) and the terms Iran and Turan originated. The consistent policies of these pre-Islamic rulers appear to have been to keep the tribal nomads of the eastern steppes at bay, so as to protect the settled communities of the plateau to the west of Khurasan. The ruling dynasts and their war machines looked invariably toward the Mediterranean west: to Greece, Rome, or Byzantium; even to the pre-Islamic Arabs.[1] It took a great conquering visionary like Alexander to venture eastward into the steppes of Central Asia and cross the Indus, bringing Hellenism in his wake to the entire region; or a *jihād*-imbued movement like Islam to carry the seeds of a new civilization eastward into the valleys of the Hindu Kush and the Tien Shan all the way to the Pamirian slopes and beyond.

81

From the Islamic invasion onwards, the orientation of the populations and governing systems faced more decidedly toward Iran, which then became the pulsating center of Islamdom. Bukhara became a "rival" to Baghdad, and Balkh (as Mazar-i-Sharif) became another burial ground of Hazrat-i ʿAlī, the first Imam of the Shiʿa. Persian literature, poetry, and prose, in the acquired "modern" script of the Arabs, appeared in Central Asia for the first time under the Samanids in the tenth/third century. Turkish steppe traditions were developing slowly; and a century later Mahmud of Kashgar, writing in Arabic, gave recognition to the local vernacular in his *Dīvān Lughāt at-Turk*, while the Turkish inhabitants gave expression in an Islamized garb to their heroic traditions in *The Book of Dede Korkut*. Already there were signs that Turkish power (*sultān*) would dominate the region.

By this time, the eleventh/fourth century, the Seljuq Turks had moved westward establishing an Islamic dynasty in which a Turk (e.g., Malik-Shah) ruled, an Iranian (Nizam al-Mulk) administered on his behalf, and a scholar of High Islam from Khurasan (Ghazzali-yi Tusi) wrote seminal treatises in Arabic synthesizing conflicting elements in the religious and theological traditions that would hold for centuries to come. The cultural unity of the Irano-Turkish world thus became secure and attracted and Islamized the next group of steppe people: the Mongol hordes. The Persian language – which by this time was in use among the literate elite from Anatolia to Bengal – served to weld together this unity: the great historians of the post-Mongol period (historians being often the true measures of social and cultural forces), Juvayni, Hamd Allah Mustawfi Qazvini, Rashid ad-Din Fazlallah, Vassaf, and others, as well as later representatives like Mirkhwand and Khwandamir, all dealt with Iran and Central Asia as one regional unit, giving equal coverage to events occurring on this or that side of Khurasan. Iranian poets, too, like the famous Hafiz, sang of the beauty of the *"Turk-i Shīrāzī"* for whose love he would gladly give away "Bukhara, yea, and Samarqand" (*pace* Timur!), and made the "black-eyed beauties of Kashmir and the *Turkān-i Samarqandī"* sing and dance to the music of his poetry. But why not let him say so himself:

Agar ān Turk-i Shīrāzī bi-dast ārad dil-i mā-rā,
Bi-khāl-i Hindu-yash bakhsham Samarqand-o-Bukhārā-rā!
(If the pretty Turkish girl of Shiraz holds my heart dearly, I would, for the Indian beauty spot on her cheek, gladly give away Samarqand and Bukhara!)

And,

Bi-shi'r-i Hāfiz-i Shīrāz mī-quyand-o-mī-raqsand
Siyāh-chishmān-i Kashmīrī-o-Turkān-i Samarqandī!
(To the accompaniment of the poetry of Hafiz of Shiraz, the black-eyed beauties of Kashmir and the Turkish girls of Samarqand will sing and dance!)

At the level of Folk Islam too, Sufis of every color and description, from the great Central Asian saint Ahmad Yasawi (twelfth/fifth century), to Baha ad-Din Naqshband (fourteenth/seventh century), not to mention their close contemporaries Ubayd Allah-i Ahrar and Hajji Bektash, satisfied the needs of Muslim piety throughout Iran and Central Asia despite the formalism of the Orthodox 'ulamā. Mention in this respect ought to be made of Mawlana Jalal ad-Din Rumi who, though born in Balkh, moved westward and finally settled (across the border?) in Seljuq Qonya, and wrote in Persian the greatest Sufi poem ever composed, the *Mathnawī-yi Ma'nawī*. Rumi certainly may be considered the best representative of the cultural unity of the Irano-Turkish world at his time. At a later period (the fifteenth century), Abd ar-Rahman Jami was another illustrious representative of this cultural unity.

Finally, it should be stressed that there is very little justification not to treat this whole region as a single cultural entity, at least till the year 1500. For a short period of a few decades immediately following the campaigns of Genghis Khan (from 1220 till Hulagu's conquest of Baghdad in 1258, and shortly afterwards) the unity of Iran and Central Asia appears to have been irrevocably shaken, and the orientation of the entire region was temporarily redirected eastward, toward Karakorum, following, if you will, in the steps of Marco Polo. But this situation did not last long; for very soon the Ilkhanid successors of Hulagu Khan decided, in a natural process, to break off their ties with the Great Khan in faraway Khanbalik and turn their attention to their newly acquired possessions and subjects. This decision produced great Islamic rulers like Ghazan Khan, Uljaytu Khudabandah, and Abu Said, who reoriented their domains toward the Islamic west. Islam also triumphed in the Chaghatai state and that of the Golden Horde, and henceforth the whole Irano-Turkish region was to remain safely within the fold of Islamic culture until today.

Having presented this introduction to the subject as a whole, I now propose to describe and evaluate Islamic culture and literature in Iran and Central Asia in the early modern period in three phases:

83

1. The period between 1500 and 1800, when the Islamic tradition was still largely independent, unadulterated with ideas originating outside its vast domains.
2. The colonial period of the nineteenth century, during which Islam fought and won its battle for survival against the Christian West.
3. The first two decades of the twentieth century, which witnessed experiments in social and constitutional reforms that came (temporarily?) to an end in Iran under the Pahlavi regime, in Central Asia under Marxism–Leninism, and in Afghanistan because of a widespread rebellion.

The discussion focuses on social and cultural developments in Iran and Central Asia. The political and chronological framework will serve to highlight the cultural continuities.

ISLAMIC CONTINUITIES DURING THE PRE-COLONIAL PERIOD

There are strong and reasonable indications that the year AD 1500, or thereabouts, ushered important and radical changes into the central lands of the Muslim world. This is the period of the sea voyages and great discoveries, of Vasco da Gama, Columbus, and Magellan, to which the modern Space Age has sometimes been compared. To quote A. J. Toynbee (1953:67–9), "Since AD 1500 the map of the oecumene has indeed been transformed out of all recognition . . . Steppe-traversing horses, not ocean-traversing sailing ships, were the sovereign means of locomotion by which the separate civilizations of the world as it was before AD 1500 were linked together . . . The Steppe ports were put out of action when the ocean-going sailing ships superseded the camel and the horse." One might add that the concept implied in the term "Mediterranean" became almost overnight anachronistic: the "center of the world" had shifted to the Atlantic.

Applied to the central Muslim lands, these momentous changes are said to have sealed the fate of Islamic civilization which, we are told, headed towards a long process of disintegration, decadence, and decline. Some have even dated this unfortunate state of affairs as beginning with the devastating Mongol invasions during the first half of the thirteenth century, if not earlier. Europe and the West, on the other hand, witnessed a great efflorescence marked by such movements as the Renaissance and the Reformation, changes in international trade and commerce, and the scientific revolution, culminating in the eighteenth-century period of the Enlightenment which led directly to the American and French Revolutions of 1776 and 1789 respectively. The two great civilizations, Western Christian and Eastern Islamic, confronted each other toward the end of the eighteenth and the beginning of the nineteenth century. Napoleon Bonaparte landed in Egypt, the heart of the Muslim world, in the summer of 1798, later sending his emissaries to Iran in search of political and commercial ties; the Russians even earlier began to push southward against Iran and Central Asia; while the British had already carved out a sizeable chunk of India, and were soon to lay claim to the entire subcontinent. Portuguese, Dutch, and other European nations had already established mercantile colonies here and there along the Asian shores.

It was clear that by 1500 the central Islamic lands had separated quite naturally at the seams, so to speak, into five entities. The Ottomans held Anatolia and the lands further to the north-west; the Mamluks, the Arabic-speaking areas of Egypt, Syria, and the Hijaz (soon to be annexed to the Ottoman empire, but nevertheless maintaining a considerable degree of independence); the newly founded state of the Safavids, the Iranian plateau; the Timurid-Uzbek successor state, Central Asia; and the Mughals, India. The system of government in all five areas was Perso-Turkic: it was based on the regulations of High Islam, Persian bureaucratic administrations, and Turk-Mongol dynastic authority.[2] Culturally, the Muslim communities in these five "states" enjoyed uniform Perso-Arabic traditions based on the fundamentals of Arabic religious literature and *adab*, and developed through Persian diplomatic *inshā'*, with Turkish language and customs gradually gaining equal prevalence. The Islamic Quran-Hadith-Sharīʿa tradition was by far the most important single rallying point, both at the High Islam level of mosque and *madrasa* (school), and at the Folk Islam level of *tarīqa* (Sufi organization) and *khāniqā* (Sufi convent). This situation prevailed roughly from 1500 to 1800, when it abruptly came to an end under the superior power of a revitalized West.

The political and dynastic history of this period has mainly focused on life at court and the interminable intrigues of the harem, but the social and intellectual history has been largely ignored. Innumerable sources wait to be edited and their contents profitably explored. The

85

dearth of studies on this period makes it difficult for the historian or social scientist to draw any meaningful conclusions.[3]

One of the most significant events that occurred during this period was the establishment in Iran of a Shi'i *ithnā'asharī* ("Twelver") state under Shah Isma'il in 1501. Shi'ism certainly was not a new phenomenon in Islamic history. Shi'i mythology, the outcome of theological and eschatological arguments propounded by great religious scholars, grew with the rise of Islam: and while Muhammad, the Prophet of the new dispensation, was (simply) a *rasūl*, a "messenger" of God, 'Ali, the founder of Shi'ism, was made to be the *walī* of God, His "friend" and "custodian" of the faith. From the beginning the Shi'i followers of 'Ali contested the leadership of the community with the mainstream Sunni majority. They failed and were endlessly persecuted, although certain branches of the Shi'a (notably, the Isma'ilis and Zaydis) enjoyed a few memorable successes.

But the largest branch of the Shi'i movement, the *ithnā'asharīs*, first seized the leadership of the Muslim community when Shah Isma'il rose up in 1501 to claim an authority going back to a Sufi *pīr* of the post-Mongol period (Sheikh Sāfi ad-Dīn Ishāq Ardabilī), and with the help of Turkmen converts to his cause (the Qizilbash tribal chieftains of the Qara-qoyunlu and Aq-qoyunlu federations of the fifteenth century) gained power in Iran, and announced the *ithnā'ashari* dawn of a new age. The origins of the Safavid movement, which under Shah Isma'il's influence turned into a powerful political and military force, have been quite extensively recounted, although certain aspects of it remain obscure.[4]

Shah Isma'il's neighbors to the east, the Uzbek successors of the Timurids, as well as his neighbors in the west, the expansionist empire of the Ottoman Turks, all ardent Sunnis, used the rise of the new Shi'i state as a pretext to attack it and try to extinguish the flame before it spread. (The rise of, and current problems facing, the Islamic Republic of Iran have been compared to those of Shah Isma'il and the Safavids.) The Ottomans almost succeeded under Sultan Selim, but Shaybani Khan (Uzbek) failed, losing his life and his head in the process. Safavid power with its distinctive Persian-Shi'i culture, however, remained a middle ground between its two mighty Turkish neighbors.

Aside from its Shi'i fervor, the Safavid state, which lasted at least until 1722, was essentially a "Turkish" dynasty, with Azeri Turkish

(Azerbaijan being the family's home base) as the language of the rulers and the court as well as the Qizilbash military establishment. Shah Isma'il wrote poetry in Turkish. The administration nevertheless was Persian, and the Persian language was the vehicle of diplomatic correspondence (*inshā*), of *belles-lettres* (*adab*), and of history (*tārīkh*). The suffocation felt as a result of excessive religious observances (the Safavid shahs were quite serious about their Shi'ism) led many writers and poets to seek shelter and more freedom outside Iran. Fazl Allah ibn Ruzbihan Khunji, for example (a great Sunni-Shāfi'ī court historian, *munshī*, of the late Aq-qoyunlu state and author of the well-known *Tārīkh-i 'ālam-ārā-yi Amīnī*, a work that contains unique information on the rise of the Safavids), escaped to Uzbek territory in Transoxiana and accepted employment at the Uzbek court. At the same time, many Iranian poets fled to the Mughal courts of Babur, Akbar, and Humayun, where a new style of Persian poetry, the so-called *sabk-i Hindī*, was developed.

It was about this time in Central Asia (when Abd ar-Rahman Jami, usually considered the last great classical Persian poet, was writing most of his work at the court of the Timurid Sultan Husayn Mirza Bayqara in Herat) that Chaghatai Turkish literature came into its own with such celebrated writers as Mir 'Alī Shir Navai and Babur. Later Uzbek rulers like Shaybani Khan, Ubayd Allah Khan, and others, wrote poems in Chaghatai – a phenomenon which, if one bears in mind similar activity by other potentates such as Shah Isma'il, Sultan Selim, Jahan-Shah Qara-qoyunlu, or Mehmed Fatih, makes one wonder how these "warrior kings" spent their leisure time. To them, campaigning seems to have been a royal sport, most probably part of their Turko-Mongol heritage from the steppes of Central Asia. These highly cultured Safavid, Ottoman, Uzbek, and Mughal rulers, as well as their contemporaries in Mamluk Egypt, were veritable "Renaissance" figures. Their capital cities – such as Istanbul, Bursa, and Edirne for the Ottomans; Tabriz, Qazvin, and Isfahan for the Safavids; Bukhara, Samarqand, and Herat for the Uzbeks; Agra, Lahore, and Delhi for the Mughals; as well as Cairo, Damascus, and Aleppo for the Mamluks – were great centers of Islamic culture that could hold their own compared with the great Renaissance cities of Western Europe. The architectural monuments in these great metropolitan centers have survived in all their beauty and splendor.

In spite of these and other cultural achievements, both Western (orientalist) and Eastern (Islamic) writers alike continue to talk of a period of decline (*ʿasr al-inhitāt*) culminating in the eighteenth century. This thesis, at least at the intellectual level, is no longer defensible. A closer look at the Muslim world, including Iran and Central Asia, during the eighteenth century (the last period of "decline" just before the West makes its long-awaited epiphany) provides a totally different picture. It is clear from a cursory review of the works of many Muslim writers (especially those that were not closely attached to the so-called Religious Institution) of this period that the Muslim world was undergoing a process comparable, if not similar, to the period of the Enlightenment in Western Europe that produced the French Revolution.[5]

A remarkable aspect of Muslim eighteenth-century intellectual activity may be seen in the continuing importance of centers of learning. We are told, for example, that "Educational institutions [of the *madrasa* type] in Khiva, together with Bukhara, had an especially high reputation. Students came to them from India and Kashmir, from Russia and eastern Turkistan. Tradition has it that the total number of theological students round about 1790 was approximately 30,000" (Spuler 1970:479). And *"The Spectator,* in describing Wolff's travels [A *Mission to Bukhara,* 1969, first published in 1845] summed it up by saying that Bukhara was the Muslim Oxford" (Wint 1969:28).

This intellectual activity could be seen in Iran where both Nimat Allah al-Jazaʾiri and Muhammad ʿAli "Hazin" left autobiographical sketches demonstrating aspects of Islamic *humanitas.* "Hazin," because of his ideological opposition to the arbitrary policies of Nadir Shah Afshar, was described as "a liberated and free person" by a British orientalist contemporary. Nadir Shah himself held at mid-century an ecumenical council in a half-hearted attempt to reconcile Sunni-Shiʿi doctrinal differences, at which a large contingent of ʿulamā from Transoxiana participated. A not exactly impartial *hakam* from Baghdad, the historian Sheikh Abd Allah as-Suwaydi, kept a diary of the deliberations – itself a very interesting document on a highly sensitive subject.

In Shiʿi studies proper (the hallmark of Islamic culture in Iran) a high point was reached at the beginning of the eighteenth century with the works of the celebrated scholar and popularizer Muhammad Baqir Majlisi. His *Bihār al-Anwār,* a veritable compendium of Shiʿi knowledge and learning (not long ago republished in more than one hundred volumes) has not been superseded. But the tradition was maintained; and works by Bihbahani (Agha Muhammad Baqir) and Bahr al-Ulum (Agha Sayyid Muhammad Mahdi) preserved the continuity between the Safavid and Qajar periods.[6] The theological struggle between traditional *akhbārī* positions and innovative *usūlī* ideas, a system peculiar to *ithnā'asharī* Shi'ism, continued unabated. Sheikh Ahmad-i Ahsai, who may be said to represent one of the highest achievements in *usūlī* dogmatics, developed at this time the extremely original concept of the *shi'ah-yi kāmil* (the perfect Shi'i) – a concept which found its natural expression at the hands of Sayyid 'Ali Muhammad the Bab, and ultimately sparked the creative impulse behind the Babi-Bahai faith in the second half of the nineteenth century.[7]

Evidence, therefore, on the eighteenth-century intellectual ferment in Iran and Central Asia (and in fact also in other regions of the Muslim world) suggests the existence of an active and productive tradition of thought and ideas which was in the process of becoming a new and unified intellectual movement, and which might be expected to have led to radical or evolutionary changes in the political, social, and cultural life of Muslim societies. At exactly this time the West came with its armies of occupation, its administrators, and its new approach to life. Muslim ideas of change had, under the circumstances, no chance to grow and develop in their own homeland away from the new and different ideas "imported" from the West. It may be that the progressive movement among the eighteenth-century Muslim intellectuals was arrested by the Western intrusion.

NINETEENTH-CENTURY SECULAR REFORMS AND ISLAMIC SURVIVAL

The nineteenth century, the height of world domination under the colonial system, witnessed the encirclement of the Muslim world from Morocco to India and from Turkey to the Yemen by the ever-expanding European powers. (The newly independent United States showed up briefly very early in the century, landed a few marines on the African shore in Tripoli, and left – not to be heard of until the two World Wars.[8] Its missionary activity, however, played a very important role during the high colonial period.)

In Iran, the French emissaries of Napoleon who rushed there as early as 1807 were soon displaced by the more ambitious British and the "neighborly" Russians; and the few French mercenaries who had

89

come to help Tippu Sultan in the last Muslim resistance on the southern tip of India were dispersed. Henceforth all India was to become the "jewel" of the British crown. To the north, the Tsarist empire, which had long before incorporated the remnants of the Golden Horde (in Kazan, the lower Volga, and Astrakhan), was pushing toward the more southerly regions of the Crimea, the Caucasus, and Central Asia. This confrontation with Russia in the north and Britain in the south was to last well into the twentieth century. Here we consider both its secular and its religious aspects in the nineteenth century.

At the secular level, the most important outcome of the growing contacts between the traditional Muslim societies in Iran and Central Asia and their neighbors to the north and south was the introduction of new ideas originating in post-French Revolution Europe. In Iran, these contacts (plus the celebrated defeat of Russian, i.e., European, armies at the hands of Asiatic Japan in 1905) eventually brought about the great Constitutional Revolution. In Central Asia, the main development was the slow but pervasive Russification of the land.

The process of change was slow but inevitable. In Iran, it started, naturally enough, with immediate steps to revamp the military establishment. This was crucial for the newly established Qajar dynasty in order, it was hoped, to stem the aggressive expansion of Russian forces in the Caucasus region (where there was a traditional enclave of Iranian presence). Although there were minor successes, the experiment failed: the Christian areas of Georgia and Armenia became "independent" under Russian orthodox tutelage; more seriously, the northern part of Muslim Azerbaijan (including Shirvan, Daghestan, and the old Islamic center of Baku) came under direct Russian control.

However, the attempt to improve the fighting power of the Persian army (training, weapons, uniforms, tactics, etc.) opened the door wide for other necessary and related changes. Young men were sent to Europe in order to "learn the ways of the West"; a translation process was started to put "the books of the West" into understandable Persian; and a movable-type printing press was devised to put the new books into wider circulation. One of the earliest books ever to be printed in Iran (perhaps the very first) was Abd ar-Razzaq Dunbuli's *Ma'āthir-i Sultāniyah*, a primary source of great importance for understanding the Western impact on Iran in the early nineteenth century.[9] Dunbuli deals primarily with the rise of the Qajar dynasty in the early nineteenth century and the reign of Fath ʿAli Shah, and the governorship in Azerbaijan of his son Abbas Mirza, the first great reformer in Iran in modern times; but his descriptions of the government systems in France, Britain, and Russia though understandably awkward are full of informative details indicating a wide knowledge of European affairs. The educational missions, returning from Europe with more Western ideas, helped create a local intelligentsia which, cooperating with the other classes of society, put an end to the arbitrary rule of the Qajar shahs, and established in 1905–6 a constitutional form of government that emulated European models.

In Central Asia, the centralizing might of the Russian Tsars and their governors-general in the Caucasus and in the steppes did not allow much change and development in the traditional Muslim regimes that came under their rule or influence. Very little in the way of transformation from absolute rule to representative government took place in the central Asian khanates of Khiva, Bukhara, and Khokand, when compared with conditions in Iran (or in the Ottoman Empire and Egypt for that matter). Autocratic Russia felt much safer with absolutist regimes under its wing. In fact, the Russian government tried to subvert the Iranian constitutional system by supporting a counter-revolution under the deposed Shah.

Rather than permitting their Central Asian appanages to experiment in constitutionalism, the Russians had for a long time attempted to bring that region and its inhabitants more closely into the Russian fold. The process of Russification of Russia's Muslim subjects was under way when Kazan (in 1552) and Astrakhan (in 1557) fell under direct Russian rule. Orthodox Russian missionaries were permitted to operate in the conquered areas and among their Muslim inhabitants. More serious than this rather ineffectual proselytizing activity (it is indeed surprising how adamant Muslims are against converting to the Christian or any other religious system!) was the tremendous influx of Russians to the occupied territories, and the ultimate dispersal of the original Muslim inhabitants to points further south and ultimately to Central Asia. This was a slow process at first, but it gained momentum when the Central Asian steppes of Kazakhstan, Uzbekistan, and Turkmenistan were opened to Russian immigrants in the nineteenth and twentieth centuries. This led gradually to Russians having substantial majorities in most areas previously inhabited totally by Muslims, especially in such great urban centers as Kazan, Astrakhan, Tashkent, Samarqand, Bukhara, Dushambe, and others.

The Russification process, naturally enough, led to a fundamental and radical change in the outlook and orientation of the people of Central Asia (and of other Muslims under Russian domination). For, whereas Iranians (Turks, Egyptians, North Africans, and Indians too) were attracted to Western Europe in search of the secrets of European progress, their Muslim brothers in Central Asia looked towards Mother Russia for learning and enlightenment. Henceforth, Russian language, literature, and culture begin to dominate the intellectual climate of opinion of Central Asian Muslims; and the two movements of nationalism and socialism (communism) that begin to grow toward the end of the nineteenth and the first decade of the twentieth century were essentially the outcome of the increasing contacts between ambitious young Central Asian figures and their counterparts in the northern Russian cities. A look into this development will be attempted below. Suffice it to say now that the radical change of direction and orientation of Central Asian Muslims from Iran and the central Muslim lands toward Russia and the north marked a serious break in the overall traditional "unity" and cultural integration of the Muslim world. A few minor and ineffectual exceptions to this directional change will be noted in due course.

At the religious level the situation was quite different. Central Asian Islam, the basic constituent in the "unity" and cultural integrity of Central Asian societies, survived the tremendous adverse forces of the colonial period, and continued to characterize the everyday life and attitudes of Central Asian Muslims. In this, Central Asia shared the same experience of Muslims in Iran, as well as colonized Muslims everywhere. Clinging to Islam (a phenomenon based primarily on the oneness of the faith during the prophetic, medieval, and later times – Shi'i Iran notwithstanding – and grounded in the tremendous weight of the nostalgic greatness of the system and its glorious history going as far back as the "golden age of Medina," a kind of collective subconscious) was essentially a formidable reaction to the hated Christian infidel, and an expression of near fatalistic satisfaction that God will provide the best for His true believers. This deep rejection, at the religious level, of Western Christian ideas and ideals, often defensive and polemical, was clearly demonstrated in the failure of conversion attempts by Christian missionaries who flooded the entire Muslim world in the wake of the colonial armies.

This fundamental oneness found political expression in what came to be known as Pan-Islamism, a movement that developed in the second half of the nineteenth century when it became progressively clear that the colonial menace could be effectively opposed only through the mobilization of the one single force that had so far withstood its formidable encroachments. The standard bearer of this movement was a certain Sayyid Jamal ad-Din "Afghani" Asadabadi – a political opportunist to his numerous detractors, but a great Muslim *jihād*-fighter to his many students and followers. Afghani moved incessantly from one Muslim capital to another (and included Western Europe and Russia among his travels), preaching the unity of Islam everywhere and opposition to Western European presence. In Iran he tried more than once to cooperate with the ruling Qajar dynast (Nasir ad-Din Shah) but found no heedful ear; and from Afghanistan, while appeals were being sent to Istanbul for assistance against Russian encroachments, he tried to reach Bukhara – "a city Afghani already cites as his goal in a poem written before he reached Afghanistan" (Keddie 1983:16).

The Muslim world probably did not need an Afghani to arouse its resistance to the Christian West at the religious level. Islam already had its redoubtable class of *'ulamā*, the most formidable religious machine and the most powerful "defenders of the faith" that ever existed. Whether they were true believers of the faith, or were defending their own selfish interests (seriously shaken by the apparent victory and unwelcome presence of the accursed infidels), the Muslim *'ulamā* rose to the occasion and, as in the case of Iran during the Tobacco Revolt, or a few years later during the Constitutional Revolution, assumed the role of leadership against both the external danger of the West and the internal "injustice" (*zulm*) amounting to oppression by the ruling monarchs. In spite of their inefficiency and, at times, their inveterate obscurantism, they continue to be the guiding light of Muslim communities everywhere. But by the end of the nineteenth and early twentieth centuries the two world-shaking movements of nationalism and socialism were fast catching up with the religious fervor heretofore exhibited in Muslim societies. The First World War was on the horizon, and the Muslim world was to be one of its major battle fronts. Islam was placed temporarily in cold storage, and secular leaders began to search for accommodation between national con-

93

sciousness and the great Islamic substratum that seemed to be out of vogue in the struggle against colonial occupation. There was also a new spirit of independence based on national sovereignty and ethnic homogeneity. The Ottomans were becoming Turks (after toying for some time with the idea of holding together their different *millets* [religious communities] under the shaky banner of Ottomanism), and the Egyptian and Syrian subjects of the Ottoman Empire were becoming Arabs. The Iranians thought that they were really Aryans; and the Tartars, Kazakhs, Uzbeks, Kirghiz, and Turkmens were becoming Central Asian Turks. The ideologies behind these various differentiations were also imported from Europe; and so the European colonialists (British, French, or Russian) had to face a new and more formidable menace.

CONSTITUTIONALISM AND RUSSIFICATION

In spite of the fact that the Prophet and the early Muslim leaders were able to create a homogeneous community of believers (*ummah*), and in spite of exhortations, Quranic, Hadithic, or otherwise, that all Muslims are equal in the eye of God and that "the best among you, in God's estimation, are those who are most pious," Islam never really obliterated differences among the various communities who embraced the new faith. Arabs, Persians, and Turks (and others), remained ethnically and linguistically different under the umbrella of Islam and within the melting pot of Islamic culture. The Arabs were proud that Islam was an Arabian invention, and the Iranians never forgot their great pre-Islamic traditions which Firdowsi sang for them, in High Islamic times, in the beautiful poetic cadences of the great *Shāhnāma*. The Turks too, the great warriors of the steppes, were almost haughty in the assumption that they inherited the *jihād* fighting spirit of the tradition and carried it half-way into Europe. But all these concepts are essentially romantic, and people's unity as members of one Islamic community remained the dominant theme for centuries.

Mention was made earlier of the gradual formation of dynastic state systems during the post-Caliphal period following the Mongol conquests. This phenomenon, it was pointed out, came into sharper focus by 1500 when five distinct dynastic empires (Ottoman, Mamluk, Safavid, Uzbek, and Mughal) shared the central regions of the Muslim

94

world among them, and continued to be dominant, each in its own area, until about 1800 and the coming of the West. Nevertheless, and in spite of these divisions (in many cases artificial), Islam remained a strong binding force among the various communities within these five empires, and Islamic intellectual activity (as was briefly argued earlier for the eighteenth century) manifested a certain degree of inventiveness and originality that might have produced a much needed change had not the West totally overwhelmed the entire Muslim world.

Among other things, the West brought with it the new and more elaborate concepts of nationalism and socialism. According to ideas originating, among other currents, with the French Revolution, man was henceforth to become a "citizen" of a nationalistically defined state with inalienable rights, duties, and responsibilities. After a period of approximately one century (the nineteenth) these ideas finally hatched among most Muslim societies and became explicitly pronounced towards the end of the nineteenth and early in the twentieth century. Muslim societies who attempted to fight the colonial powers with the sword of Islam (e.g., Afghani and his Pan-Islamic movement), now found a much sharper weapon, this time borrowed from the West itself. Nationalism and national consciousness were destined to dig the grave in which colonialism was to find its resting place.

The clearest manifestation of nationalist consciousness in the Muslim world appeared in the Ottoman Empire, first in the form of Ottomanism (an amorphous concept aimed at including all the *millets* that constituted the empire), and soon afterwards in the form of the more doctrinaire concept of Turkism (to which only "Turks", properly defined, could belong). These movements, the most significant aspect of which was the distinct attraction they had for the "Turks" of Central Asia and those of Iranian and Russian Azerbaijan, were drowned in the torrent of the First World War, especially when the Arab subjects of the Ottoman Empire seceded, soon to fall prey to the last phase of Western colonial rule. Immediately thereafter, one of these movements (Turkish nationalism) was effectively utilized as the rallying point for the creation of a new Turkey by one of the most notable nationalist figures of modern times, Ghazi Mustafa Kemal "Ataturk."

The other, and perhaps more complex, manifestation of nationalism was that which grew among the Arab communities of the Middle East at about the same time. This movement (which coalesced in the so-called Arab Revolt of 1916) was also extinguished by the secret policies of the victors of the First World War (in this case Britain and France). Since then, much blood has been spilled on the altar of Arab nationalism, and countless books written to discuss and explain its course; but its future remains uncertain.

In Iran and Central Asia, the road to nationalism took slightly different turns. Iran as a continuously independent country (at least since 1500) did not seem to need the spirit of nationalism to fight a physically non-existent colonialist power (although Britain and Russia behaved as occupying powers in everything except in name). Iran's problems were internal, and the need at the turn of the century was for some form of constitutional government. A healthy spirit of "constitutionalism" rather than "nationalism" seemed to pervade the country around 1900. So, working together, the Iranian intellectuals, religious scholars, and merchant groups (*rūshanfikrān*, *ʿulamā*, and *bāzārīs*) wrested their prized *mashrūtiyat* (constitution) from the teeth of their indolent shahs and established, against tremendous odds, a constitutional form of government. The system worked hesitantly at the early stages, voting down the Anglo-Russian Agreement of 1907, which would have placed Iran firmly in the colonized camp (the term used was the ubiquitous "spheres of influence"), and successfully resisting the Russian-inspired counter-revolution of Muhammad ʿAli Shah (condoned, some say, by the British Foreign Office). But then the experiment faltered: after all, it was a novel thing in an Islamic country, although the Shiʿi establishment accepted the theory of constitutional government in the absence of the "occulted" Twelfth Imam, and participated actively in its course.[10] The complete disruption of life and institutions during the First World War, and the interventionalist policies of the Allies against Russia's October Revolution after it, brought the constitutional experiment in Iran to a halt. This led directly to the rise of Reza Shah, who based his rule on nationalist policies and effectively stifled the constitutional spirit of the people until his abdication in 1941.

The ideology of nationalism in Central Asia, on the other hand, came from the north where Central Asian intellectuals had gone after their countries were annexed to Russia during the nineteenth century. This nationalism differed from the nationalism that grew in the Ottoman Empire and in the Arab lands, and from the constitutionalism that we saw in Iran, in that it came down to the Central Asian Turks diluted with ideas of socialism already prevalent in Russia. Still in its early stages, it shared with the rest of the Muslim world many of its basic components.[11] Ideas of religious reform, national consciousness, and socialist justice seemed to go hand in hand among the various Muslim communities of Central Asia. Thus, the Central Asian poet Abd ar-Rauf Fitrat exclaimed in a poem "which became almost a popular anthem" among Central Asian Muslims:

Turkic people, oh great people, open your eyes!
Open your eyes and see the world for the first time!
Kindle the glowing fire into flames:
Not one tyrant in Turkistan!

And another poet, Hamzah Hakim-zadah Niyazi, "also expressed the spirit of protest in a poem called 'Turkistan' which was sung 'in every street, square, and theatre in the land' ":

The tyrants are pouring from the skies,
But my people sleep for ever.
They are inert, like a lifeless body;
They don't bleed if you stab them![12]

This sentiment was shared by a poet from Iran (Mirza Agha Khan Kirmani, in 1896), a country resisting encroachments from both Russia and Britain:

Ne'er may that evil-omened day befall
When Iran shall become the stranger's thrall!
Ne'er may I see that virgin fair and pure
Fall victim to some Russian gallant's lure!
And ne'er may Fate this angel-bride award
As serving-maiden to some English Lord!

(Translated by Browne 1910:xi).

Innumerable poets sang similar songs almost in unison, and their voices rang throughout the length and breadth of the Muslim world. Islamic religious fervor, followed by the growth of national consciousness and cries for social justice, paved the way for ultimate national sovereignty and independence.

The concept of Islamic unity, however, suffered an irretrievable loss. This was because the fate of Central Asian Muslims and of other Muslims in Russia was affected by policies, events, and developments peculiar to the northern context. The main influences were the following.

First, the areas inhabited by Muslims were colonized, Russified, and acculturated. This process started with the beginning of Russia's expansion, and ultimately, on the basis of the well-known colonial policy of "divide and rule," created serious differences among the various Muslim groups themselves, specifically among the Volga and Crimean Tartars, the Azerbaijani Turks in the Caucasus, the Kazakhs, and the Turks and Tajiks in Eastern and Western Turkistan. The schisms among these groups worked against any possible collective action by them against the Russians. And while it has been asserted that "the capitals of the south had little to learn from Moscow" (Allworth 1967:35), the statement made by Engels in a letter to Marx in 1851, that "For all its baseness and Slavonic dirt, Russian domination is a civilizing element . . . in Central Asia" (quoted in Allworth 1967:37) is perhaps a more applicable assessment of the encounter between the two cultures.

Perhaps the most significant aspect of this Russification process is the attraction of young Muslim scholars from the south to study in the Russian cities of the north. This process was similar to, but intrinsically different from, what was going on at the same time in other Muslim countries, e.g., Turkey, Iran, Egypt, North Africa, India, etc., as the students from these countries received their ideas directly from Western Europe whereas those from Muslim Central Asia received them only as they were perceived and assimilated through Russian culture. The "civilizing mission" of Mother Russia was expressed in its strongest terms by the conquering generals of the Russian armies of occupation. General Gorchakov, for example, called the conquest of Tashkent in 1865 "a civilized mission," as "Asiatic peoples respect nothing but visible and palpable force" (quoted in Rywkin 1982:11). The great Tolstoy said in 1850 what many Russians took as their civilizing responsibility: "With all my strength, I will assist with the aid of a cannon in destroying the predatory and turbulent Asiatics" (Wolff, quoted by Wint 1969:23).

Having noted certain Russian colonialist views on imperial Russia's "civilizing mission" among the Turkish peoples of Central Asia, I must stress, however, that the resultant Russification was essentially a veneer under which the inhabitants of this region (Kazakh, Uzbek, Kirghiz, Turkmen, and Tajik, as well as the Azerbaijanis this side of the Caucasus) remained, and continue to be, true to their Islamic traditions and nationalist aspirations.[13]

Islamic reformers arose under the influence of the Pan-Islamic ideas propagated by Jamal ad-Din Afghani elsewhere in the Islamic world.

One of the early figures was Ahmad Mahdum (Makhdum), 1827–97, who, according to a very good authority, was "one of the greatest nineteenth century thinkers of Central Asia and theoretical precursor of the local reformists" (Carrère d'Encausse 1967a:172, and see ff.). This Islamic reform movement, which gradually included ideas of Turkic nationalism within the Russian empire, found its best-known representative in the person of Isma'il Gasprali (Gasprinski), 1851–1914, and his so-called *Jadīd* movement. Gasprali preached "a real Russian-Muslim-Turkic alliance . . . to be established for the mutual benefit of both parties."[14] His newspaper, *Terjumān*, "the best and most widely read Muslim paper of its time" (Bennigsen 1969:196), was published from 1882 to 1914. According to Bennigsen and Wimbush, "Gasprinski was the leading figure in the Muslim liberal national movement. He advocated the cooperation between the Muslim world and Russian liberals. After 1908, his prestige began to lose its hold over the younger generation of Muslim intellectuals, who had lost all hope to cooperate with Russian liberals and were turning themselves toward socialism."[15]

The Russian Revolution of 1905 opened the way for participation by Muslims in the new system of government. Some Muslim representatives were elected to the first Duma, and as many as thirty-one delegates were present when the second Duma met in 1907. An editor of a Muslim newspaper explained the new realities to his readers as follows:

The aim of our newspaper was simply to make the local population understand the activity of the Duma and its significance; also to prepare this population adequately [for] . . . the next elections . . . My intention was not to propagate anti-government ideas, but to devote my efforts to calming passions, to preparing tranquil and useful elections. (quoted by Carrère d'Encausse 1967b:191)

Meanwhile Muslim congresses were held in 1905 and 1906 to discuss matters relating to Muslim nationality groups and their position in the new government. The parliamentary experience was no doubt useful, although it did not last long. Instead, ideas of socialism and social democracy began to filter among Muslim intellectuals and gradually were to change the attitudes of Muslim societies in the Russian Empire. In fact, these socialist ideas were already coming in by the late nineteenth century, "thanks to the czarist political deportees whose numbers kept on swelling" (Carrère d'Encausse 1967a:181). They were nurtured by the steady growth of secret societies, by the

99

Tajik, Uzbek, and Kazakh press, and finally through the formation of social democratic groups in such places as Ashkabad, Tashkent, and elsewhere.

In addition to socialism, doctrinaire Marxism was also finding its way to Central Asia as early as the 1905 Revolution. This was to grow during the period immediately preceding the First World War and during the war itself. With the outbreak of the October Revolution in 1917, activist Muslim leaders (e.g., Mir-Said Sultan Galiev), joined the Bolshevik Communist Party and began to work for a special position within the new system: "the synthesis of socialism, nationalism, and Islam into a new dynamic ideology – national communism" (Bennigsen and Wimbush 1979:xx).

CONCLUDING REMARKS

Islamic culture and literature in Iran and Central Asia in early modern times (from the early fifteenth century to the early twentieth) passed through several stages of change and development shared to a considerable extent by Islamic regions lying to the west (the Ottoman Empire and the Arab world) and to the east (Muslim India and Chinese Turkistan).

At the beginning of this period, dynastic states were established on the Iranian plateau and the Central Asian steppes by Safavid-Qizilbash warriors in the one, and Chaghatai-Uzbek chieftains in the other – both descendants of the great Turko-Mongol tribal groups who pushed westward into the Muslim heartlands from the mid-eleventh century on. In both these states, Muslim cultural traditions, the heritage of centuries of Islamic predominance, prevailed at the level of High Islamic norms and Folk Islamic popular beliefs. In Iran, Shi'ism of the *ithnā'asharī* persuasion was officially proclaimed as the Islamic religion of the land, while in Central Asia the Sunni persuasion predominated. And whereas the Arabic and Persian languages retained their special place in matters of religion and administration, Chaghatai Turkish was gradually gaining ground as the literary vehicle in the Central Asian region. Also a common Turkish vernacular was the spoken language at court and among the military. A striking example of cultural uniformity in both regions are the Registan Square in Samarqand and the Meydan-e Shah in Isfahan – both containing Islamic architectural marvels that continue to impress and please the

100

modern traveler. Islamic cultural and intellectual activity continued unabated until the end of the eighteenth century with discernable signs of further developments that would argue against unsubstantiated theories of decline and decadence adumbrated by many uninformed modern scholars.

The coming of the colonialist West towards the end of the eighteenth and early nineteenth century shook the entire region of Iran and Central Asia to its foundations as it did the rest of the Islamic world. But in spite of political and other material changes imported from the West, Islam, the religion and culture, came out almost totally unscathed, thanks to a redoubtable group of Muslim scholars (the *ʿulamā*) who protected the faith and the people from the heavy-handed encroachments of Western civilization. The nineteenth century, however, did end up with experiments in constitutional forms of government in Iran along European models, and with pervasive and systematic Russification of the Muslim communities of Central Asia. Soon, however, nationalism and socialism (two more European imports) created more problems to Islamic culture in the region, which had survived the colonial nightmare.

In Iran, the first decades of the twentieth century witnessed experimentation in constitutional government which ultimately collapsed under the military might of Reza Shah Pahlavi, the nationalist founder of modern Iran. In Central Asia, nationalism among the predominantly Turkish population was not allowed to grow; and instead, a watered-down "Russian-Muslim-Turkic alliance" was preached by such figures as Ismaʿil Gasprali (Gasprinski), while Russification of the region continued. Finally, during the period before and immediately after the First World War, Marxist socialism (communism) swept everything before it including even "national communism" preached by such activist Central Asian Muslim leaders as Mir-Said Sultan Galiev and his group.

In the midst of these earth-shaking movements that befell the peoples of Iran and Central Asia, Islam, the religion and culture, remained the only distinctive characteristic that withstood the ravages of time. The period under investigation ended (arbitrarily perhaps) with the outcome of the First World War. Since then, however, more changes have taken place, and in the last few years an Islamic "revival" of sorts has pervaded the entire Muslim world. In Iran it brought about the Islamic Republic dominated by the religious class; in Afghanistan an Islamic religious opposition to Soviet encroachments goes on; and though the Muslim peoples of Central Asia may have accepted Russian communism, still among themselves they continue to adhere to the precepts of Islam and observe an Islamic cultural tradition which the Russians of the north find it difficult if not impossible to stamp out.

NOTES

1. The western orientation of Iran is expressed, a bit poetically perhaps, by the late Iranian writer Jalal Al-Ahmad: "History reveals that we have always had our gaze fixed firmly on the west . . . the shores of the Mediterranean, Greece, the Nile valley, Libya, and the far-west. We, the inhabitants of the Iranian plateau, have been but a small portion of this great entity, and as such have always set our sights on the west . . . Perhaps our westward orientation arises from the fact that we have always been waiting expectantly, in this dry expanse of ours, for Mediterranean clouds. Although the east is the source of enlightenment, still, for us, inhabitants of the Iranian plateau, the rain-bearing clouds have come always from the west." Quoted by Millward (1976:170).

2. The steppe state system, "based on a confederation of appanages under the sovereignty of a kind of dual kingship . . . with a nominal khan elected by virtue of seniority within the ruling clan and a paramount or 'real' khan" (McChesney 1980:9).

3. There are a few exceptions, e.g., Gibb and Bowen (1950, 1957); Naff and Owen (1977).

4. For an introduction to the subject see Mazzaoui (1972).

5. The present writer has for some time been engaged in researching religious-intellectual activity in many parts of the Islamic world during the eighteenth century. Several Muslim scholars, representative of this period, have been carefully studied. A monograph on this subject is in preparation. For a short presentation see Mazzaoui (1983).

6. On Bihbahani and Bahr al-Ulum, see Tanakabuni (n.d.:167–75, 199–204).

7. On Ahsai see Bausani (1956a) and Algar (1969:66–7). On the Babi-Bahai movement see several works by E. G. Browne.

8. Not quite! J. A. MacGahan, correspondent of the *New York Herald*, for example, "accompanied at the start by Eugene Schuyler the American chargé d'affaires at St. Petersburg, then on an official tour of Russia's dominions in Central Asia," reported on the fall of Khiva in 1873. See the account in de Gaury and Winstone (1982:149–61).

9. The translation of Dunbuli's *Ma'āthir* by Harford Jones Brydges (1833) is not trustworthy.
10. For a Shi'i "defense" of constitutional government see Naini's *Tanbīh al-Ummah* reviewed in Algar (1979:238ff.).
11. Bennigsen and Quelquejay (1961) use the famous Marxist paradigm, originally expounded by Stalin in 1913, to explain the origin and development of nationalism among the Central Asian Turks.
12. The two poems are in Edward Allworth (1964:39) with quotations from Arslan Subatay (1930–1).
13. The question of "Russification" dealt with here in the broadest sense evidently needs further clarification which goes too far beyond the terms of reference of the present discussion. For more on this, the reader is referred to the following works: Bennigsen and Lemercier-Quelquejay (1967); Pipes (1954); Rorlich (1986); Demko (1969); Bennigsen and Wimbush (1979 and 1986); Bennigsen and Broxup (1983). I wish to thank one of the anonymous reviewers for several points related to this question of "Russification."
14. Bennigsen and Broxup (1983:79). For contrasting Marxist views see the translation of an article on Uzbek literature by S. S. Kasymov (originally appearing in *Bol'shaia Sovetskaia Entsiklopediia*, 1956) by Allworth (1964:256–7); and see Kaushik (1970:79).
15. Gasprali's biography is summarized in Appendix H, "Biographies," of Bennigsen and Wimbush (1979:197–8).

5
Perso-Islamic culture in India from the seventeenth to the early twentieth century

FRANCIS ROBINSON

From the eleventh century the elites of India came increasingly to share in the high culture, which we shall term Perso-Islamic culture, fashioned by the Iranian and Turkish peoples of Central and Western Asia. Men in Lahore and Delhi, in Jaunpur and Bijapur, came to speak the same languages, read the same books, delight in the same verses, follow the same laws and cherish the same values as men in Herat and Samarqand, in Shiraz and even Istanbul.[1] But from the eighteenth century it began to become less likely that such men would have things in common. In India, as elsewhere throughout the Perso-Islamic cultural region, this shared culture came either to be transformed as it interacted with local cultures or to be overwhelmed by a new elite culture imposed from outside. We aim to look briefly at the nature of Perso-Islamic culture and its relationship to Indian society. We shall go on to examine the main strengths of the culture in the high Mughal period. And then we shall devote especial attention to its fortunes from 1700 onwards, from the continuing processes of consolidation in the eighteenth century to the rapid decline of the nineteenth and early twentieth centuries.

Perso-Islamic culture formed the second great cultural nexus of the Islamic world. As Arab-Islamic culture covered, at various times, the regions of Spain, North Africa, the Fertile Crescent, Arabia and South-East Asia, so the Perso-Islamic covered the remainder of Muslim Asia, reaching at its furthest stretch from the Aegean and the Euphrates in the west to Sinkiang and the Bay of Bengal in the east, from the Russian steppe in the north to the Indian Ocean in the south. The ingredients of this culture came together between the ninth and the thirteenth centuries when several cities, for instance, Bukhara, Isfahan, and Baghdad, became great centers of government and the civilized arts. Islam provided a common framework of law and values; sweet and sibilant Persian became the language of the courts; the Turkish, and later the Mongol, genius for warfare and administration upheld state power; the Iranian genius in matters of intellect and the arts oiled the wheels of government and nourished courtly cultivation.

In describing the second great culture of the Islamic world as Perso-Islamic we do not wish to play down the considerable contribution of the Turkish peoples to its military and political success, nor do we wish to suggest that it is particularly the achievement of the great cities of the Iranian plateau. We adopt this term because it seems best to describe that culture raised both by and under the influence of Muslims who used Persian as a major cultural vehicle. The net is cast wide enough to include those Iranians whose contributions to Islamic scholarship in Arabic formed such a substantial part of the region's educational system, those Turks who placed their own very distinctive mark on the development of Islamic mysticism, and those Hindus whose contributions to poetry and history in Persian were considerable.

This Perso-Islamic culture was fundamentally the culture of those who ruled. It was not, for instance, that of all Muslims in India, but that of the *Ashraf*,[2] the honorable people, those whose ancestors came, or those who were in a position to claim that their ancestors had come from outside the subcontinent, men of Arab, Iranian, Turkish, or Afghan descent. The *Ashraf* shared a well-defined vision of themselves. They had come from abroad to rule; the wielding of power was their birthright. They cherished what they felt were the international Perso-Islamic standards of cultivation and behavior. They were prepared to accept as part of their world those Hindu castes, Kayasths and Kashmiri Brahmins, who joined them in the business of government and absorbed their culture. They were not, by and large, prepared to accept those low-caste Hindus who were slowly being drawn into the Islamic milieu, that is converting to Islam, as having anything to do with their world.[3]

Perso-Islamic culture was also the culture, as we might expect, of the town-dweller. Indeed, one way in which we might see this cultural region as having some unity is to see it in terms of the world of the towns and that of the countryside. Throughout the region, most large towns were places of Perso-Islamic culture, whether great capital cities, seats of provincial government, or centers of Muslim pilgrimage. So, too, were many small towns, those *qasbahs* whose world and whose significance in the context of northern India Christopher Bayly has done so much to alert us to.[4] It may help to see these towns as islands of international Perso-Islamic civilization set in countrysides dominated by local cultures, some barely Islamic, others not Islamic at all. As Zand Shiraz subsisted amidst the territories of nomadic Iranian tribes, as Janid Bukhara subsisted amongst the Uzbek tribes of Transoxiana, so the Indian *qasbahs* subsisted amongst the bazaars, *gunjes*, and villages of a mainly Hindu countryside. In these towns, great and small, the work of government was conducted, Islamic arts and letters were cultivated, Islamic knowledge was preserved and transmitted. Their existence as the bases of a great regional cultural system was affirmed by the way in which soldiers and administrators, scholars and artisans, were able to travel from one to the other to gain patronage and employment, and to feel at home.

THE PILLARS OF PERSO-ISLAMIC CULTURE IN MUGHAL INDIA

In 1700 Perso-Islamic culture had never been so well placed or so influential in India. Behind it lay a century or more of the highest achievement in art and architecture, thought and letters, which had been sustained both by magnificent and discerning patronage and by a constant flow of men and ideas from Central Asia and Iran. To consider the fate of this cultural system in the eighteenth and nineteenth centuries we need a sense of what it primarily consisted of, or where its great strengths lay.

The first pillar of the culture was the Persian language and the literature which it expressed. Persian had been the language of government everywhere except the far south for at least a century, in some areas for several centuries. Through it, Hindus as well as Muslims had

106

come to explore the riches of Perso-Islamic civilization; it became the main language of their intellectual and artistic life. Moreover, through those Indians who came to use it in their work and in their art, it came to lay its impress on the various regional cultures: on the forms of Bengali verse, on Marathi vocabulary and grammar, on the script, the vocabulary, and the literary content of Pushtu, Sindhi, Baluchi, Kashmiri, and above all Urdu. The major forms of Persian literature had also come to be widely cultivated. For much of the high Mughal period there was a strong tradition of historiography. Notable too was the writing of biographical dictionaries, or *tazkīrahs*, the recording of the alleged sayings of Sufi sheikhs, *malfuzāt*, and the art of official letter-writing, *insha'*, which was so vital to the diplomatic prestige of courts in the Perso-Islamic world. Most important, as in all Muslim societies, was poetry. In the late sixteenth and seventeenth centuries poets from Iran and Central Asia had created a golden age at the courts of both Mughal emperors and Deccan sultans. At the beginning of the eighteenth century one outstanding representative of this period of achievement still lived, Mirza ʿAbd al-Qadir Bedil (d. 1721), who was to have great influence in India and even greater influence in Afghanistan and Central Asia (Siddiqi 1979:14–31).

The second pillar of the culture was Islamic knowledge, both formal and mystical. In formal knowledge the rational sciences, *maʿqulāt*, had gained increasing attention. Their study had been greatly encouraged by the leading intellectual at Akbar's court, Fadl Allah Shirazi (d. 1589), who promoted the philosophical traditions of his countryman Jalal al-Din Dawani (1427–1502/3), which led to great interest in the contemporary philosophers Mir Baqir Damad of Isfahan (d. 1631) and his distinguished pupil Mullah Sadra of Shiraz (1571–1640) (Rizvi 1975:191–2). The interest had been strengthened by the arrival of scholars from Central Asia who found the growing orthodoxy of the Shaibanid state increasingly hostile to their rationalist thought. Then, in the seventeenth century, both Sialkot and Jaunpur had become leading centers of scholarship in the field; scholars began to explore non-Islamic philosophical traditions, Hindu, Zoroastrian, and European; and influential work was produced, most notably Mullah Mahmud Jaunpuri's *al-Shams al-Bazigha* (Rizvi 1980:63–73).

Some scholars, however, were disturbed by the increasing prominence of rationalist studies; they feared the free thinking and free behavior of the emperors Akbar and Jahangir with which it seemed to be associated. This led to new interest in the revealed sciences *manqulāt*, in particular the study of Hadiths. The study was firmly established by Sheikh ʿAbd al-Haqq of Delhi (1551–1642) who had fled to the Hijaz in 1587 to escape the lax atmosphere of Akbar's court. Here he benefited from that powerful school of Hadiths scholarship which was to have such widespread influence in the seventeenth- and eighteenth-century Islamic world (Voll 1982:57–9; Robinson 1982:120).

These different emphases in Islamic scholarship came quite naturally to be reflected in the syllabuses of the *madrasas*. By the beginning of the eighteenth century the concern for the rational sciences in the tradition of Dawani and Sadra had come to be represented by the teaching of the learned men of Farangi Mahal Lucknow, and their pupils. They had consolidated a new style of teaching in their Dars-i Nizami syllabus, which was instinct with the rationalist tradition. By encouraging students to think rather than merely to learn by rote the syllabus enabled them to get through the usual run of *madrasa* learning with greater speed, while they came to be noted for their capacity to get to the heart of a matter, to present an argument, and to be flexible in their approach to jurisprudence.[5]

The concern to develop the study of the revealed sciences, on the other hand, was represented by the syllabus of the Madrasa Rahimiyah, founded by Shah ʿAbd al-Rahim (d. 1718) in Delhi. Here much more attention was paid to the Quran and Hadiths than in the Nizami syllabus, logic and philosophy being studied more to ensure that students had a rounded education than because they were greatly valued in themselves. Through teaching the student as much as poss- ible about the Prophet's life and the earliest traditions of the Islamic community in Medina it was hoped that Muslims might be fashioned who were better able to resist the dangers of mystical and philosophical experiment (Nizami 1983:18–20).

In mystical knowledge men were divided much as they were in formal knowledge. At the beginning of the eighteenth century most Sufis followed Ibn al-ʿArabi's (d. 1240) doctrines of the unity of being, *wahdat al-wujūd*, which had dominated Sufi thought for the previous four hundred years. His argument that all phenomena are manifes- tations of a single being, which was encapsulated in the dictum "all is God," had made it possible for Muslims not only to tolerate Hindus but also to search for what common ground they might share. Dara

108

Shikoh, that gifted but unfortunate Mughal prince, had been the most prominent amongst those recently to explore in this direction. But, Ibn al-ʿArabi's teaching had come to be challenged by Sufis of the Naqshbandi order who feared the potential for permissiveness which it offered and detested the free-thinking habits of the Mughal emperors. Their leader was Sheikh Ahmad Sirhindi (1563–1624) who refuted Ibn al-ʿArabi, arguing in favor of the unity of experience, *wahdat al-shuhūd*, the utter transcendence of God, and the need to be guided by His revelation. Instead of declaring "all is God" men should now declare "all is from God." Sirhindi's teaching seems to have had limited impact on Mughal society until the time of Awrangzeb. But it was of great significance as it prepared the ground for a market reorientation of mystical understanding not just in India but also in the wider Islamic world.

As formal learning was transmitted from teacher to pupil, so mystical learning was transmitted from master to disciple in chains of spiritual succession. At the beginning of the eighteenth century, these chains of succession existed in three main orders; the Chishti, which divided into the Nizami and the Sabiri branches, the Qadiri, and the Naqshbandi. All had sheikhs of prestige and vigor, and seemed almost subconsciously to be adjusting to the slackening of Muslim power, to a time, in fact, when they might be called upon to play a more prominent role in the leadership of Muslim affairs. The Nizami branch of the Chishti order had, after centuries of decline, just begun to revive under Shah Kalim Allah of Delhi (d. 1729), whose disciples were spreading through north-western India and into the Deccan. The Sabiri branch of the Chishti order was just coming to the end of a period in which Shah Muhibb Allah Allahabadi (d. 1648), its most prominent sheikh, and his disciple, Saiyid Muhammadi (d. 1685), had strongly defended the teaching of Ibn al-ʿArabi against the bitter assaults of the Naqshbandis. The leading Naqshbandi sheikhs themselves had had considerable influence over the emperor, Awrangzeb, while their disciples were to be found not only in most towns in India but also in West Asia and in Africa. Finally, the Qadiri order, which had enjoyed considerable prestige during the time of Dara Shikoh, was about to experience a period of new vitality as a result of Saiyid Shah ʿAbd al-Razzaq of Bansa (d. 1724) and his successors (Nizami 1983:71–126).

Here, then, are the pillars of Perso-Islamic culture in India: first,

Persian language and literature; second, formal and mystical learning together with their systems of transmission. We are struck by how much in the seventeenth century they owe to the world beyond India, by how very much they seem to be part of an imperial culture projected into India. Almost all the books, commentaries, and supercommentaries normally used in teaching had been written in Iran or Central Asia between 1100 and 1600. To list their authors is to parade the great names of Perso-Islamic scholarship: ʿAbd Allah al-Nasafi (d. 1310), Burhan al-Din ʿAli al-Marghinani (1135–97), Jalal al-Din Dawani, and those great rivals at the court of Timur, Saʿad al-Din al Taftazani (1322–89) and Saiyid Sharif al-Jurjani (1339–1413). In the same way, the Sufi orders, their teachings and their teachers, were all intrinsic parts of Perso-Islamic civilization on the subcontinent. The Chishti way, which was followed only in India, had been carried by Muʿin al Din Sijzi from the area around Herat at the end of the twelfth century; the Qadiri path was first introduced by Muhammad Ghauth who traveled through much of the Perso-Islamic world before establishing himself in fifteenth-century Uch; that of the Naqshbandis was brought by Khwaja Baqi Billah from Central Asia in the late sixteenth century. Their *maktubāt* were in Persian, as were their *malfuzāt*. Moreover, the teachings of Ibn al-ʿArabi, which even some Naqshbandis followed, were to be found everywhere in the work of the greatest Persian poets. It was not possible to recite the verses of Rumi or Hafiz, Jami or Nizami, as the *Ashraf* loved to do, without also absorbing the ideas of this great mystic. Likewise Persian poetry written on Indian soil was remarkable for a complete rejection of Indian life and landscape as acceptable poetic resources, which in part explains the success of Bedil elsewhere in the Perso-Islamic world. Its images would all have been immediately recognizable to the great poets of Isfahan or Shiraz; they were all tulips and roses, there were no *champaks* and lotuses. Their work was remarkable, too, for its "Indian style" which did not mean a style generated through interaction with Sanskrit verse, or a particular regional tradition, but one which grew out of a strong reaction to all which seemed Indian. "Indian style" was characterized by a highly intellectualized imagery, a mental withdrawal from the immediate physical environment. Indeed, the tenor of the Persian literary tradition in India was that of a world which wished to distance itself from the polluting influences of the subject peoples. It was what we might expect from a proud governing elite concerned to preserve intact its high cultural tradition (A. Ahmad 1964:223–34; 1969:71–89).

This said, we would not for a moment wish to convey the impression that Perso-Islamic culture somehow floated above the world of Hindustan, never mingling with it, never interacting with it. Of course it did. There had been fruitful interactions, on occasion complete transformations. From the thirteenth century, Persian musical traditions, for instance, had harmonized closely with those of the Hindus, being fostered in the process both by the Chishtis for whom music and ecstasy were inextricably intertwined and by Muslim courts like those at Jaunpur and Bijapur. As time passed, the Persian traditions came increasingly to be absorbed amongst those of the Hindus. Then, from the mid-sixteenth century, there had been that striking encounter between the formal and highly decorated styles of Central Asian painting and the warm, realistic, and vital ones of Hindu artists which produced the great achievements of the Mughal studios. By the beginning of the eighteenth century, however, an essentially Hindu school had broken away from the Mughal tradition and come to flourish at the Rajput courts of Jaipur, Jodhpur, and Bikanir, whence it was itself to set a standard for the Perso-Islamic styles in their decline.

Likewise, the Sufi world, for all the Persian or *Ashraf* quality of the high Sufi culture, mixed most intimately in the workings of Indian society, finding local functions, adopting local forms of expression. Thus, as Richard Eaton (1978) has shown us, Muslim holy men became established in the interstices of Indian life. The sheikhs of the leading orders danced, sang, chanted, and held their breath, as Sufis did elsewhere in the world, to achieve ecstatic communion with God; sometimes they did so in ways which betrayed the influence of Hindu ascetic practices. Where Sufi culture embraced Hindu converts to Islam, or Hindus themselves, the evidence of Hindu practices was much greater. There were the irreligious Sufis, like the Jalalis, who took hashish and ate scorpions, or the Madaris who got themselves up like Hindu sannyasis, or the Haydaris who pierced their sexual organs. There were the thousands of shrines dotting the Indian landscape. Some, like that of Saiyid Salar Masud at Bahraich or Zinda Shah Madar at Makanpur, were places where Islamic content had been given to an already existing local cult. Others were the resting places of the sainted Muslim dead. If the *Ashraf* tended to see them as sources of grace because in them lay those who were already close to God, the

111

masses saw them as places of magical power, where illness might be cured, the barren become fertile, and evil spirits cast out. In India, as throughout the Muslim world, there were many steps on the ladder of Islamic understanding.

In the seventeenth century, therefore, there were strands of Perso-Islamic culture which still stood out from the Indian environment; there were also strands which had come to be closely interwoven with the fabric of the land. We would like to suggest that in the ideas and the mix of those who contributed to the finest architectural achievement of Perso-Islamic civilization, the Taj Mahal, there is a paradigm of what made up that civilization in seventeenth-century India. The underlying ideas came from abroad; the garden tomb was a Mughal development of a Central Asian tradition. The skilled craftsmen came fro·ᶜ all over the Perso-Islamic world: the draughtsmen and calligraphers from Shiraz, the clerk of works from Qandahar, the finial makers from Samarqand, the dome builder from Ottoman Turkey, the stone- and flower-cutters from Bukhara. Their skills were blended with those of Indian craftsmen: Muslim masons from Delhi and Multan, Hindu inlayers largely from Multan, the Hindu garden expert from Kashmir. At the behest of all sweated thousands of Indian laborers. Such was the relationship of Perso-Islamic civilization to India in general. A clearly identifiable Perso-Islamic structure stood proud, and, as yet, mingled only in part with the Indian world in which it was placed (Nath 1979:1–18; Moynihan 1980:100).

PERSO-ISLAMIC CULTURE IN THE EIGHTEENTH AND EARLY NINETEENTH CENTURIES

In the eighteenth century the bases on which Perso-Islamic culture rested in India began to weaken. Not much more than half a century after the death of Awrangzeb in 1707 the Mughal empire was reduced to a few pathetic square miles around Delhi. By the beginning of the nineteenth century Muslim power itself was reduced to Awadh, Hyderabad and the north-western borderlands. Instead, there now ruled confident non-Muslim powers: the Sikhs in Punjab, the Marathas across a great swathe of territory from Gujarat almost to the eastern seaboard, and the British in most of the Gangetic basin, Bengal, and Madras. The end of Mughal power and wealth meant the

112

end of large-scale patronage for the highest cultural achievement; it also meant the drying up of that stream of administrators, artists, and craftsmen from Iran and Central Asia which had fed the growth of Perso-Islamic culture for many centuries past. The rise of non-Muslim powers, on the other hand, in particular the Marathas with their Hindu revivalism and the British with their aggressive Christian civilization, threatened the existence of Perso-Islamic culture itself. But these developments did not mean that its progress was immediately blocked. Far from it. There continued to be enough patronage and creativity for the eighteenth and early nineteenth centuries to be regarded as the period of the "highest refinement" of Persianate culture, a period to be compared with the late Renaissance in Italy, the golden age of Spain and the era of French rococo (Goetz 1938:6–7).

Consider Persian. Until the 1830s Persian was the language of government in most of the subcontinent. This was the case not just at the provincial Muslim courts which sprang up as Mughal power ebbed – Murshidabad, Hyderabad, Arcot, Mysore, Awadh, Shahjahanpur, Rampur; it was also the case under the Sikhs, the Marathas, and even under the British. All these successor governments rested on the established systems of Mughal administration and the skills of its service classes. Thus, there continued to be a substantial Persian-speaking bureaucratic class. Indeed, the British were in the forefront of maintaining government-sponsored learning for this class when in 1781 they set up the Calcutta Madrasa. Gifted administrators and artists could find positions throughout the land. Men from the great service families of northern India travelled to Calcutta, Hyderabad, and Arcot. Men from Kashmir, Brahmin pandits and Muslims forced out by Afghan or Sikh rule, found work in northern India. It was thus that notable Kashmiri families, like the Dars and Chaks, the Saprus and Nehrus, became established. Iranians who wished to come could still find a ready outlet for their talents, while a Hindu convert to Islam who was skilled in Persian, like Mirza Qatil (d. 1817), could make a home for himself for years in Shiraz, Isfahan, Tehran and Azerbaijan (Sharar 1974:99). In the 1790s, when Tipu Sultan talked to his courtiers in Seringapatam, he did so in Persian (Hasan 1971:379); in the 1830s, when the poet Ghalib (d. 1869) wrote to his friends in Delhi or Calcutta or Banda, he did so in Persian (Tirmizi 1969:9–120).

There is reason to believe that in the eighteenth century Persian came to be more widely used than before. This was the time when

113

FRANCIS ROBINSON

Hindu involvement in the language reached its peak. The Hindu Raja
of Benares gave substantial patronage to the greatest Iranian scholar to
migrate to India in the century, Sheikh Muhammad ʿAli "Hazin"
Gilani (1692–1766) (Cole 1984:34–7). Hindus, moreover, came not
just to use the Persian language, but Persian forms of mystical verse,
the *mathnawī* form, for instance, to express Hindu religious themes.
Inshaʾ became a Kayasth monopoly, Hindu lexicography of Persian
was thought the best, while the considerable Hindu tradition of historiography in Persian reached its peak. Indeed, one author had so
absorbed the Persian style that in describing the death of the great
Hindu hero, Shivaji, he consigned him "to hell" (A. Ahmad
1969:234–8). Persian was evidently understood outside the *Ashraf*
class. When in 1826 the leading Hindu intellectual of Calcutta, Raja
Ram Mohun Roy, chose to propagate his views, he did so in a Persian
language newspaper. In particular localities it penetrated to the common people. "Knowledge of Persian language in the late eighteenth
and nineteenth centuries," declared the literary historian ʿAbd al-
Halim Sharar (d. 1926), "was greater in India than in Persia itself . . .
this was particularly the case in the last [nineteenth] century when
Lucknow was famed throughout the world for its progress and education, when every child could speak Persian, when ghazals [lyric
poems] were on the lips of all, even the uneducated, courtesans and
bazaar workers, and when even a bhand [entertainer] would jest in
Persian" (Sharar 1974:100).

Consider the second pillar of Perso-Islamic culture, Islamic knowledge and the systems which transmitted it. In formal learning the
rational sciences remained dominant, as they were to be until the mid-
nineteenth century (Rizvi 1980:398). They were cultivated with most
vigor and distinction in Awadh, the "Shiraz of India" as the emperor,
Shah Jahan, had so aptly called it. The Farangi Mahal family were the
focus of scholastic activity in the region. The descendants, pupils, and
pupils' pupils of Mullah Qutb al-Din Sehalwi, whose murder in 1691
had led Awrangzeb to bestow Farangi Mahal upon his sons, were the
great names in the field: Muhibb Allah Bihari (d. 1707), for instance,
whose texts on jurisprudence and logic came to have an international
following; Mullahs Nizam al-Din (d. 1740), Hasan (d. 1794) and
Mubin (d. 1810), whose exposition of Bihari's work helped to spread its
fame; and Mullah Nizam al-Din Sehalwi (d. 1761), whose pupil,
ʿAlim Sandilwi, founded the influential Khayrabad school of logic and

114

philosophy. Such was the standing of this scholastic tradition that it came to be investigated at al-Azhar (Gran 1979:146) and in the nineteenth century its books were used to try to revive the rational sciences in Cairo (Cole 1984:22).

In the eighteenth and early nineteenth centuries this rationalist tradition came to be consolidated and spread throughout much of India. Here again the activities of the Farangi Mahal family were significant. Their Dars-i Nizami teaching methods were widely adopted because of the new speed with which they enabled students to learn. Their emphasis on the rational sciences was widely accepted because of the training it gave those who hoped for posts in government, a tendency which was reinforced when Warren Hastings adopted the Dars-i Nizami as the curriculum for the Calcutta Madrasa, thereby setting the standard expected for service under the East India Company. Indeed, such was the influence of the Company that British ideas of the desirability of a set curriculum led to specific books being fixed in the Nizami syllabus and so the prevailing bias towards the rational sciences came to be reinforced (Nizami 1983:31). Long before this, however, the Farangi Mahalis and their pupils had begun to spread their traditions throughout India. In the early eighteenth century they made Lucknow the greatest center of learning in northern India; students from outside were boarded in the city's Tila mosque which had room for 700. Later they traveled from court to court, from patron to patron, in search of teaching opportunities. Mullah Hasan went from Lucknow to Shahjahanpur, and thence to Rampur via Delhi; Mawlana ʿAbd ʿAli Bahr al-ʿUlum (1731–1810) from Lucknow to Shahjahanpur, to Rampur, to Buhar in Bengal and finally to Madras; Mullah Haydar (d. 1840) established the Nizami course in Hyderabad. The family's pupils numbered many hundreds; they came to be scattered throughout India and the wider Islamic world. Most of the chains of teaching, declared Azad Bilgrami towards the end of the eighteenth century, go back to Mullah Qutb al-Din Sehalwi; all the educational centers from Calcutta to Peshawar, declared Shibli Numani at the beginning of the twentieth century, are mere offshoots of the Dars-i Nizami (Ansari 1973:43; Shibli Numani 1955:104).

In mystic knowledge the orders closest to those Perso-Islamic mystical traditions, which stretched back through Mughal to pre-Mughal India, were widely followed. In common with Sufi orders elsewhere in the Islamic world, and not least in Central Asia and Chinese

115

Turkistan, as Muslim power declined they sought to give leadership to Muslim affairs. The Chishti-Nizamis, through the energy of the Shah Kalim Allah and his successors, became once more a vigorous all-India order, their hospices springing up most thickly in the region from Awadh to the Punjab. The Chishti-Sabiris became extremely active in the many *qasbahs* of the Ganges-Jumna Doab, and eventually produced Hajji Imdad Allah (d. 1899), spiritual inspiration of more than one nineteenth-century reformist movement and most influential Sufi of his time. The Qadiris were active mainly in the Punjab; there were only two major centers in Awadh, and one in Madras whence the brotherhood was carried by ʿAbd al-ʿAli Bahr al-ʿUlum. With this new vigor there also came significant developments in practices and attitudes. Sufis began to be initiated in more than one order; there was some softening of the Naqshbandi stance towards Ibn al-ʿArabi; Sufis began to place greater emphasis on formal knowledge, scholars on spiritual development. All was part of a coming together of the transmitters of the central messages of Islam to preserve what was essential in a time of growing weakness. The Sufi aspect of those messages, however, remained predominantly in the Persianate tradition. Bahr al-ʿUlum's magisterial study of Rumi's *Mathnawī* in the light of Ibn al-ʿArabi's *Fusus* and *Futuhāt* is a representative Sufi classic of the period.

In addition to the strengthening of acknowledged pillars of Perso-Islamic culture in the eighteenth century there was also the establishment of a new one. This took the form of the emergence of a powerful and self-confident Shiʿite culture in constant interaction with the Shiʿa heartlands in Iraq and Iran. The platforms of this development were the Shiʿa satrapies which, as Mughal power declined, came forward as increasingly independent states. First Murshidabad arose as a major commercial center and seat of the governors of Bengal; at the same time Hughli came to be favored by long-distance traders from Iran. Bengal offered growing opportunities to emigrants from Iran. When the East India Company took power in the 1760s, these Iranians turned to Awadh where from 1722 another Shiʿa satrapy had begun to flourish. This court, which was established by Saiyids from Nishapur, grew steadily more Shiʿite in its institutions and in its culture. From the 1760s the Nishapuri Nawabs began to gather Shiʿite *ulamā* about them. In May 1768 Shiʿa congregational prayers were held for the first time. By the early nineteenth century 2,000 *imambaras* and 6,000

116

taziehkanas had been built in Lucknow, many of whose citizens threw themselves into *mohurram* celebrations of a distinctly Safavid kind. Shiʿa ʿulamā led prayers, acted as *muftis*, collected the *khums* tax and distributed it as charity. The evolution of this Shiʿa state reached its climax in the 1840s when a formal Shiʿa judicial system was established and a large royal *madrasa* was set up. Court and capital sustained a highly developed Persianate culture which two generations later Abd al-Halim Sharar was both to celebrate and to mourn in his noted series of articles on Lucknow as the last expression of an oriental culture[6] (Cole 1984:95–101, 127–67, 377–416).

The Shiʿa world of Murshidabad and Lucknow was continually refreshed by emigrants from the cultural centers of Iran and the shrine cities of Iraq. Sheikh Muhammad ʿAli "Hazin" Gilani fled the wreck of the Safavid Empire to finish his life teaching the rational sciences and verse composition in Benares. Descendants of the Majlisi family which had provided leaders of Friday prayers in Isfahan and the Sheikh al-Islam of the Safavid Empire came to serve ʿAli Vardi Khan in Murshidabad, their descendants later moving on to Lucknow. These men had a vast network of cousins who were scholars in the shrine cities of Iraq and high religious officials in the towns of the Iranian plateau. From the early nineteenth century the numbers of Iranian scholars who succeeded in establishing themselves in northern India began to dwindle, but physicians, poets, and architects still came in numbers and settled with success (Cole 1984:95–101, 315).

With the movement of men there also moved ideas and money. Ideas by and large traveled from the Shiʿa heartlands to India. When, for instance, the millenarian Sheikhist movement developed in early-nineteenth-century Iran, its impact was soon felt in Awadh. More important, the changing balance of influence in jurisprudence, and therefore in theology, between the fundamentalist Akhbaris and the rationalist Usulis[7] in Iran and Iraq was also reflected in India. The Akhbaris dominated in the first half of the eighteenth century, helped by the crumbling of the Safavid state; and so they did in India. When, from the 1760s, the Usulis rose again assisted by the Zand peace in Iran, Indian Akhbaris seeking knowledge at the Najaf and Karbala found themselves in a world of Usuli thought. One of them, Sailyid Dildar ʿAli Nasirabadi, converted to Usulism and was almost entirely responsible for establishing it within the growing Awadhi state (Cole 1984:102–67).

117

It was money, on the other hand, which traveled from India west-wards. From 1786 large sums flowed from Awadh to the shrine cities. After 1815 the amounts lessened somewhat because of the East India Company's demands, but from the late 1830s they became substantial once more. In the 1780s half a million rupees were sent to dig a canal, the Asafiyah canal, from the Euphrates to the perpetually dry city of Najaf. Further Awadh subventions built a pilgrim hostel and a library, embellished the shrine of Imam Husayn, repaired the holy cities after the Wahhabi invasion, and supported scholars. In consequence the leading men of Awadh had long-standing ties with the most influential Shi'a scholars of Iraq (Cole 1984:153–4, 357–72).

This period, then, up to the early nineteenth century offers a picture of the continuing growth and consolidation of Perso-Islamic culture. Indeed, in Shi'a Lucknow we sense we have the ultimate location of Hermann Goetz's "highest refinement," his French rococo stage of Perso-Islamic culture.

There were, nevertheless, emerging challenges to the dominance of Perso-Islamic culture. Indigenous languages were coming increasingly to be cultivated and hence to challenge the cultural sway of Persian outside the world of government. By the end of the eighteenth century Bengali, whose flowering had long been held back by the dominance of the Persian language, was beginning to develop new and vigorous Sanskritized forms, Punjabi had produced its two greatest poets, Bulhe and Warith Shah, and Sindhi, under the patronage of the Kalhoras and now the Talpurs, was flourishing as never before. But it was the rise of Urdu which presented the real challenge to Persian. Urdu was the creation of the Muslims in India, the language they had developed to communicate with the Indian world about them, often the language of their households and their harems. It combined regional grammar and syntax with Persian nouns, adjectives, and images. Two streams had developed over the centuries of Muslim rule, one in the Deccan, another around Delhi. After Awrangzeb's conquest of the Deccan these came togther to form the medium which the *Ashraf* were to come to feel would give more scope for the expression of their poetic genius than a Persian language, which had become exhausted by extremes of intellectualism and which was no longer as often refreshed by new blood from Iran. Within a generation, Aziz Ahmad tells us, the Muslims of Delhi had discarded Persian as their main poetic language in favor of Urdu (A. Ahmad 1964:252).

118

From the moment that Persian was no longer the prime conveyor of the forms of artistic speech through which Muslims have delighted to probe the secrets of the heart, it began to slip from the center of Indo-Muslim civilization. Nevertheless, this heralded the dilution, not the destruction, of Persianate literary culture. Until the mid-nineteenth century much Urdu poetry like Indo–Persian poetry before it, rejected Indian life and images, drawing all its symbols from "the unseen and unexperienced sights, sounds and smells of Persia and Central Asia." It strove to maintain its artistic solidarity with the external world of Islam with which it was losing touch (A. Ahmad 1964:252–3). Moreover, this was a dilution which enabled Perso-Islamic culture to be spread more widely. With its Indian roots, Urdu was accessible to all, both Hindu and Muslim, who spoke the vernaculars of northern India.

In formal learning the counter-tradition of Hadiths scholarship, which Shah 'Abd al-Haqq had inspired in the sixteenth century and Shah 'Abd al-Rahim had cherished in the seventeenth, began to grow with vigor in the eighteenth. The cause was 'Abd al-Rahim's son, Shah Wali Allah (1703–62) who, like 'Abd al-Haqq, had sat at the feet of the masters of Hadiths scholarship in the Hijaz. Distressed by the waning of Muslim power and by the disintegration of Muslim society, Wali Allah strove to clarify and to harmonize the entire body of the Islamic tradition in the hope that, once truth was clearly revealed, divisions would end and power would return. He attacked the rationalist scholastic traditions of Iran and Central Asia as a source of arid intellectualism and confusion. Muslims should turn to study the revealed sciences; only these could bring them closer to the central teachings of the faith. To draw society nearer to religious truth he urged that the decisions of the law schools should only be adopted in the light of the Hadiths. To draw people nearer to religious truth he took the immensely courageous step of translating the Quran into Persian. His work was consolidated by his four sons. The eldest, Shah 'Abd al-Aziz (d. 1824), used *fatawa* in a new way as a source of guidance in all matters of life (Metcalf 1982:49–52), another son, Shah Rafi al-Din (d. 1818), produced a literal translation of the Quran in Urdu, and yet another, Shah 'Abd al-Qadir (d. 1813), an idiomatic translation. All taught in the Madrasa Rahimiyah and other Delhi *madrasas*; an extensive network of pupils and connections was established with the learned and holy families of the *qasbahs* of the upper Doab and further afield. Their reputation reached into the

119

Islamic world beyond Hindustan; Shah ʿAbd al-Aziz, according to one
visitor from Bukhara, was a great scholar from whom "rivers of *sharīʿat*
would flow into the world" (Metcalf 1982:47). They provided much of
the intellectual platform from which Saiyid Ahmad Barelwi's (d. 1831)
reformist movement of *jihād* was to be launched. They were
determined to overthrow those Iranian and Central Asian traditions of
rationalist scholarship which had flourished so long.

In mystical learning the Naqshbandi challenge to Ibn al-ʿArabi's
teaching that God is immanent in all things, which had first been
voiced by Sheikh Ahmad Sirhindi, came to be voiced once more, and
with increasing stridency. As Muslim power declined, the
Naqshbandiyah became increasingly loud in their opposition to those
practices threatening the unity of God, which a Persianate Sufism
seemed to tolerate; they became increasingly concerned that the
sharīʿa should be most assiduously observed. As we might expect from
Sufis who were concerned in particular to influence those who wielded
power, their efforts were concentrated in the Mughal capital of Delhi.
One great sustainer of this challenge was Mirza Mazhar Jan-i Janan (d.
1781), poet and eighteenth-century pivot of the order, in whom all the
chains of succession from Sirhindi combined. He left the unusual
number of forty-nine successors and a Sufi hospice which under his
leading successor, Shah Ghulam ʿAli (d. 1824), was famed through
much of Asia. He asserted the *sharīʿa*, attacked practices which
threatened the unity of God, and held aloof from the growing British
presence; he also waged bitter battles against the Shiʿas, one of whom
was to kill him as, somewhat unwisely, he mocked a *mohurram* pro-
cession. Further sustainers of the challenge were the family of Shah
Wali Allah. Under the influence of Shah ʿAbd al-ʿAziz's disciple,
Saiyid Ahmad Barelwi, moreover, this challenge became both more
aggressive and more extreme. The Saiyid, raising support amongst the
lower ranks of Muslims as well as the *Ashraf*, created his own *Tarīqa-i
Muhammadīyah*. In 1826, he declared *jihād* against the Sikhs and
established a state in the Pathan country of the North-west Frontier.
Here his supporters could follow the *sharīʿa* and repudiate, as he had
declared in his testament, all those "Indian, Persian and Roman
customs which were contrary to the Prophet's teaching" (A. Ahmad
1964:211).

The Naqshbandi assault on the Sufi culture of the Perso-Islamic
world was severe. It was, however, not without aspects of irony which

120

deserve notice. It should be clear that the Naqshbandiyah were quin-
tessentially a product of that world. In sixteenth-century Central Asia
the order had been imbued with the ideas of Ibn al-ʿArabi and it was
only under Sirhindi's guidance in India that an element had been
implanted in it which brought conflict with Persianate Sufi culture.
Moreover, it was only when power began to slip away from the
Mughal ruling elite that some Muslims began to find it really attrac-
tive. It should also be clear that in the eighteenth and nineteenth
centuries, Naqshbandi ideas, as they had developed in India, were a
major Indian export to the rest of the Perso-Islamic region. Shah
Ghulam ʿAli's hospice welcomed many disciples from Samarqand,
Bukhara, Tashkent, Qandahar and Kabul (Fusfeld 1981:172). Most
important among these disciples was Mawlana Khalid of Baghdad (d.
1826–7), who not only led the third phase in the order's development
but spread its influence through West Asia, East Africa and into
South-East Asia. Whether or not there were also connections with the
considerable Naqshbandi activity in the nineteenth-century Caucasus
and Chinese Turkistan only further research can tell. But we know
enough already to see how the Naqshbandiyah, Shiʿite Iran apart, were
able to give some new life to the old Perso-Islamic unities.[8] Finally,
we should note that Sirhindi's Naqshbandi message, which raised what
were assumed to be the earlier Islamic traditions of Arabia over the
later ones of the Perso-Islamic empires, appealed to the *Ashraf*
because it reassured them of their distinctiveness, of their apartness
from the peoples of the land, at a time when they feared being sucked
into the maw of Hindu India. "We are Arab people," declared Shah
Wali Allah, "whose fathers have fallen in exile in the country of
Hindustan, and Arabic genealogy and Arabic language are our pride"
(Schimmel 1980:157).

Nevertheless, however severe the Naqshbandi assault, however significant both this development and developments in formal learning
and in the indigenous languages, it should be clear that in the
eighteenth and early nineteenth centuries they were no more than
emerging challenges to the primacy of Perso-Islamic culture. This
understanding calls into question the emphasis of much historical
writing since the emergence of the modern states of India and
Pakistan. Historians have tended to focus on those eighteenth-century
developments which have been thought to be the forerunners both of
the movement for Pakistan and of Muslim support for Indian national-

121

ism. In each case the story has seemed to begin with Shah Wali Allah and has been carried forward in the activities of his sons and of Saiyid Ahmad Barelwi. In consequence, a distorted picture of eighteenth-century Indian Islam has grown up, which has tended to obscure the dominance of rationalist scholarship after the fashion of Farangi Mahal and mysticism in the tradition of Ibn al-ʿArabi, the dominance in fact of established Perso-Islamic ways. This picture, drawn largely from the perspective of the emerging challengers, sacrifices eighteenth-century realities to twentieth-century concerns.

PERSO-ISLAMIC CULTURE FROM THE EARLY NINETEENTH TO THE EARLY TWENTIETH CENTURY

From the 1820s and 1830s Perso-Islamic culture dissolved with almost shocking speed. The prime cause was, of course, the increasingly confident assertion of the new imperial power and culture of Britain in the administration of the land. But not all was British doing, at least, directly. While they dismantled the cultural fabric from without, Hindus and Muslims also undermined it from within. We can see the shape of the transformation by tracing the fate of what we have termed the pillars of the culture.

Support for Persian quickly declined. Before the Mutiny uprising of 1857 the poet Ghalib was full of aristocratic contempt for Urdu: Persian was the only fit literary language. Yet he came to grieve most over the Urdu verse which he lost in the sack of Delhi (Russell and Islam 1969:82–3, 182); it was as though, with the last Timurid emperor gone, with the last symbol of Perso-Islamic power dethroned, he knew that he had lost what was now the best means of speaking to his fellow countrymen. Saiyid Ahmad Khan (1817–98) started his Muhammadan Anglo-Oriental College in the 1870s to teach Arabic and Persian subjects alongside English ones; but within a few years he had to close down the two "oriental departments" as few showed any interest in them. By the end of the century Persian was cherished by a few small groups: the Shiʿa, the more learned amongst the Sunni ʿulamā, the Kashmiri Brahmins, the Armenian community of Calcutta. Beyond these narrow circles it was just an academic language. In the first decade of the twentieth century a mere 281 Persian-language books were published in the United Provinces, the heartland of Perso-

Islamic civilization, as compared with 3,547 Urdu-language books. Moreover, there was not one significant newspaper in Persian as compared with 116 in Urdu (Robinson 1974:77–8).

One reason for this decline was that the British replaced Persian as the language of government. In 1835 English became the official state language and the medium of the higher courts of law; in 1837 the regional languages became the mediums of the lower courts. At one stroke the major reason for learning Persian was wiped out. English was raised up as the new language in which the discourse of power would take place; the vernaculars were given a boost which would enable some at least to become increasingly effective vehicles of elite expression in the various regions. Opportunities for those educated in Persian did not immediately disappear. Openings still existed in states such as Sikh Punjab, Awadh, Kashmir, and Hyderabad; they still existed, too, in those north Indian areas where Urdu became the language of government. But, as the century progressed, these oases of comfort disappeared. Sikh Punjab was conquered, Awadh annexed; new entrance requirements, demanding achievement in the government educational system, increasingly limited the opportunities for the Persian-educated in the Urdu language areas. By the end of the century even Hyderabad (in 1883) and Kashmir (in 1889) had deserted Persian for Urdu. The former, nevertheless, remained the one really significant unit of government in which members of the *Ashraf*, educated amongst Persian poets and sharpened by the rationalist treatises of al-Taftazani and al-Jurjani, could hope to climb to the highest reaches of power.

This body blow to Persian was accompanied by further battering. The general assertion of British power attacked the language's material bases on a wider front. Poets and scholars had long depended on the revenue-free grants which Hindu and Muslim rulers had made to support their skills: these were steadily reduced. All this, moreover, took place in a context in which, as C. A. Bayly tells us, "almost everywhere political change, the rise of monied men or the resurgence of Hindu landholding communities put pressure on the Islamic gentry" (Bayly 1982:355). We should not be surprised at Ghalib's lifelong obsession with his pension. The finest Persian poet of his day did but voice the prevailing anxiety of his class.

The process of decline was then compounded by ʿulamā and Sufis, in particular those of a reformist bent who had long been challenging the old Perso-Islamic ways; they began to transmit Islamic knowledge more and more in regional languages. The more widely knowledge was spread, the argument went, the better the community would be able to protect itself against innovations stemming either from the Hindus or from the British; the better too they would be able to lead the community when it was without power. Urdu benefited considerably, as it did from the change in the court language. It became the recipient not just of many translations of the Quran and the Hadiths but also of dozens of classics of Islamic scholarship from al-Ghazali to Ibn Khaldun. Sufis followed suit, translating more and more of their *malfuzāt* and *maktubāt* from Persian into Urdu so that the example of the saints could reach fresh generations. Towards the end of the century Bengali benefited from a similar process. This shift away from the old imperial language coincided with the introduction of the lithographic printing press. Admittedly many Persian classics were published, but from the beginning books, magazines, and newspapers published large scale were published in the regional languages. It was a coincidence which only served to hasten the decline of Persian (Metcalf 1982:198–215; Ahmed 1981:72–105).

As Persian slipped towards oblivion so did its influence over the regional languages and literatures. Powerful forces helped it on its way. Christian missionaries concerned to speak to as wide an audience as possible, and government schools concerned to teach as effectively as possible, were bound to favor the demotic forms of speech. At the same time Hindu revivalists, concerned to reassert their culture after centuries of Muslim domination, sought to purge their tongues of all Muslim words and Sanskritize them. They began in Bengal where from the early nineteenth century Brahmo Samajists and their intellectual descendants fashioned a purely Hindu literature in Sanskritized Bengali. Later the movement was carried into Upper India where from the 1870s Haris Chandra and his circle, encouraged by Bengalis, developed a literature in a de-Persianized Urdu – that is, Hindi – which was written not in the Persian but in the Nagri script. Hindu revivalists demanded that this Sanskritic script should replace that of Persian as the script of government. In 1873 they had their way in the Central Provinces, in 1881 in Bihar, and in 1900 they had a partial success in the United Provinces where Nagri was given equal standing with the Persian script. By the beginning of the twentieth century, Perso-Islamic sounds were greatly muted in literary Hindu language; the Perso-Islamic look was disappearing from the written face of government. We should not be surprised that Upper India's greatest novelist, Prem Chand, was soon to switch from Urdu to Hindi.

Urdu remained the one major carrier of Persian influences. Even here, however, although the vocabulary and the script remained, Persian style and inspiration were to a large extent abandoned. There were harbingers of these changes in the first half of the nineteenth century, when Nazir Akbarabadi (d. 1830) wrote poetry revelling in Indian life and atmosphere, and Saiyid Ahmad Khan examined the archaeology of Delhi in simple and straightforward prose. The Mutiny uprising and its suppression, the shattering of the illusion of Perso-Islamic power, smashed the grip of Persianate aesthetics. Poets forsook the highly structured and atomistic forms of verse; they no longer strove for those Persianate effects which might transform the humble Indian roasted betel nut into "the black musk in the navel of the deer of Khotan" (A. Ahmad 1964:253). Instead, they adopted freer forms which offered continuity of ideas unhindered by schemes of rhyme, and they began to write with a stronger and stronger sense of realism. They dealt no longer just with love and with faith, but with the great issues of the moment: the decline of Islam, the rule of the West, the position of women. By the era of the Progressive Writers' Movement of the 1930s and 1940s they had come to deal with social and political revolution. Prose writers followed a similar path, forsaking ornament, intricacy, and escapism for the new workmanlike style which Saiyid Ahmad Khan had already begun to adopt. Indeed, by the Saiyid's death in 1898, he and his Aligarh followers had completed a revolution in Urdu prose style which made it a highly flexible medium. The inspiration for these developments came almost entirely from the West. Saiyid Ahmad Khan modeled himself on Mill, Addison, and Steele, the historian and novelist Sharar, on Walter Scott. Hali (d. 1914) found guidance in Milton and Ruskin, Iqbal (d. 1938) in Shelley and Renan, the Progressive Writers in Auden and Day Lewis, Gorky and Chekhov (Sadiq 1964:247–87; Ansari 1984:chs.3, 6). As time went on Urdu seemed more and more to be just a Persianate mold into which foreign substances were poured.

Turning to the second pillar of Perso-Islamic culture, Islamic knowledge and the systems which transmitted it, we find that the Persianate elements slip away almost as quickly. The rational sciences, that distinctive contribution of Iran and Central Asia to Indian Islam, were cultivated less and less. As Muslim courts disappeared and

Western knowledge was increasingly required for service under the British, the demand for men trained in the skills which had administered Muslim empires declined. The platform which supported the rational sciences crumbled; their glamor faded. The last outstanding scholar in the field was ʿAbd al-Hayy of Farangi Mahal, who died in 1886. By the twentieth century they formed a minor subject in men's minds and in the curriculum. Instead, the tradition which emphasized the study of the Quran and the Hadiths, and which mingled with the Naqshbandi thrust for reform, came uppermost in religious thinking. The seeds planted long before by ʿAbd al-Haqq of Delhi and Sheikh Ahmad Sirhindi at last began to flower. Indian Islam came to be orientated more to its Arab sources and to the Arab world; it was to acquire a deepening fundamentalist hue. The heirs to the scholars of the rational sciences, as far as there were any, were the Islamic modernists, who learned the skills of the new imperial civilization, and who, from Saiyid Ahmad Khan to Fazlur Rahman, sometime head of Pakistan's Institute of Islamic Research, have striven to reconcile Islamic revelation with modern knowledge. In their rejection of dogma and in their determination to use reason to enable Islam to live comfortably, if not fruitfully, in the modern world, they have sustained and still sustain some of the spirit of the old Persianate tradition.[9]

With the decline of scholarship in the rational sciences, there was also a decline in the systems by which they were transmitted. Boys no longer pressed to sit at the feet of ʿulamā. By the late nineteenth century the learned men of Farangi Mahal themselves were struggling to keep their teaching traditions alive. Their Nizami style of teaching was still used through much of India, but the Nizami syllabus, in the form in which it had ossified in the late eighteenth century, was coming under heavy fire. Indeed, in the 1890s a conference of ʿulamā made it the subject of a substantial and unfavorable report (Husain n.d.). As the twentieth century progressed, Farangi Mahalis still taught the syllabus in their Lucknow madrasa but increasingly few even of their own children came to follow it (Robinson 1983). On the other hand, madrasas adjusted their syllabuses to take account of the heightened interest in these subjects. New madrasas were founded. At the leading edge of this institutionalization of Islamic reform in the education of the Indo-Muslim young was the Dar al-ʿUlum at Deoband, founded in 1867 by ʿulamā imbued with the traditions of Shah Wali Allah's family. By 1880 it had spawned over a dozen schools, by 1900 nearly forty, and at its centenary it claimed nearly 9,000. Thus Islamic education was transformed. The training for empire built up over 800 years faded away to be replaced, as Barbara Metcalf has so ably demonstrated, by a training for Islamic survival in a world where Muslims had no power (Metcalf 1982:3–15, 87–137, 348–60).

Developments in Sufi thought and amongst the Sufi brotherhoods are hard to assess because as yet we know little of them. Certainly, Persianate traditions were maintained, at least amongst the Chishtis and the Qadiris. Farangi Mahalis taught the Mathnawi in their *madrasa* where in the twentieth century they welcomed children from the holy families of northern India from Ajmer to Phulwari. Ahmad Raza Khan (d. 1921), the founder of the Barelwi movement which had a large following in the rural areas, maintained a strong pantheistic position in the widely accepted interpretation of Ibn al-ʿArabi.[10] Even his opponent, the reformist Ashraf ʿAli Thanwi (d. 1943), the most influential Sufi of his day, wrote to prove that Ibn al-ʿArabi and the *sharīʿa* need not be irreconcilable. Nevertheless, we sense that the climate of thought amongst the *Ashraf* was becoming less favorable, not just to Persianate Sufism but to Sufism itself. Persianate Sufism faced a strong movement of religious revival and reform which was, of course, dead set against all pantheistic tendencies. Sufism itself was threatened in part by the extremists amongst the reformers, the aristocratic *Ahl-i Hadīths*,[11] but in the main by the growing numbers of *Ashraf* educated in the sceptical, rationalizing, and materialistic culture of the West. Whereas their forefathers saw the resting places of the sainted dead as inviting havens of spiritual warmth where they might come close to God, they tended to see them as homes of mumbo-jumbo and of parasites who lived off the gullible. Such men were both less willing and less able to understand the elaborate architecture of higher Sufi thought which joined tried sources of immediate relief and hope in every village and *qasbah* to Muhammad's revelation.

RETROSPECT AND PROSPECT, 1900

Looking back to the seventeenth century from the vantage point of the twentieth century, we can see how Perso-Islamic culture has been transformed. The language element, Persian, has mingled with Indian languages and brought forth Urdu, a purely Indian tongue, which has come to have for Muslims resonances of communal identity much as Persian had resonances of the old imperial identity. The Islamic element, Islamic knowledge and its systems of transmission, has changed from knowledge designed to support Islam in power to knowledge designed to support Islam without power. In place of a Perso-Islamic culture drawing its inspiration from Iran and Central Asia, there is an Indo-Muslim culture deriving its inspiration increasingly from India, Arabia, and the West. No longer is the Taj Mahal, that Mughal ideal made real by craftsmen from throughout the Perso-Islamic world, the appropriate paradigm. The paradigms of the new cultural orientation are not nearly so magnificent; they are school buildings, like those of the Dar al-ʿUlum at Deoband and Saiyid Ahmad Khan's Aligarh College, which express a Muslim identity, which absorb to varying degrees the messages of the West, and which house institutions in their various ways committed to a Muslim future on the Indian subcontinent (Metcalf 1982:112–13, 327; Lelyveld 1978:147–66).

Looking forward into the twentieth century we find traces of Perso-Islamic influences still lingering in the living culture of India: in the Persian script, the Persian words of Indian languages, and the various Shiʿa enclaves; in aspects of Sufi thought, of the landlord culture of Awadh, and of the film culture of Bombay; in the store of Timurid political idioms on which the British drew with skill in fashioning their system of imperial rule (Cohn 1983:165–209). All around were relics of a once-dominant Perso-Islamic culture: the domes and minarets which soar above city rooflines, the gardens and palaces, the Friday mosques and imperial mausoleums. "The footprints in the sands of India still say," as Hali mourned in his *Musaddas*, "a glorious caravan has passed this way" (Minault 1974:462).

There were still some striking expressions of the old Perso-Islamic unities, but they were full of paradox. There were those bright-eyed Muslims who, during and after World War I, fled to Afghanistan and Central Asia to seek help against the British; they were the last of those who from Shah Wali Allah onwards sought help for Islam in India from the Perso-Islamic heartland. They were quickly disillusioned by the opportunism of the Afghans and the brutality of the Turkmen. Easy prey for communist propaganda, many returned in the early 1920s to become the organizers of the Communist Party in India (Ansari 1984:chs. 1, 2).

There was the poet, Muhammad Iqbal, who, in order to speak to the Perso-Islamic world, wrote his intellectually most sustained verse in Persian; his historical vision encompassed much of the Perso-Islamic past and his imagery with its tulips and *saqis* shared in its great tradition. But his inspiration was derived as much from Nietzsche, Bergson, and Schopenhauer as it was from Ghalib, Bedil, and Rumi. Arabian Islam, moreover, was his ideal, not that which had "gone astray in the scented rose-gardens of Iran." He waged war on the "Persian encrustation of Islam," on the pantheistic Sufism of Ibn al-ʿArabi, which robbed Muslims of the ability to move, to act, to over-power the forces of nature (Kamali 1971:211–14). He spoke for those *Ashraf* who had already turned for their religious inspiration towards Arabia. He spoke for those who were grappling with a framework of government which was no longer that of the Perso-Islamic patrimonial systems but that of the modern national state.

As they grappled, the *Ashraf* drew on their memory of the Perso-Islamic past to sustain them in the present. Many recalled that their forebears had come to India to rule. Power, and its management, was in their blood. It was their birthright. This feeling was at the heart of modern Muslim politics as they developed in northern India. It was instinct in the writings of the Aligarh movement, in the All-India Muslim League's insistence on the "political importance" of Muslims, in the power worship which runs through Iqbal's poetry, and in the development of the demand for Pakistan. While not forgetting the many other elements which helped to give birth to this new state, we would suggest that the emergence of Pakistan was the last striking expression of Perso-Islamic values in India, and one which has been revealed to be, like others in the twentieth century, not without its elements of paradox.

NOTES

1. No aspect of this culture was more widely enjoyed than poetry in Persian. In 1940, Sadriddin Aini, the Tajik writer, recalling his upbringing in the Bukharan village of Soktare, declared "Saʿadi, Hafiz, Bedil, Saʿib, Navai and Fuzuli and other classical poets I regarded as saints" (Aini 1958:5). The areas from which these poets come reveal a Perso-Islamic culture still living in late-nineteenth-century Central Asia: Saʿadi and Hafiz from Shiraz, and Saʿib from Isfahan, all from Iran, Bedil from Patna in India,

Navai from Herat in Afghanistan and Fuzuli from Najaf in Ottoman Iraq.

2. For the meaning in a social sense of the term *Ashraf* (sing.) *sharīf*, see Ansari (1960:35–68) and Dumont (1972:251–4). For some of the dangers in using the term see Ahmad (1966:268–78; 1973:xvii–xxxii, 157–94).

3. The special quality of an *Ashraf* upbringing has been most felicitously evoked by David Lelyveld in "Growing up *Sharīf*" (1978:35–68). Lelyveld also tells much about the ethos of these Muslims as a ruling class. They cherished all that they regarded as Perso-Islamic culture from styles of dress, manners, architecture, painting, and literature to manly sports and amusements. If their family trees confirmed to their own satisfaction their respectable origin, they announced their standing to the world in their personal style of "dignified temperament, self-confident but not overly aggressive, appreciative of good literature, music and art, but not flamboyant, familiar with mystical experience but not immersed in it," and in their education as men widely read in "Persian literature, able to quote a verse . . . who knew how to be polite, witty, and when appropriate, pious" (Lelyveld 1978:26–34).

4. In this period northern India boasted many small towns with populations of less than 5,000. Some were focuses of Hindu commercial activity, often known as *gunjes*, others were the Islamic gentry towns or *qasbahs*, which acted to an even greater extent than the cities as deep reservoirs of Perso-Islamic culture and the *Ashraf* tradition. For an examination of the development and the significance of these towns from the high Mughal period into the twentieth century see Bayly (1980; 1982:189–93, 364–8).

5. For the early development of the Dars-i Nizami see Ansari (1973). For its place in the development of Muslim education in India see Sufi (1977:89–152). For a discussion of the specific books established in the course of the early twentieth century and how they should be taught see Qidwai (1924).

6. Sharar was a native of Lucknow and a student at Farangi Mahal. Essayist, novelist, and historian, his articles on aspects of Perso-Islamic culture in eighteenth- and nineteenth-century Lucknow were published under the title *Hindustan men Mashriqī Tamaddun ka Ākhrī Namūna* ("The last example of oriental culture in India") over several years in the second decade of the twentieth century in his Urdu literary journal *Dil Gudaz*.

7. The differences between the Akhbaris and the Usulis revolved around two issues. First, regarding the sources of law, the Akhbaris restricted them to the Quran, the Hadiths, and the Imams, while the Usulis asserted that both the consensus (*ijmā'*) of the jurisprudents (*mujtāhids*), as well as the independent

reason (*ijtihad*) of a jurisprudent, could also serve as a source of legal judgment. Second, regarding the capacity to represent the Hidden Imam, Akhbaris agreed in principle that a relater of Hadiths from the Imams could act as a judge, but often forbad such action in practice in the absence of an infallible Imam. Usulis, on the other hand, asserted that the *mujtahids*, as general representatives of the Hidden Imam, could substitute for him in giving legal judgments, collecting and distributing alms, ordering defensive holy war, and leading Friday prayers.

8. Much work needs to be done on the role of the Naqshbandiyah in eighteenth- and nineteenth-century Asia. For an overview of their significance and a bibliography see Robinson (1982:118–25, 230), and for a summary of the range of work currently being done, CNRS Jeune Equipe, La Transmission du savoir dans le monde musulman périphérique (1984).

9. For a survey of this strand of thought, its heritage and the path of its development see Ahmad 1967; Rahman 1970; 1982.

10. Ahmad Raza Khan Barelwi's movement was a mass movement, defending popular Sufism, which grew in response to the influence of Deoband in the late nineteenth century. It should not be confused with Saiyid Ahmad Barelwi's *jihād* movement of the early nineteenth century. Note, too, that Ahmad Raza came from Bareilly, Saiyid Ahmad from Rai Bareli (Metcalf 1982:52–68, 296–314).

11. The *Ahl-i Hadiths* were an aristocratic and intellectual reformist movement of the nineteenth century, which sought guidance almost entirely from the Quran and the Hadiths. They opposed almost all Sufi practices (Metcalf 1982:268–96).

6
Theological "extremism" and social movements in Turko-Persia

ROBERT L. CANFIELD

PROBLEM AND ISSUES[1]

Islam encompasses many distinguishable subtraditions, and in the early centuries of Islam alternative viewpoints existed in abundance. Through dispute and debate, and sometimes by war and negotiation, some of the diverse ideas were discarded; others were rephrased to fit the accepted understandings of the majority of Muslims. Eventually a cluster of views congealed into a set of dogmas considered "orthodox." Unacceptable beliefs persisted, however, and became a means of expressing dissent from the central authorities, with whom "orthodox" views were identified. In this chapter I examine a series of social movements that made doctrinal claims that were rejected by the majority of Muslims and declared "heresy" by most Islamic theologians. As orthodox Islam hardened in response to these movements, their doctrines were suppressed. Even then, however, they persisted, eventually being sublimated into other doctrinal traditions that were more politically "moderate."

The central belief in these movements was that certain individuals had an exalted spiritual status because God was incarnated in them. The belief was called "exaggeration" or "extremism" (*ghulūw*) by

132

Islamic heresiographers. The earliest extremists, for example, deified ʿAli. The first person to be accused of *ghulūw*, ʿAbd Allah b. Saba', declared that ʿAli was the incarnation of God, that he "would one day return in the clouds, with thunder as his voice, and lightning as the radiance of his whip" (Moosa 1988:69). According to some of the sources ʿAli repulsed the followers of Ibn Saba' and banished him. Ibn Saba' nevertheless persisted in deifying ʿAli, and when ʿAli was assassinated he and his followers preached that he had not died and would some day return in the clouds.[2]

These ideas presumably had their origin in pre-Islamic gnosticism, which emphasized esoteric knowledge, cosmogony, and the secret powers of the alphabet (Wasserstrom 1985). They are "extreme" in a theologically defined sense, and differ from the exoteric extremism of the "orthodox" Islamic dogmatists, such as Ibn Hanbal, Ibn Taimiya, the Wahhabis, and other Islamic reformers, who advocated a formal adherence to Islamic regulations but despised esoterism. Indeed, it was the popularity of the esoteric extremist movements (the *ghulūw*) that prompted the exoteric extremists to formulate and defend their own views as "orthodox" (Wasserstrom 1985:2). The *ghulāt* (esoteric extremists) were accused by the "orthodox" heresiographers not only of theological heresy but also of moral debauchery: they were said to disregard conventional morality and to practice all sorts of repulsive and illicit acts, including incest.[3] These accusations were probably unjust: most of what we know about the *ghulāt* comes from their critics, whose own interests were often threatened by the popularity of the *ghulāt*. It is evident that the heresiographers at least sometimes overdrew the moral excesses of the extremists. The extremists did "exaggerate" in theological matters and some of them turned their extreme ideas into political rebellions, but few of them, if any, practiced or condoned the moral excesses attributed to them. Contrary to the accusations of their detractors, some of them observed ritual and moral requirements more carefully than the majority of Muslims around them.

However offensive esoteric extremist ideas may have been to the Islamic heresiographers, they were clearly popular among some elements of the population. A number of social movements that burst forth against the Muslim Caliphs in the early years of Islam were informed by extremist ideas. In that period dogmatic positions had not yet hardened among the Islamic authorities and many pre-Islamic traditions were still in place. Zoroastrianism was still strong, of course; but many syncretic faiths had intermingled in Iran and Central Asia: Marcionistic blends of gnosticism and Christianity; Manichaean syntheses of Buddhism, Christianity, Mithraism, gnosticism, and Zoroastrianism; and various other gnostic traditions, Jewish and animist. In the midst of this cacophony of ideological voices esoteric extremist ideas were notable for their appeal among the Muslim peoples of the eastern Caliphate. In periods of social disorder such ideas repeatedly surfaced as the ideological cover for popular expressions of discontent. Hopes for a divinely inspired savior persisted, passing from generation to generation, awakened from time to time into social movements by claims that the awaited savior had appeared.

In this concept a spiritually endowed hero was expected to bring social well-being. The concept naturally implied certain conceptions about what the hero would be like, and so constituted a kind of institutionalized anticipation, a formally defined hope for a heroic leader and a Utopian world that he would bring into being. The concept of course also entailed some abstract notions about the nature of leadership as well as some assumptions about the obligations of followers, about the nature and uses of knowledge, about the way God accomplishes His will in the world, and about the trajectory of history. It was this elaborate hope that was manifested in the responsiveness of people to the "heretical" claims of the *ghulūw*.

It is the appeal of this concept that interests us here. The appeal of the *ghulāt* exposes something of the nature of that institutional anticipation:

what attracts people to political leaders in times of high drama is more than calculation of utilitarian programs and strategies; it is something more emotional. And insofar as it is social – that is, does not attract only isolated individuals – it is composed of a configuration of cultural or symbolic forms, a "condensation of meanings into a symbolic figure" . . . which tacitly resonates with deeply felt understandings about the world . . . these tacit understandings, as well as much of language and culture in general, are metaphorical representations of experience. That is, their formulation and their validity resides not in verifiable science-like propositions but in their aptness for capturing or expressing experience. (Fischer 1980a:101, 103)

In this review of the *ghulūw* movements I want to draw attention to the emotional, symbolically condensed power of the eschatological hope for a savior that has been perpetuated for generations among the

134

Muslims of the eastern Islamic world. This hope was particularly intense in the eastern lands of Islam, where in the early centuries there were a number of "extremist" movements. Eventually, this eschatological vision spread to other parts of the Islamic world; social movements inspired by "extremist" notions have appeared in many places, especially in the later centuries of Islam. We will here follow the stirrings of this hope in the Turko-Persian Islamicate world, where it first arose among Muslim peoples, and where it was, especially in the early centuries of Islam, manifest in a number of radical social movements. Eventually it would be sublimated into other less opprobrious religious movements and through those means become a part of the heritage of many Muslims. It has persisted up to the present time. It was one of the inspirational impulses in the Islamic Revolution of Iran in which Ayatollah Khomeini was the object of popular veneration.

THE MORAL IMAGERY OF EXTREMISM

Two words, "Imam" and "Mahdi," enshrined special nuances for the esoteric extremists. Both took on a rich moral and eschatological content among the Shi'ites, and one of them, mahdi, although never in its broader eschatological sense formally accepted into Sunni dogma, was fully absorbed into the moral ideals of the Sunni populace.

The original meaning of "imam" was of course "leader," as it still is among the Sunnis, and it thus had obvious political implications, but it took on special meanings for the Shi'ites. The early Shi'ites became distinguishable in opposition to the Caliphs, who had grown richer and more worldly in their manner of living. As the times of the original Imam, Muhammad, receded into a golden past and his spiritual and moral stature acquired more splendor, the word "imam" became the Shi'ite term for the right kind of leader – just, wise, noble in birth (i.e., a descendant from the Prophet's lineage) – in contrast to the Caliph, who was manifestly a secular and political leader. Among the Shi'ites, and notably those in the eastern regions of the Caliphate, the imamate was a moral office, worthy of supreme deference, even if the incumbent never actually held the political office he deserved. The imamate also took on a mystical and spiritual ambiance: Imams were thought to have a deeper, more spiritual understanding of the Quran, to be custodians of cosmological secrets, and to be capable of miracu-

135

lous works. They were also regarded as personally sinless and their judgements as infallible; to many they were thought to be imbued with the divine light, infused with a spirit that had indwelt the sacred heroes of the past.[4] For many Shi'ites the crucial requirement of the believer was rightly to identify and venerate the true Imam of the times – a particularly difficult task in the first few Islamic centuries, in view of the plethora of voices claiming the imamate (Sachedina 1981:5ff.; Moosa 1988:94ff.).

Early Shi'ites with esoteric extremist tendencies probably affected the popular concept of "mahdi."[5] The term precisely meant "a rightly guided one" and was used very early with reference to 'Ali and Hosayn to mean a just and righteous ruler (Sachedina 1981:9). But as the Shi'ites were increasingly frustrated in their attempts to gain political power (and indeed sometimes, by their insurrections, brought upon themselves crueler oppressions) their conception of the righteous ruler for whom they longed became more vivid, and among some, notably those of the eastern Islamic territories, more imbued with Zoroastrian heroic nuances.[6] They awaited a savior, a "rightly guided one" who would "fill the earth with equity and justice as it [was] filled with injustice, oppression and tyranny" (Sachedina 1981:3). The term "Mahdi" was actually first applied in this sense to an unwilling candidate, Muhammad, a son of 'Ali by his wife al-Hanafiyya. Muhammad ibn al-Hanafiyya (as he is called) declined the mahdistic qualities ascribed to him but the times were fluid and coalitions in quest of someone to lead in opposition to the unpopular Umayyad Caliphs were numerous. People responded to the extravagant claims made for him by one of his more zealous admirers, and a movement gathered in Kufa in which he himself took no part. So strong was the movement, so vivid the popular hope for a mahdi, that after his death in 81/700 some people refused to believe that he had died; they claimed that he had merely gone into hiding and would eventually reappear to bring peace to the world (Sachedina 1981:11, 165).

The concept of a Mahdi has enshrined the hopes of many Muslims for a deliverer and a restorer of social order, whose appearance would mark the climax of history. Ibn Khaldun stated the notion as it was widely held among Sunnis, even though it was never formally endorsed by the Sunni 'ulamā: "It has been commonly accepted among the masses of the people of Islam, as the ages have passed, that there must needs appear in the End of Time a man of the family of Muhammad who will aid the Faith and make justice triumph; that the Muslims will follow him and that he will reign over the Muslim kingdoms and be called al-Mahdi" (quoted in Gibb and Kramers 1953:311).

EXTREMIST MOVEMENTS IN TURKO-PERSIA

Some early Shi'ite populations eagerly awaited the coming of such a deliverer, conceived as an "Imam" or a "Mahdi." In the Iranian heartland these concepts provided the ideological framework for a variety of popular movements. Some of them, especially the earlier ones, were essentially rebellions, but others were tempered by politically moderate influences, although in fact they remained essentially "extreme" in their theology.

Radical extremism in the high Caliphal period

Many of the uprisings against the Umayyad and Abbasid Caliphs were informed by esoteric extremist ideas, and in the second Islamic century (our eighth) most of the notable ones took place in Khurasan. The Islamic caliphs, situated in the Arab Near East, were some distance from Khurasan, and this region, naturally divided by deserts and a severe topography, became a caldron for the development of locally based discontent. Although subjected by Muslim Arabs in the first Islamic century (our seventh), the Iranian populations of Khurasan were never fully assimilated into the culture of their rulers. Their recalcitrance repeatedly erupted in local uprisings in the second/eighth century, and in the next century it brought forth the first Muslim dynasty of Khurasan, the Tahirids.

One of the earliest of these movements was organized by the Abbasids, a lineage identified by their eponymous ancestor, an uncle of Muhammad, al-'Abbas. The Abbasids were agitating well before the turn of the second Islamic century, although they did not emerge as a political force until much later. In 78/716 Muhammad b. 'Ali, the first politically active member of the Abbasid family, began to send out missionaries who were to solicit followings on his behalf. They went to various parts of the Muslim domains, but mostly into Khurasan. It would be thirty-four years, and Muhammad b. 'Ali would himself be dead, before an Abbasid would ascend to the Caliphate, and in the

137

intervening years several abortive uprisings presaged the massive convulsion that would bring the Abbasids to power. One of these abortive uprisings was led by ʿAbd Allah b. Al-Harb, or Ibn Harb, who rose up claiming that he had been inspired by the spirit of the great Muslim Imams of the past. These he identified as Muhammad, ʿAli (Muhammad's cousin and son-in-law), Hasan and Hosayn (sons of ʿAli by Muhammad's daughter Fatima), Muhammad ibn Hanafiyya, and finally Abu Hashem (the latter's son). Ibn Harb claimed that by the transmigration of the divine spirit he had received this spirit from Abu Hashem. (This may have been the earliest Muslim movement to have been inspired by a Buddhist-like notion of the transmigration of divinity.) But the uprising was soon to fail, for although Ibn Harb immediately attracted a loyal following, it soon dissolved, for his followers discovered that he as not omniscient, as they had supposed (Madelung 1973).

But the popular elements that had followed him found another object of veneration in ʿAbd Allah b. Muawiya, a great grandson of ʿAli's brother, Jaʿfar. ʿAbd Allah claimed to possess both divinity and prophethood, a combination of spiritual qualities that had inspired other great moral figures before him. Moreover, say the heresiographers, he denied the existence of heaven and hell, or any obligations to perform the ritual acts of piety – prayer, fasting, pilgrimage, and almsgiving – and he authorized wine, "the eating of corpses" (presumably meat slaughtered without the proper rituals), adultery, and sodomy (Daniel 1979:80ff.). In 129/746–7 a coup attempt in Kufa under his leadership failed and he and his followers fled to Khurasan, seeking a new locus of power, but he was executed there by a popular Abbasid missionary, Abu Muslim. Some of his followers, however, denied his death and expressed the hope that he would soon reappear. Some also differed among themselves over which of his successors had received his divine spirit, and they formed several competing movements (Zettersteen 1954).

At about the same time there arose another group in support of a man named Khidash who had been an Abbasid missionary in the eastern Islamic lands. Appealing to "the esoteric religion and social beliefs of the Khurasani masses,"[7] Khidash was extremely successful at gathering devotees to the Abbasid family, who were living in seclusion in Syria until the planned uprising was to be set in motion. But Khidash began to attribute to himself supernatural qualities. Affirming that the imamate had been transferred directly to him by his ancestor, al-ʿAbbas, he declared himself to be the incarnation of God. He also (according to the heresiographers) reinstituted libertine practices once associated with the Mazdakite rebellion in Iran a few generations before Islam, authorizing his followers "to enjoy each other's wives." This was why, according to one critic, "people hastened to him and accepted what he told them. They listened and obeyed." After he was killed – according to one source, crucified in Amul, and according to another, nailed to the gates of Kabul – some of his followers denied he was dead (Daniel 1979:36–7; Madelung 1979; Rekaya 1984).

Another uprising, in 131/748–9, revealed more clearly than others before it how strongly pre-Islamic eschatological hopes informed the popular unrest that was in the air, for it focused on a man who explicitly sought to blend Zoroastrian and Islamic practices. This was Bihafarid b. Maharwardin. He claimed to have been raised from death and to be imbued with miraculous power. He opposed Mazdakite libertinism, but instituted prayers that resembled those of the Zoroastrian/Magian religion suppressed in Iran by the Muslims. When he died – executed for being a Magian – his ideas and rituals persisted for centuries among groups who believed he had ascended to heaven "on a common dark brown horse" and would eventually return (Daniel 1979:92).

Only a few months after Bihafarid's death, the Abbasids, who had been active only in secret, issued the call for rebellion, and the peoples of Khurasan set it in motion. A truly popular movement, it appealed "to every area [of Khurasan] and every social group, [including] . . . some of the highest ruling elite" (Daniel 1979:37). The various local factions of Khurasan no doubt had their own reasons for rising up in support of the Abbasids; but they also shared certain concepts of authority and legitimacy that the Abbasids were able to exploit. The strength of the response to the Abbasid call to arms in Khurasan revealed, as the responses of these peoples to previous appeals had done, how ready these people were for a charismatic leader. The Abbasids had by that time exposed little about themselves: their doctrines were vague, their whereabouts obscure, and their plans secret; but through the agency of their missionary, Abu Muslim, they succeeded in generating strong support from many elements of Khurasan society. The Khurasanis were to become disillusioned and would, in fact, rise up against the Abbasids several times in the succeeding

139

century and eventually establish locally based Islamic powers of their own. The same mahdistic hope that had galvanized the first stirrings of the Abbasid movement was in each case placed on other persons who claimed unique rights to authority on grounds similar to those of the Abbasids.

The qualities for which the people of Khurasan looked were probably those that the Abbasids tried to appeal to in the stories they circulated about their reasons for seeking the Caliphate in the first place. One of these stories was that the Abbasids had descended from the Prophet's lineage, specifically from his uncle, al-ʿAbbas, whom they (untruthfully) represented as a loyal and righteous follower of Muhammad. This was a basis of authority that the Umayyad Caliphs, who had only a distant connection with the Prophet, and whose ancestors in any case had opposed him, could not match. But as other lineages had closer lineal ties with Muhammad through Fatima, his daughter, and her husband (and Muhammad's cousin) ʿAli, the Abbasids in addition claimed to have been especially designated to lead the Muslim community. This designation derived, according to one of their assertions, from the Prophet's promise to al-ʿAbbas that he and his descendants should be the leaders of the Muslim community; and according to another of their assertions, it came from Abu Hashem, the son of ʿAli's son Muhammad ibn al-Hanafiyya – a claim that thus presumed the propriety of the movement that arose around Muhammad ibn al-Hanafiyya in Kufa. They claimed that Abu Hashem's designating Muhammad b. ʿAli leader of the Abbasid house gave the family of ʿAbbas an additional legitimacy. But this appeal to authority was linked to another, that is, the knowledge of (vaguely defined) secrets, for it was said that Abu Hashem, as he lay dying of poison, passed on to Muhammad b. ʿAli certain secrets and instructions (Daniel 1979:28, 29). Another basis, according to the Abbasids, for their right to rule was that Muhammad b. ʿAli had been approached by a delegation from Khurasan who, in the attempt to organize an uprising against the Umayyads, were seeking someone "noble, pious, and generous" to lead their revolt. They first approached the leading personage of ʿAli's lineage, but he declined and referred him to Muhammad b. ʿAli, who took up the cause (Daniel 1979:29).

All these reasons for claiming the Caliphate the Abbasids gave after the fact; probably the reasons contained only grains of truth. But that such reasons were used at all suggests the grounds of authority that

140

were respected during this period: piety; noble descent (that is, as the Abbasids put it, descent from the Prophet's lineage);[8] designation by the previous Imam; possession of secret information on, as people supposed (it was never clear), such matters as future events, the rightful successor, and magic; generosity (which implied more than magnanimity, as the Arabic word for generosity, *karām*, was taking on the aura of miraculous power, *karāmāt*) – these were the qualities on which legitimate power was based in the early caliphal period in the eastern realms of Islam. A ground of authority that especially interested the esoteric extremists was direct revelation or direct inspiration by God. This source of authority was not explicitly claimed by the Abbasids; it was, however, implied in, for instance, broad hints that they had in visions received special gifts of understanding and insight.[9]

As already mentioned, the Abbasid movement was not the only one active at the turn of the first Islamic century. In the eastern Muslim lands – that is, in most of the territories of Khurasan and neighboring areas – rebellion was in the air. Many of the uprisings in Khurasan were inspired by an intense devotion to the Abbasids' own missionary-general, Abu Muslim. The responsive chord that was struck among the masses by Abbasid claims to the imamate was largely indebted to his genius. But tempted by his own vast popularity, Abu Muslim began to set up an independent rulership, and the Abbasids had him assassinated. This event was, however, only the beginning of Abbasid troubles with Abu Muslim, for his name became the battle cry of many subsequent rebellions. Many people supposed that Abu Muslim had not died but would return to lead his devotees against their enemies.

Among those that arose in his name was Sunbadh, a magian who two months after Abu Muslim's death in 135/753 led an uprising in Nishapur and Rayy that lasted only seventy days. Sunbadh believed that Abu Muslim had escaped death by reciting "God's greatest name," one known only by a sacred few. Transformed into a white dove, Abu Muslim had hidden in a secret fortress with Mazdak and the Mahdi and would return with them (Daniel 1979:126ff.). Besides Sunbadh's uprising there were others that were informed by the belief that Abu Muslim was still alive. Some people believed that he had been the last in a long series of incarnations of God. These people supposed that the same divine spirit would continue with Abu Muslim's descendants, in some of whom signs of supernatural power

141

were expected. Other groups – at least according to their critics – combined libertine ideas with the veneration of Abu Muslim, under the belief that the recognition of the Imam of their time was the only religious requirement, and they, as it was said, abandoned all Islamic proscriptions (Daniel 1979:130ff.; Madelung 1979). One group followed an associate of Abu Muslim, Ishaq al-Turk (d. circa 140/758–9), who led a revolt in Transoxiana, claiming that Abu Muslim was concealed in the mountains of Rayy and would bring Zoroaster with him when he returned (Barthold 1968 [1900]:199; Daniel 1979:130). And in about 141/759 a group formed around a native of Balkh known best by his title, Al-Muqanna', "The Veiled One." This man taught, like others before him, that Abu Muslim had been endowed with the divine spirit, having received it from other sacred heroes of the past. The chain Al-Muqanna' identified was the following: Adam, Seth, Noah, Abraham, Moses, Jesus, Muhammad, 'Ali, Muhammad ibn al-Hanafiyya, Abu Hashim, Muhammad b. 'Ali (the initiator of the Abbasid revolt), Al-Saffah, and Abu Muslim, from whom Al-Muqanna' claimed to have received the divine spirit. At first he declared himself a prophet, but soon began to call himself "a god who has the power to take his followers to paradise and revive the dead," supporting his extravagant pretensions with magical tricks. After his death his followers persisted in the belief that he "would someday return, riding on a gray horse, to restore his rule" (Daniel 1979:138–46). Another group of insurgents known as the Muhammira ("wearers of red") arose in 162/778–9 in Jurjan with the cry that Abu Muslim was alive and that the kingdom should be seized on his behalf. And nearly a century after Abu Muslim's death, Babak al-Khurrami and a successor named 'Ali b. Mazdak generated a movement in western Iran with the assertion that they had received Abu Muslim's powers by virtue of their descent from Abu Muslim's daughter (Madelung 1979). The hope for Abu Muslim's return persisted until as late as 345/956 when a group of men in western Iran rose up in veneration of a precocious child, "Kudak-i Dana" (translated by Madelung, "omniscient boy"), a great-great-grandson of Abu Muslim, who was believed to have received the divine spirit (Madelung 1979).

Politically moderate Shi'ism and extremist hopes

The imputation of divinity to certain leaders, and the belief of some groups in the transmigration of the divine spirit, served as part of the ideology of some rebellions, and as a consequence were viciously suppressed by the caliphal governments and severely criticized by "orthodox" Islamic authorities. Nevertheless, esoteric extremist ideas persisted and provided the justification for radical uprisings well into the ninth/fifteenth century. They also persisted in the form of eschatological hopes for a deliverer that have lasted much longer, even to the present, in politically moderate forms. They were even eventually incorporated, although sometimes under other guises, into the "orthodox" dogmatic traditions. In Sunnism they found a place as it became more self-conscious after the fourth/tenth century, and in "orthodox" Shi'ism they were absorbed in a politically moderate position that avoided persecutions by the Sunnis.

The Shi'ite sects that survived – of which the Imamis and Isma'ilis were the most important – placed esoteric extremist notions at the core of their theologies but clothed them in innocuous forms. Esoteric extremist ideas were, from the beginning, intrinsic to Shi'ism, and, despite the opposition of many eminent Islamic authorities, they continued from generation to generation to capture the popular imagination of Shi'ites. This may be why extremist notions were never expunged from Imamism. Even so, Imamism survived by projecting an image of political moderation, fostered by the Shi'ite Imams themselves. The most important Imam to sublimate extremist notions into less politically threatening forms was Ja'far al-Sadiq (d. 148/765). Ja'far, like other Imams before him, was approached by activist factions seeking a leader for a revolt against the Abbasid caliphs; and like most others he refused. Moreover, he used his considerable influence – which was based on his descent from Hosayn and his authority as a jurist and theologian – to persuade his devotees to control their rebellious impulses. They should wait for the appearance of the Mahdi, he said, who would then summon the faithful to arms and launch an insurrection that would deliver the Shi'ites from their misery and distress.[10] The notion of the Mahdi was not essentially changed under Ja'far's influence, only its practical application. While still allowing the eschatological expectations of the Imami believers, with their explosive revolutionary potential, he taught that the Mahdi must be awaited; until the Mahdi appeared, people should refrain from actively seeking him and, until his appearance is clear, from making any move on his behalf.

Imami Shi'ite dogmatic formulations, while hedging the concept of the Mahdi into a content less alarming to a central government, also reshaped the concept of the Imam. Imamis retained some extremist notions in their concept of the Imam but also gave it a certain formal elegance, in particular with respect to 'Ali. The formal Imami Shi'ite position became that 'Ali was a morally superior being, possessing "sainthood" (*wilāyat*), which entailed the esoteric function of revealing the secret meaning of God's revelation; Muhammad possessed only "prophethood" (*nubuwah*). When he died, the revelation remained essentially intact in its esoteric aspect, but it was God's will (Shi'ites say) that no generation afterward should lack a saint (*walī*) who would keep alive the inner, esoteric understanding of Islam. This was 'Ali's function. Through him God supplied the spiritual impulse for the right practice of Islam in the hearts of the believers (Vaglieri 1956; Nasr 1974). 'Ali was the proper teacher of religious law and the proper example and guide in worship and religious understanding. Shi'ite hadith emphasized 'Ali's sacred status: he was supreme above all others, the "noblest in merit and religion," "the tongue of the word of God," "the door of knowledge" (Gibb and Kramers 1953:534–41). But under the influence of popular suppositions 'Ali was granted an even more elevated moral essence: he was considered infallible in judgment, the critical link into the cosmos (because he knew its esoteric secrets); he was not only the guarantor of true faith on earth but also the "pole" (*qutb*) of the cosmos, around whom the spheres of existence rotated, without whom the world could not have existed, in whom all the processes of nature found their essence (Madelung 1971; Nasr 1974). 'Ali, then, became to the Imami Shi'ites the spiritual essence of God. As an esoteric truth this belief was hidden from most, only known to the believers who understood the deeper essence of Islam.

'Ali's function as the supreme saint of the Islamic community was taken over, according to Shi'ite theologians, by his heirs after him in a line of designated male descendants, the Imams, who successively received, like 'Ali, the sacred quality of sainthood (*wilāyat*) and therefore became the rightful leaders, the accurate teachers of Islamic dogma, and the spiritual guides for the community. In principle, the

144

spiritual essence of sainthood which was enshrined in the imamate for the benefit of the Islamic community would never cease until the Day of Judgment. This principle was, however, challenged by events, for the twelfth Imam vanished without issue. Shiʿite theologians came to regard the twelfth Imam as having gone into concealment, like other claimants to the imamate before him, until the time when he would return to bring justice and salvation to his devotees. The concepts of the Imam and the Mahdi thus were merged into a condensed core of eschatological hope for the Imami Shiʿites.

The Ismaʿilis, like the Imamis, also found ways to sublimate extremist ideas into their formal dogma. In the eleventh century they had mounted radical movements against the established rulers, notably from Hasan-i Sabah's hideout at Alamut. But after Hasan-i Sabah and the Alamut fortress were reduced, the Ismaʿili elements moderated their political profile. Like most of the Shiʿite factions, they held that every believer must know the Imam of the time, and that no generation could exist without an Imam. As was wont among the Shiʿites generally, the Ismaʿilis repeatedly divided over the succession to the imamate, and the subgroups developed some distinctive teachings. The Ismaʿilis in most of the eastern Islamic lands followed the Nizari subsect which formed in the fifth/eleventh century, holding that the only authoritative source of instruction was the Imam of the age and that the resurrection was essentially a spiritual discovery – namely, that the Imam was, in his essence, divine, and thus greater than the prophets. They believed, as had some pre-Islamic groups, that history was cyclic, and that in each cycle, marked by the appearance of a Prophet, there was an ancillary figure who, despite a shadowy secondary position, was in fact, the divinity. ʿAli, not Muhammad, was the greatest figure of the Islamic past, for he was the incarnation of God. In addition, just as there was in every age a prominent figure and a humble figure who masked the divine incarnation, there was an outward truth and an inward esoteric truth enshrining the spiritual essence of truth. Muhammad gave the outward meaning in the form of the Quran; but ʿAli knew its inner meaning and passed it on to his heirs. Thus was preserved under divine oversight the secret for the protection and guidance of the believing community by the living Imams.

This is the formal doctrine of the Ismaʿilis. But it should not be regarded merely as a teaching that the Ismaʿili authorities imposed

145

upon the popular conscience; for the popular readiness to impute such powers – that is, to insist that their Imams were the repositories of divine insight and power – sometimes welled up in the face of the Imams' own protestations. In the seventh/thirteenth century Imam Jalal al-Din Hasan, in order to ally himself with the Caliph against the Crusaders, distanced himself from the extremist notions of the Isma'ilis and announced that he was a Sunni. Requiring his followers to practice the Sunni rite, he brought in Sunni scholars to instruct both him and his followers. The Isma'ilis obeyed him faithfully, apparently becoming Sunnis; but within a generation Isma'ili theologians were teaching that, for reasons known only to him through his divine insight, Jalal al-Din Hasan had introduced a period of dissimulation among the Isma'ilis to bracket a new period marking the beginning of the last cycle of history (Madelung 1973). This doctrine probably did not originate among these learned authorities, for the common Isma'ili believers appear to have persisted in the belief that divine insight and power remained inherent in their Imam. The theological formulation seems to have followed – or perhaps, better, given formal expression to – what had persisted, in a less formalized shape, in the popular imagination.

The Isma'ilis had by then been dispersed after the destruction of Alamut by the Mongols, and Isma'ilism had become an esoteric religion, secretly propagated and preserved among scattered populations in the isolated regions of Islamdom. But its extremist notions permeated other traditions, notably the Sufi orders, whose moral imagery readily lent itself to Isma'ili teaching. The Isma'ili missionary, Nasir-i Khusraw, for example, was often taken as a Sufi, and his poetry, with its emphasis on the importance of interior piety, is still widely appreciated among Sunnis.[11]

Sufi extremism

But esoteric extremism percolated into Sufism from other sources than Isma'ilism, and Sufism provided the institutional framework for attracting numbers of people to Sunnism at the expense of Shi'ism. What would later be called Sufism was at first the pietism of a worship-minded few in contrast to the administratively minded rulers and the legally minded clergy. The early pietists attended to the worship of God in informal rituals and routines of self-abnegation, but they were

146

undistinguished from the rest of the Muslims.[12] By the third/ninth
century, however, they had a name for what they did, *tasawwuf,*
"Sufism," although some of the more pious individuals felt that true
worship had already by that time decayed; in the words of one,
"Today Sufism is a name without a reality, but formerly it was a
reality without a name" (Sufi al Fushanji, quoted in Lings 1969:253).
Sufism was taught formally as a method of worship and spiritual
realization by venerated sheikhs, and in Baghdad and elsewhere
growing numbers of people in search of a deeper religious reality
attended the lectures.

But there was a further development. What was initially a withdrawal from the gathering formalism of the Islamic scholars turned
into a form of popular resistance against the legalism of the jurists and
the erudition of the theologians in the third/ninth century. By the
fifth/eleventh century Sufism had become, in some places, an agency
of outright protest against oppressive rulers, and in other places, those
where the social fabric was weakening, a social and political shelter
(Gibb 1961:134–6; Rahman 1966:151). But the Sufi orders were not
then as solidified as they would later become in the aftermath of the
Mongol invasions in the seventh/thirteenth century. That was a time
when, in the words of one Anatolian observer, "the affairs of the world
lost order and organization," or, in the words of someone else, there
was "utter darkness, disunity, and corruption."[13] In such a context the
Sufi brotherhoods provided a necessary semblance of social and political structure.

Sufi sheikhs (or *pīrs*) enjoyed authority because of the widespread
belief that they might be special friends of God, *walīs.* This term had
no such implications in Quranic times,[14] but had acquired them by
the third/tenth century under the influence of gnosticism (Rahman
1966:136). Hujwiri, a Sufi from Ghazni, writing in Persian in the
fifth/eleventh century, expressed the grand and glorious qualities associated with the *walīs*:

God has chosen [them] to be the governors of his kingdom and has marked
them out to manifest his actions and has favored [them] with diverse kinds of
miracles [*karāmāt*] and has purged [them] of natural corruptions and has
delivered [them] from subjection to their lower soul and passion, so that all
their thoughts are of Him alone . . . Through [the] blessing of their advent the
rain falls from heaven, and through the purity of their lives the plants spring
from the earth, and through their spiritual influence the Moslems gain vic-
tories over unbelievers. (al-Hujwiri 1910 [originally *c.* 450/1050]:212–13.)

147

Indeed, in the opinion of the great Islamic poets from the seventh/
thirteenth century onward, *walīs* were – as the Imams had been to the
Shiʿite esoteric extremists – the mouthpiece of God, even the incarnations of God. Jalaludin-i Rumi spoke of his own sheikh, Shams-i
Tabrizi (who may have had connections with the radical Ismaʿilis at
Alamut), as "a chosen organ and mouthpiece of the Deity" (Nicholson
1898:xviii).

Esoteric notions of divine inspiration, sublimated to the formal
requirements of Sunni jurisprudence by al-Ghazali's theological dis-
courses in the eleventh century, were accepted, even if reluctantly,
into main-line Sunnism. It is to such notions of mystical inspiration
that the term "Sufism" normally has applied. Esoteric ideas had by
that time long been part of Shiʿite thought. They were evident already
in the notion that ʿAli was a *walī* with even greater power and insight
than Muhammad, and that his saintly power (*wilāyat*) was passed to
his descendants; and after the sixth/twelfth century in the notion that
this power had passed to some Shiʿite sheikhs. Thus, the esoteric ideas
formerly associated with extremism persisted, with variations, among
Shiʿites and Sunnis alike.

Extremism under the Safavids

The esoteric extremist notions implicit in the claims of the Sufi masters seemed especially to grip the imaginations of the Turkic populations who had been for several centuries pushing in greater numbers
into Western Asia and who became the source of the military power of
the Safavid dynasty in Iran. "Turkish popular Islam was . . . from the
first intimately associated with the Sufis and their organizations" (Gibb
1970:224–5).

One of the notable Sufi orders to attract the intense loyalty of the
Turkish populations collected around the descendants of Sheikh Safi
ud-Din (650–735/1252–1334). Regarded as the "unique one in the
world," he was venerated by the Turkish peoples in the towns and
countryside of eastern Anatolia, and even by their Mongol rulers. He
was reputed for his knowledge of both secular and religious matters,
and his ability to work miracles (Mazzaoui 1972:49–52). He was a
quiet man, pious and scholarly, widely trusted among the people, as
were his heirs for several generations after him. But his great great
grandson, Sheikh Junaid, transformed the pious collection of Sufi

148

devotees that had formed around himself as a descendant and heir to the spiritual eminence of Sheikh Safi ud-Din into a political movement that would acquire lands and wealth and eventually dominate Iran. Shiekh Junaid and his descendants were known as the Safavid dynasty. They combined both religious and secular powers, and "forsook poverty and humility for the throne of a kingdom" (Fadl Allah ibn Ruzbihan Khunji, quoted in Mazzaoui 1972:72). To effect his political objectives Junaid encouraged his followers to ascribe to him divinity. They called him "the Living One – there is no God but he," and killed anyone who challenged their claim (Mazzaoui 1972:73). When his son Haidar acceded to the throne he was announced as the divinity and his Turkmen Sufi followers prostrated themselves before him. Isma'il I, Haidar's son (r. 1501–24), explicitly courted the abject devotion of his followers, although he seemed at the same time to be repelled by it. In his poetry he falsely claimed descent from 'Ali and Fatima and averred that he was the reincarnation of 'Ali's divine substance and had formerly abode with God; now he had appeared in the world, the hallowed powers of the Prophets and the Imams having combined in him. He explicitly claimed to be God, light, the Seal of the Prophets, the perfect guide (Mazzaoui 1972:73). These claims were merely reflections of a practice of adoration already in place: "From the time of Isma'il's grandfather, the heads of the Safavid Sufi order were worshipped as saviors and incarnations of God by their Turkmen followers" (Arjomand 1981:4).

This tradition of worship became the basis for the establishment of a politico-military administrative structure. In Isma'il's time there was "a thorough permeation of the military pillar of the state with extremist religion in the form of millenarian savior worship" (Arjomand 1981:4). This system provided advantages to both the Shah and his followers: to him it provided an ideology for appealing to their loyalty as bodyguards and administrative servants; to them it represented their special access and privileges as his personal servants. But once Shah Isma'il's position was secure, stabilized by an embryonic but loyal bureaucracy, he became distrustful of his most zealous devotees and he recoiled from the ideology that bound them to him. A visitor to his court reported that he was "not pleased with being called a god or a prophet . . . [and] put to death several of his disorderly fanatical devotees" (Arjomand 1981:4).

Isma'il's son, Shah Tahmasb (r. 1524–76), "whom they continued

149

to venerate as God," similarly tried to suppress the ritual expressions of devotion by his Turkmen followers; by this time the ruling institution was in place and Shah Tahmasb was more threatened than reassured by the extremist notions of his devoted followers. He removed from the works of his ancestors all claims to being the Mahdi or the Mahdi's precursor, "ordered the bloody suppression" of esoteric extremists in one of the Turkish tribes, "put down the heresy of a group of Sufis who proclaimed him the Mahdi," and put to death or imprisoned devotees in another tribe (Arjomand 1981:5). Eventually, Shah Tahmasb managed to strip away any image of divine inspiration, but the mahd-istic hope entailed in the concept persisted: the Turkish esoteric extremists imputed the "divine charisma" to the Khalifas, the "assistants" of the Sufi sect. Eventually this imputation of divine power to the Khalifas brought upon them the wrath of the Shah. Isma'il II (r. 1576–7) blinded the chief Khalifa and at the same time "massacred a large number of his Sufis in Qazvin" (Arjomand 1981:5).

Again, however, in the time of Shah 'Abbas I (r. 1587–1629), when the foundations of the regime were cracking, the Shah turned back to his Turkish followers, and exploited their "sincere loyalty and unques-tioning obedience to the King as the supreme spiritual leader." However, again, when it was possible to do without them, he replaced his *sufigari* corps with a secularized corps whom he called the Shah-savani ("King lovers"). The tension between his Sufi servants and the bureaucracy he was installing in their place led him to extreme measures. In 1614–15 he massacred the "old Sufis of Lahijan" who "had priority over other Sufis as the oldest adherents of the Safavid order" (Arjomand 1981:6). The rest of his Sufi followers he made guards and gate-keepers for his palace, and jailers and executioners for his prisons. By 1660 the word "sufi" simply meant "trooper" and had overtones of "riff-raff" (Arjomand 1981:6).

Other extremist movements

Esoteric extremism provided the moral imagery that informed some marginal movements in the fourteenth through the sixteenth cen-turies. There arose, for example, in the eighth/fourteenth century an esoteric extremist movement in Iran, Transoxiana, and Anatolia led by a putative descendant of 'Ali named 'Abd al-Rahman, who took for himself the title "Fadl Allah," "the Grace of God." Fadl Allah claimed

150

to be "the Lord of Time" and "the Sultan of all the prophets," and the exact "theophany of the inaccessible divine treasure." He claimed to have received in visions and dreams the revelation that he had appeared at "a time of divine glory," and would be the innovator of a new cycle of revelation. He supported these claims by portraying his own dreams as revelations, by interpreting the dreams of his followers and by, as they believed, reading their thoughts. Moreover, he claimed to know the esoteric meanings of the letters of the alphabet through which hallowed secrets could be understood – a knowledge, it was presumed, that existed in the mythical book *Jafr*, believed possessed by the descendants of the Prophet, "containing all they needed to know and all that was to happen until the Judgment Day" (Gibb and Kramers 1953:80–1); or, as was also said, a knowledge that may have come "through vision and with the aid of divine intervention" (Fahd 1967). His followers believed, in fact, that the divine name, Allah, was traced on the lines of his face; and as part of the cult rituals they recited, "There is no God but *f ' h*," a cryptogram for Fadl Allah (Bausani 1956b). Fadl Allah founded an esoteric Sufi-like order, known as the Hurufiyya, that became distinctive for its practice of divination on the basis of the numerical value of words. And their preoccupation with the esoteric meanings of names and numbers was acquired by other groups, many of them less extreme. Much later, in 999/1590–1, a Hurufiyya group would rise up in rebellion in Shiraz under the leadership of a blind poet, Amri, who claimed to be the incarnation of God, like the great sacred heroes of the past (Arjomand 1981:8–9).

Two other movements in the ninth/fifteenth century manifesting extremist notions had their origins in the teachings of Ahmad ibn Fahd al-Hilli, a leading Imami Shiʿite scholar, who was said to know magic and miracle working. He was eventually embarrassed by uses made of his magical teachings by his students, but the power of the movements that sprang up in response to their ideas displayed the responsiveness of people to claims of extraordinary powers. One of Ibn Fahd's students was Muhammad ibn Falah, better known as al-Mushaʿsha.[15] Al-Mushaʿsha declared himself to be the Mahdi, claiming descent from Muhammad, and made use of magical devices learned from his teacher to attract a following, most of whom were Arab tribes in southern Iraq. Another was Muhammad Nurbakhsh (795–869/1393–1477) founder of the Nurbakhshiyya Sufi order in

151

eastern Iran and Transoxiana.[16] Nurbakhsh was called "the Imam and Caliph" and "the Mahdi," and claimed to have mastered all sacred and secular sciences. He taught that the Imam should be a descendant of ʿAli and Fatima, which he claimed to be, and to have accomplished the "greater holy war" of purifying the soul, which he claimed to have done (Gibb and Kramers 1953:452–4; Algar 1976).

At about the same time a similar extremist movement arose in Baluchistan. The Zikris identified the Mahdi as someone named Nur Pak, who was taken to be the possessor of pure light created by God before Adam, given, it was believed, in the last days of mankind to restore the faith. The mahdistic hope was explicit in the Zikri creed: "There is no god but God, and Nur Pak, the Mahdi, is the Prophet of God" (Pastner 1978:233ff.).

During this period an esoteric extremist rebellion also took place on the margins of the dominant powers. The Rowshaniyya was a sect that arose in the Pushtun-speaking environs of Peshawar in the middle part of the sixteenth century. They formed around Bayazid Ansari whose teachings were "largely based on a pantheistic Sufism to which he added a belief in the transmigration of souls, ingrafting thereon various eclectic and syncretic features, of which the most notable, according to his critics, was that the complete manifestation of the Godhead was to be seen in the persons of the holy men, more particularly in his own" (Caroe 1965 [1958]:201). Bayazid attracted many converts and tried to mobilize the Pushtun tribes to overthrow the Moghul emperor, Akbar, but was eventually defeated in battle and killed in 1585. The movement continued, led for several generations by his descendants, and may be the basis of the Shiʿism still followed by some of the Orakzai and Turi Pushtuns.

Extremism in the modern period

Extremist notions have continued into the modern period, after Western influences intruded into Central and South-West Asia, but largely in the form of the movements already mentioned. Ismaʿilis still exist in various parts of the region, and of course they continue to believe their Imam is the repository of divinity. (Actually, the Ismaʿilis that I knew in Afghanistan never quite admitted this to me. What they said was that the Imam, Prince Karim Khan, was "completely near to God"; he of course did not sin. Moreover, his *mukki* or representative to them – that is, their *pīr* – also did not sin, they said.) Similarly, the Zikris persist in Baluchistan, with the esoteric extremist beliefs already mentioned. And although the Sufi orders most often mentioned are politically moderate, extremist notions exist among some of them. An unsympathetic Afghan once told me that the son of a great sheikh in Afghanistan was regarded by his clients as the incarnation of God even though he was an alcoholic. His followers believed, my informant said, that he was drinking the wine of heaven. Another observer has noted signs of extremism among the Naqshbandi Kurds of Turkey, implicit in their notion that a certain Naqshbandi sheikh was the *ghawth* – the highest single *walī* – of their time. The belief has usually implied merely a close association with divinity, but an "extreme" version of the belief was explicitly proposed in 1927 when an over-zealous disciple declared Sheikh Ahmed Bazani to be an incarnation of God. The Sheikh himself made nothing of it and the idea died (as well as the disciple) soon afterward (Van Bruinessen 1978:439 n.).[17] Another recent expression of the eschatological hope associated with esoteric extremism has been the claim by the Nurjus in Turkey that their founder, Saidi Nursi, had not died on March 23, 1960, as was announced, but had only gone into hiding and would eventually return (Dumont 1986).

The most notable expression of extremist eschatological hopes in modern times has of course been the Islamic Revolution in Iran. There were many impulses behind this massive social convulsion and it would be unwise to overdraw the importance of any one influence, but esoteric extremist hopes were clearly expressed in the movement. Such hopes were apparently sparked first among the students of Khomeini but they were also aroused among the laity by Khomeini's interest in mysticism. Khomeini was an unusual teacher in Qum, in that he taught (among other things) courses in esoteric mysticism, a subject regarded with suspicion by the Shi'ite clergy. Indeed, he is said to have experimented with mystical exercises (Fischer 1980a:110). Khomeini's interest in mysticism and his publications on subjects of wide interest, such as the proper form of worship at shrines, and his open opposition to the Shah made him a notable theological figure (Fischer 1983:152).

As public resentment against the Shah rose in the 1970s Khomeini's reputation rose with it. Rumors about his special mystical insights further added to his influence. A sense of divine purpose was ascribed to him by some of his students, and in the period when Khomeini was in exile in Iraq they let out that he had learned through divination that he was destined to return to Qum (which of course he did, after the flight of the Shah in 1979; Fischer 1980b:177). In the early 1970s, when resentment against the Shah was gathering, Khomeini's students began to refer to him as "Imam" Khomeini, and this title was apparently first ascribed to him publicly in 1975 (Fischer 1980b:127). It was a pointed usage, for the eschatological nuances of the term were evident to the theological students, as well as to many of the laity.

A transformation in the image of the acceptable national leadership for Iran was taking place in the 1970s: as the awe of Persian kingship slowly left the Shah the aura of the Shi'ite imamate gathered upon Khomeini (Mottahdeh 1985:374). By 1978, the excitement was growing; more people were referring to the exiled cleric as "Imam Khomeini" (Fischer 1980b:183) and some wondered if Khomeini were the long-awaited Twelfth Imam returning from occultation (Robinson 1982:168). He was also called by some the "Saheb-i Zaman" (master of the era), another term used for the Mahdi (Moosa 1988:99). Khomeini apparently first applied the term "Imam" to himself in 1977 (Taheri 1985:170–1). He was called "Imam" in a widely known ode to him that was reproduced at the beginning of his biography:

The throne is yours in the whole Islamic world
From the Nile Valley to the banks of the Shatt al-Arab
You are the Imam among the ulema . . .
Your thought is victorious by the glory of the Quran
And your name is everlasting, we swear by your name.
(quoted in Fischer 1983:150)

In a regular television program, the general prosecutor, Ayatollah Muhammad Gilani, began each program by praising God and Muhammad, adding a similar benediction on Khomeini: "Peace be upon our leader and guide, the Mahdi and his representation and Wali al-Amr [ruler in charge], the Imam, Khomeini" (Moosa 1988:99).

The use of the terms "Imam" and "Mahdi" in these expressions allowed several possible meanings, and in fact not everyone took Khomeini to be the Imam in the established Shi'ite sense. There were several distinguishable views on Khomeini among the Iranian peoples. Besides the devotees who ascribed to him the imamate, many more recognized him as merely the supreme jurist of the law. This implied a person who is just and "better than any other" (Khomeini's term;

Mottahedeh 1985:243), one who thus has the right (and obligation) to serve as the guardian of the Islamic community on behalf of the Imam. This was a concept developed by Khomeini, and it would eventually add special nuances to popular notions of the imamate (Taheri 1985:318); it became a central concept in the constitution of the Islamic Republic of Iran. In the fervor of the revolutionary struggle in 1978 many of the educated middle class accepted Khomeini as such a jurist and argued that whatever he said should be done without question (Fischer 1980b:212). Many Iranians, nevertheless, even in the moment of his highest popularity, granted him no supernatural authority: a rival ayatollah remarked that the Twelfth Imam was not expected to arrive by jumbo jet (Robinson 1982:168). And some people refused to accept the new call to prayer established after Khomeini's accession to power: "God is Great!" (twice), followed by "Khomeini is the Mahdi!" (twice) (Moosa 1988:99).

At no time was Khomeini universally accepted as the Imam or as his deputy, but in the high enthusiasm of the revolution the support for him, although driven by various motives from pious to practical, was evidently huge. The urgency of popular discontent and the strength of popular hopes for deliverance combined with an exalted concept of authority that was ambiguous enough to encompass a diversity of opinions. The concepts of the Imam and the Mahdi, and the esoteric notions of the guardianship of the jurist, were with various understandings applied to Khomeini, enabling him to mobilize one of the most dramatic revolutionary movements of modern times.

EXTREMISM AS A CULTURAL PHENOMENON

The common thread in these diverse social and cultural movements has been the imputation of divinity, in some form, to the leaders of these movements. The eschatological expectation it enshrined was not so much "messianic" (a common analytical term I have avoided) as mahdistic; the hope was for a Mahdi. It was not usual, for instance – Bihafarid being the only exception mentioned here – for a leader to be acclaimed risen from the dead, as the Christians did of Christ; rather, as in the Quranic version of the story of Christ, the leader had never died. In this kind of "messianism" the leader usually does not die but disappears until a time when he will return to launch "a great social

transformation ... and adjust all things under divine guidance"
(Sachedina 1981:2). Besides the concept of Mahdi the other concepts
mentioned here – Imam, *walī*, sheikh – also imply Mahdi-like qualities, for these sacred leaders were also believed to be divinely inspired,
capable of bringing order and direction to a disordered society.
Through discussion and debate about such subjects as the nature of
leadership, the trajectory of history, and the social obligations of
believers, extremist ideas about the incarnation of divinity were shaped
and contained, although never really quenched. They were brought
into the orthodox Islamic traditions – in particular, in the Shi'ite
concepts of Mahdi and Imam, the Sunni concept of the awaited
Mahdi, and the Sufi concepts of the divinely inspired *walī* and sheikh
– and they continue, in some form, to represent a certain widely held
hope for social and personal deliverance.

For the people who have held these notions there has been a practical difficulty in applying them, for such leaders are not easily identified. Some qualities are rather easily recognized, such as descent from
a sacred leader, personal piety, and miraculous power; but the relation
of these qualities to sacred authority is never precisely specified, so that
the ideal images of the sacred leader are never easily attached to real
men. Even a *walī* himself, according to Hujwiri, may be unaware of
his sacred status, so engrossed in the worship of God is he. The
identification of a sacred leader – Mahdi, Imam, *walī*, or sheikh – can
thus be subject to rumor and the whims of public opinion. The
'ulamā, the trained authorities of Islam, have claimed a strategic role
in the public recognition of sacred leadership, designating themselves
as the only experts qualified to distinguish true sacred leadership from
its counterfeit and authentic miracle signs from spurious ones. By
virtue of this authority the *'ulamā* and the mullahs – the less well-
trained specialists of Islamic knowledge, who are sometimes the only
authorities available on the local level – have had a powerful influence
on the public response to those leaders who have claimed sacred
authority. The *'ulamā* and mullahs form a loose network of specialists
who, in distinguishable subsets, perpetuate distinctive traditions of
interpretation and application. They constitute a key institution of
social influence, not only for the perpetuation of abstract notions
about sacred leadership but also for the recognition of sacred leaders.
The social movements chronicled here demonstrate not only that
extremist ideas have been perpetuated for generations in stories,

156

legends, sermons, and other media of popular imagery, but also that certain learned authorities, perhaps of many sorts, have for generations tolerated, if not supported, the extremist ideas that galvanized these movements.

The pool of ideas about sacred leadership already in place among these peoples supplied the underlying cultural resource for the rise of sacred leaders. Those who aspired to sacred leadership were able to capture popular support by invoking extant concepts of sacred authority. Even if most of the leaders of these movements actively sought to lead, it was the response of people to the ideals and images they invoked that set collective activities in motion. The people who followed showed by their behavior that the notions invoked were for them vivid enough to be potential realities. Some of the followings behaved, in fact, as if they believed their world to be imperfect without a Mahdi-like hero, for they imputed to their leaders more than was actually claimed. Even death could not, in some cases, destroy their leaders, whom they sometimes regarded as only concealed for a time. Some people insisted on imputing authority even after it was repudiated; for example, when Jalal al-Din Hasan tried to convert his Isma'ili followers to Sunnism, they not only continued to venerate him as the Isma'ili Imam but also developed a dogma to explain his unusual behavior. And when the Safavid Shahs tried to destroy their Turkmen Sufi devotees, the Sufis continued to treat them as incarnations of God, and only under great pressure redirected their worship to the Khalifas – who may not have relished the honor, as it placed their own lives in jeopardy. It is true that the Turkmen Sufis' rites of homage masked a practical motive: to protect their special access to the Shahs. But what is significant for our purposes was the exaggerated imagery of the mask; for it represented their practical interests as devotion to a god. As in other cases of extremism, a human being was given a spiritually elevated status, an office. The incumbent of the office was considered a uniquely endowed, divinely inspired personage commissioned to lead the faithful and to bring order to social affairs. This notion was so vivid to some groups that it persisted in the face of the leader's own denials and repudiations. It is hardly surprising that such a notion served well as the idiom of social movements.

Political power is often said to be claimed. Our cases here – and especially the more dramatic ones – draw attention to the other side of political power, legitimacy. Legitimacy is enshrined in moral images

157

that are already generally understood. It is a public phenomenon, made of concepts of value and significance that exist in the public imagination. The uprisings described here were presumably, like many movements, attempts of distressed people to gain relief and to set straight worlds that had "lost order." But the relief that was sought and the ordered worlds that were desired were constructs entailing hopes and ideals that persisted for other reasons than the mere manipulative designs of leaders. Those ideal constructs had an appeal in their own right. Imposed on the discursive circumstances of human affairs, they helped people understand their circumstances and organize to respond to them. In these cases, whether or not legitimacy was claimed, it was in the end essentially a status granted, a quality imputed on the basis of ideal constructs already in place. The granting and the imputation were done by people who followed. Divine statuses and Mahdi-like qualities had a social impact because they belonged to the structured world of imagination that informed the life and experience of multitudes of ordinary people.

THE INTRACTABILITY OF TRANSCENDENT IMAGES

The social movements we have examined here were overt manifestations of people's attempts to match their ineffable notions of virtue and hope with the real and changing conditions of practical experience. Notions of that sort never quite match the conditions they are applied to; they only more or less work as mechanisms for understanding the discursive affairs of life. Ideas are gradually revised or emended over time as they are pressed into service to explain situations. Because the situations are always changing, structured constructs established in the past acquire fresh nuances, constrained by circumstances to conform more closely to the exigencies of new experience. But the constructs that make up human understanding are changed differentially. Some ideas are more affected by changing conditions, those that are more directly tested by experience; but the notions that are more abstract, that refer to virtual, transcendent, and enduring entities, are less affected by the vicissitudes of daily life.[18] As a consequence, notions of virtue, sublimity, and permanence resist change, while less abstract notions are more susceptible to the influence of actual experience.

158

The moral imagery of esoteric extremism has persisted because it is not easily tested by experience. The popular image of the qualities of the Imam and the Mahdi have been little affected by the discursive succession of events. Such virtual notions about sacred leadership, referring to an immutable order of existence, have not only persisted for many centuries but for that very reason have also served to place the disparate events of the past into a meaningful context. It is an abstract and ineffable context, and one that gave to many generations of Muslims in this region a sense of place in an orderly and meaningful cosmos.

NOTES

1. I want to thank the participants in the School of American Research Seminar on "Greater Central Asia as a Culture Area" for their comments on the first draft of the paper; also the following people who have given the text special attention: Elisabeth Case, Dale Eickelman, Jean Ensminger, Michael Fischer, Cornell Fleischer, Matti Moosa, John Perry, Daniel Sherburne, Rebecca Torstrick, Stephen Wasserstrom.
2. Hodgson (1954) believes that Ibn Saba' may have actually been several persons. Moosa (1988) is the most recent statement on Ibn Saba', and is the most extensive source in a Western language on most other *ghulūw* movements. I have refrained from citing him except where he has been particularly useful; he provides extensive discussions of many *ghulūw* movements. See him and the other works cited here for guidance to the extensive original sources in Arabic and Persian.
3. The term is still in use in Afghanistan as a term of opprobrium for the Isma'ilis.
4. The similarity of this belief to the Buddhist notion of the transmigration of souls will be evident in the cases given below (Anesaki 1922:430).
5. Here I follow Hodgson (1965). Blichfeldt (1985) does not associate the Mahdi concept with the *ghulūw*.
6. Michael Fischer has pointed out (in a personal communication) that the concepts of savior in Islam and Zoroastrianism influenced each other; under the influence of Islam Zoroastrian heroes were increasingly formed into the mold of the Islamic prophet.
7. Daniel 1979:36. Sharon (1983:165–86) has an extensive treatment of Khidash.
8. On descent, see Gibb and Kramers (1953:529–33); Mottahedeh 1980:98–104.

9. Muhammad b. ʿAli, the first politically ambitious Abbasid, made allusions, for example, to "certain prophecies known to him about black banners [a symbol of Abbasid uprisings] advancing from the East [Khurasan] to strike down 'the Umayyad pharoah.'" (Daniel 1979:31).
10. Sachedina 1981:15. On the encorporation of *ghulūw* ideas into Shiʿism see Halm (1978).
11. Madelung (1973) and Hodgson (1974, I:378–84) disagree over how much extremism carried forward into succeeding cults. Madelung doubts that it had much influence on succeeding sects; Hodgson is sure it did.
12. Gibb 1961:128–32; Lings 1969; Gibb and Kramers 1953:634. Moosa (1988) contains an extensive treatment of esoteric extremism among the Sufis.
13. The first quotation was by Ibn Fadl Allah al-Umri (d. 749/1349), paraphrased by Mazzaoui (1972:53); the second was by Yahyah Qazwini, quoted by Mazzaoui (1972:83).
14. Gibb and Kramers (1953:629–31). In Sura 17:33 the word means a near relative; in 10:62 and 2:257 a friendly relation between God and believers generally.
15. Although teacher and student would personally withdraw from each other they became closely related. Ibn Fahd married Ibn Falah's widowed mother and gave his own daughter in marriage to Ibn Falah (Mazzaoui 1972:68).
16. This follows Mazzaoui (1972:68), but Gibb and Kramers (1953:452–3) make no reference to any connection to Ibn Fahd. Nurbakhsh's ideas, however, do resemble those of Ibn Fahd as well as al-Mushaʿshaʾs.
17. Van Bruinessen (1978:251) has noted a similar zeal among the Kurdish Naqshbandi for their current sheikh: "Seyyid Nesredin ... does not make any claims to divinity himself – to the contrary, he is a most unassuming and humble person – but all his followers recognize in him a divine spark."
18. I have not seen this concept developed elsewhere. It is mentioned by Fischer (1980b:11).

7
Local knowledge of Islam and social discourse in Afghanistan and Turkistan in the modern period

M. NAZIF SHAHRANI

The inhabitants of Afghanistan and Turkistan (i.e., the Turkic- and Tajik-speaking Muslim territories of Soviet and Chinese Central Asia), have in the modern period consistently had to bear the burdens of military conquest and political domination by alien powers.[1] Western Turkistan was subjugated by the Tsarist Russians prior to 1917; Eastern Turkistan by the Chinese before 1949; and Afghanistan by the British before 1920. But there has been a particular irony in the oppressive intrusions of alien powers on these people in recent years. At a time when most other colonized nations of the world achieved political independence, the Soviets were solidifying their grip on Western Turkistan and the Chinese Communists theirs on Eastern Turkistan, and in 1979 the Soviets, firmly ensconced in Central Asia, extended their reach into Afghanistan. The regimes that now control the heartland of Central Asia not only aim to control and exploit available resources in the region, but also are opposed to the age-old systems of thought and social institutions of the subjugated Muslim peoples and are inclined to replace them with a different set of ideologies and social forms.

In this prolonged colonial encounter Islam has been, and remains, at the center of political and ideological opposition to the particular

161

brands of Marxism imposed by the Soviet and Chinese Communists. The imposition of Communist rule has been marked by violent suppression of any opposition by the peoples of Afghanistan and Turkistan. Islamic traditions in Turkistan have been under particularly severe and systematic attack for many decades. With the exception of a few token *madrasas* (Islamic centers of higher learning) and *'ulamā* (Islamic scholars) as part of "official" Islam in Soviet Turkistan, all Islamic educational establishments (*maktabs* and *madrasas*) have been shut down; religious scholars and teachers (*'ulamā* and mullahs) have been killed, persecuted, co-opted or suppressed; publication, dissemination, and reading of all religious materials have been banned; application of Islamic *sharī'a* laws and customary practices abolished; prayers and acts of worship forbidden, and mosques and shrines destroyed or closed. Although fewer details are known about the Chinese anti-Islamic policies in Eastern Turkistan, they seem to be comparable to those of the Soviet policies in Western Turkistan (see e.g., Mann 1985:10). And in spite of public promises made by the puppet regime in Kabul after the Soviet invasion of 1979 to protect Islam, it implemented policies similar to those carried out earlier in Turkistan by the Soviets and the Chinese (see Arnold and Arnold 1985:149–50).

The persistent attacks on Islam and Islamic beliefs and institutions in Western and Eastern Turkistan may have weakened certain ideological and institutional elements of Islam in these societies; but many Turkistanis continue to adhere to a core of Islamic doctrine. Institutional structures may be weakened or destroyed, but Islamic values and beliefs continue, and are constantly implicated in the day-to-day interactions of Turkistanis.[2] The Islamic basis of the stiff resistance against the Soviet occupation forces in Afghanistan, the Islamic *jihād*, is beyond any doubt (see Canfield 1985a; Roy 1983, 1984; Shahrani and Canfield 1984).

What we will call the "local or popular knowledge of Islam"[3] has persisted among a large segment of the Muslim populations of Turkistan. Given the virtual unavailability of any formal institutional means of transmitting Islamic knowledge in the area, how have the basic principles and ethos of Islamic faith been socially produced, reproduced, and sustained? The most readily available answer to this question in the literature is the activities of Sufi *tarīqas* (paths or brotherhoods) led by the *pīrs* and *īshāns*, the so-called "sectarian underground" or "unofficial" Islam, in Turkistan. While the Sufi brotherhoods no doubt play a crucial part in the perpetuation of the local knowledge of Islam in the area, there has been little serious investigation and analysis of the means by which they achieve such a task.[4]

The unequivocal and overwhelmingly enthusiastic support and participation of the majority of the illiterate masses of Afghan people in the current struggle against the Marxist regimes of Kabul and the Soviet invaders pose another set of problems concerning the behavior of the Afghan masses, especially in view of the ways in which Islam in Afghanistan is often characterized in the literature. Louis Dupree has stated that:

The Islam practiced in Afghan villages, nomad camps, and most urban areas (the ninety to ninety-five percent non-literate) would be almost unrecognizable to a sophisticated Muslim scholar. Aside from faith in Allah and Mohammad as the Messenger of Allah, most beliefs relate to localized pre-Islamic customs. (Dupree 1980:104; also see 1966:270, 274)

Elsewhere Dupree suggests that while Islam is a sophisticated religion, "few non-literates in Afghanistan know the philosophical niceties of the religion they practice" (1967:196). Furthermore, he asserts that because of the prevalence of many pre-Islamic beliefs and rituals, the "village and nomadic Islam becomes, in essence, non-Islamic or, at best, a local, bastardized version of Islam" (1967:196).[5]

Other scholars have expressed similar views. For example: "Remote from the intellectual centers of the Islamic world and lacking strong urban institutions, Afghans have developed local variations on Islam's major doctrines incorporating distinctive beliefs and cults that predate Islam" (Newell and Newell 1981:22; also see R. Newell 1980:256).[6] Olivier Roy (1983:49–50) claims that a major gap exists in Afghanistan between the illiterate village mullahs who often "recite the set phrases without always fully comprehending them," and the Cairo-educated urban theologians and intellectuals.

Assumptions of such radical differences are not new. However, if the statements above are taken to have any sociological merit, then it is incumbent upon us to raise and respond to the following questions. If the divide between the literate Islam of the urban sophisticated theologians and the highly diluted knowledge and practices of village mullahs and masses of their illiterate followers is as great as suggested, then how are the two sides able not only to communicate but to cooperate in a common endeavor, that of an Islamic *jihād*, which is expressed entirely in an Islamic language of discourse? Alternatively, and more significantly, how can we explain the fact that an overwhelming majority of the illiterate peoples of Afghanistan have, in effect, chosen to support one segment of the literate urban-based intellectuals against another, especially when those they oppose command the power of the state and promise them greater social justice and liberty? On the other hand, if the divide is not so great then how is the Islamic vision of the world socially produced, reproduced, communicated, and sustained among the peoples of Afghanistan, both literate and urban as well as illiterate and rural? That is, how is the received Islamic knowledge contained in the "Great" literate traditions of *madrasa* and *ʿulamā* mediated, appropriated, and transformed into popular sources of knowledge easily accessible to the majority of illiterate Afghans and, for that matter, Turkistanis and other Muslims? It is the principal intent of this paper to explore these questions.

Statements by scholars on the seemingly great divide between the "textual" Islam of the *ʿulamā* and urban literati, on the one hand, and the "corrupted" Islam of illiterate mullahs and the rural masses in Afghanistan, on the other, appear to result from a flawed distinction between literacy and illiteracy,[7] and between modernization and traditionalism.[8] Such assertions are often the result of uncritical acceptance of the views of a very small segment of urban-based, secular, educated and/or religious scholars who believe in the presence of such a divide between themselves and most of their rural and urban compatriots.[9] In some instances these assertions are also the product of generalizations about the nature of rural Islam in the absence of adequate systematic data (see e.g., Dupree 1961:376–80; 1967:199–202). An important consequence of such points of view has been an unnecessary bifurcation in Islamic studies. Many students of Islamic studies, until very recently, devoted their efforts either to the study of the high tradition of Islamic scholarship – that pertaining to the study of the Quran and the *sharīʿa*, and the later interpreters of formal Islamic norms for proper social conduct – or to the study of local, popular manifestations of Islam, often referred to as "pre-Islamic" and "non-Islamic."

The studies of the high tradition of Islam have focused for the most part on the description of the institutional structure and organization of the *madrasas*, their curricula and pedagogic styles; the status and role of the educated elite, the *mudarris* (teachers and professors), the imams, or prayer leaders of the mosques; and *qāzīs* and *muftīs* of the *mahkamas*, or the judges and functionaries of the courts. Much emphasis is placed upon the methods of the transmission of normative and orthodox aspects of Islamic doctrine within the learned community. Economic and political ties between the *ʿulamā* and the government authorities, as well as the relatively formal and detached relations of the *ʿulamā* with the Muslim populace also receive attention. In much of this literature, the normative and textual Islam, and its possessors and transmitters, the *ʿulamā*, are treated as forces acting upon the masses of Muslim faithful, who can neither comprehend nor control them. The lower levels of traditional Islamic educational establishments, the *maktabs* and mullahs, are given either a cursory treatment or ignored altogether, even though they are the critical link between the populace and the formal corpus of Islamic knowledge and the *ʿulamā*.

Studies of popular Islam, in contrast, have focused almost exclusively on the behavioral, rather than normative, aspects of the Islam of poorly educated or non-literate peoples. Behavioral patterns, whether manifested during life-crisis rituals or in the activities of voluntary associations, are thought to address the immediate affective needs of the individuals and groups. Participation in these rituals is thought to provide a greater emotional depth and meaning to the religious experience of individual Muslims. Finely tuned into local social-structural principles and the political and economic structure of the community, such Islamic practices are often said to exist in a state of constant tension with the normative, legalistic, and textual orthodoxy of the *ʿulamā* and the larger external political power structures. While this body of literature provides us with information about some important aspects of religious practices in local contexts, we are left with no indication of whether or how these local practices are related to the larger corpus of normative and textual Islam of the *ʿulamā*.

Students of the high tradition of Islam assume that the practices of illiterate Muslim believers are either poorly informed or uninformed by the true and authentic knowledge of Islam. The students of popular Islam, on the other hand, assume knowledgeability, but they point out that it is often conditioned by social, economic, and political contexts. With the exception of some recent studies (e.g., Eickelman 1985; Hefner 1985; Metcalf 1984; Israel and Wagle 1983), the nature of

165

Islamic knowledge displayed by the people is often assumed rather than explored; the question of how illiterate Muslims come to acquire and display Islamic knowledge, discursively or non-discursively, is not well studied. It is contended in this essay that exploring the question of how the local knowledge of Islam is appropriated, socially produced, reproduced, sustained, and perpetuated is critical to an understanding of the existing ties between local Islamic practices and the normative and formal Islam of *madrasa*, *khānaqā*, *ʿulamā* and *mashāyikh*. It is argued that the masses of Muslim believers acquire their local knowledge of Islam from various "textual" sources by literary and oral means, and learn a language of discourse which enables them to communicate with and therefore monitor and evaluate the claims of the *ʿulamā* and *mashāyikh* (e.g., see Gilsenan 1982:132, 136–7).

LOCAL KNOWLEDGE OF ISLAM IN AFGHANISTAN AND TURKISTAN

The local knowledge of Islam in Afghanistan and Turkistan is made up of elements of both *sharīʿa* and *tarīqa* traditions. A large portion exists in standardized texts (both written and oral) widely used in the Turkic, Persian, and Pushtu languages. These written and oral texts represent what Robert LeVine (1984:81) calls the "reflective discourse, that is, indigenous cultural description and analysis within a culture." As such these texts are "conventionalized formats for commenting on cultural beliefs and norms in themselves and their influence on social behavior." The most widely used written texts may be categorized under the following four major genres:

1. The basic popular Islamic "guide-books," which are compiled from a variety of other written and oral sources. Although the authors of some of the materials included in them are identified, the compilers are not always known. Such texts are highly normative in character and very persuasive in tone. Among the Sunni communities in the region two of the best known books in this category are commonly referred to as *Panj Ganj* ("Five Treasures") and *Kulliyāt-i Chahār Kitāb* ("The Complete Four Books").[10] A more recent addition to this genre is *Muʿalim al-Dīn* (Teacher of Religion), compiled and edited by Qari Sharif Ahmad, a preacher at a major mosque in Karachi, Pakistan. The first two are in Persian and the third is translated into Persian, probably from Urdu.[11]

2. Narratives of the lives, extraordinary adventures, pious deeds and attributes of the prophets, other noted heroes, and saints. These include such widely known texts as: *Mi'rāj-i Muhammadī* ("The Prophet Muhammad's Ascension to the Heavens"), *Qasas ul Anbiyā* ("Story of the Prophets"), *Tazkīrāt ul Awliyā* ("Biographies of the Saints"), *Safīnat ul Awliyā* ("The Ship of Saints") and *Qiyāmat Nāmah* ("Book of Resurrection"). They are all in Persian.

3. *Dīwāns* (collections of poetry) and *munājāts* (invocations). These include works of Hafiz, Bedil, Ahmad Jami, Shah Mashrab (in Turki, a literary form of Uzbek), Huwayda (in Turki), Nawayi (in Turki and Persian), Sufi Allahyar (in Turki), Khawjah Abdullah Ansari, and Sa'adi, among others.[12]

4. Heroic tales and/or love stories. At least one such story is based on the Quranic story of Joseph (*Yūsuf wa Zulaykhā*). There are others, such as *Haydar Bēk, Najmā-i Sherāzī, Amīr Hamzah, Sikandar Nāmah, Laylā wa Majnūn,* and *Farhād wa Shīrīn,* which are basically secular in nature, but the narratives are studded with clearly articulated Islamic values and normative principles.[13]

In addition to written texts serving as a means of perpetuating knowledge and popular Islamic beliefs and values, there are two predominant forms of oral reflective discourse that have a crucial role in this process. They are the proverbs (*zarbulmasals*) and *afsānah-hā, qisa-hā, hikāyāt* (tales and stories).[14]

SOCIAL PRODUCTION AND DISSEMINATION

Copies of most of these written texts have long existed in most rural areas in the region: first in hand-written form, and since the late nineteenth and early twentieth centuries in lithograph, and more recently in printed editions. Much of this material was traditionally produced in Lahore and Peshawar or in Bukhara and other Central Asian cities. It was, however, readily available in almost any town, and itinerant traders and sometimes professional book pedlars often sold them in the villages along with copies of the Quran and other reading materials.

For all youths who passed the stage of learning how to read the *haftyak*[15] and the Quran, the *Panj Ganj* and *Kulliyāt* texts provided the primary reading materials in the traditional system of *maktab* or mosque schools, both in urban and in rural areas. The use of these and of other Persian poetry texts was as widespread in Turkic- and Pushtu-speaking communities as in those whose native language was Persian (see Elphinstone 1815, I:248–61; Khanikoff 1845:275–96; Becka 1966; and Jarring 1951, IV:117–26). The *Panj Ganj* and *Kulliyāt* are the "primary" texts in both senses of the word. That is, they are collections of very simple but elegant and highly rhythmic Persian prose and poetry, which are relatively easily understood by the uneducated public; and they contain the essential and fundamental facts and nor-mative principles of Islamic beliefs and practices. For example, they detail the basic tenets of the faith, ritual purity and pollution, pro-cedures for ritual cleansing and the correct and appropriate perform-ance of prayers and other religious duties. They address issues ranging from the maintenance of personal hygiene to regulation of relations between members of a family, from standards for the performance of public duties to the conditions of the prosperity or downfall of rulers, and from the praise of learning and condemnation of ignorance to such theological concerns as the truthfulness of Muhammad's proph-ecy and the existence of the unitary God.

Much of this critical information is not otherwise readily accessible to the public. The editors and compilers of these texts have used many important and well-known literary devices to enhance memory reten-tion. Some of the devices are repetition, recapitulation, analogies, and catechisms. Many of these literary devices are combined in the presen-tation of much of the materials in narrative forms – i.e., a story with a beginning, middle, and end – both in poetry and prose.

While these texts are an essential part of the *maktab* curriculum for the young, their function is by no means restricted to the mosque or school grounds. They are widely read aloud to all kinds of audiences in a variety of contexts, such as at family gatherings in the evenings during the long winter months; in guest houses, especially if a guest is a literate person or a religious functionary such as a mullah or *mawlawi*; in reading sessions specially arranged by pious individuals; in the mosques; in tea houses; by certain professional singers; at wed-dings and other festivities; in public places in larger towns by pro-fessional *naʿt khawns* (panegyrists of the Prophet).[16] The primary texts such as *Panj Ganj* and *Kulliyāt* repeatedly encourage frequent read-ings, memorization, retelling and enactment of what the books admonish. For those who take heed and obey, there are promises of assured spiritual reward (i.e., *sawāb*) in both this life and, especially, the life hereafter.[17]

Before the availability of large numbers of portable cassette tape recorders in the rural areas, most of the public readings were for male audiences of all ages. Occasionally readings were given in the women's gatherings, but most of their exposure to Islamic knowledge came through male members of their own immediate natal or conjugal households.[18] More significantly, access and exposure to the contents of the popular written Islamic texts of all categories was much larger than the availability of competent readers. Because large portions of these texts are memorized verbatim and often assimilated by some individual, the written texts entered the realm of the oral tradition, thus facilitating to a greater degree the dissemination of the knowledge, not only across time and space but across local vernaculars as well.[19] The dynamic exchange between written and oral texts in the social production of Islamic knowledge in societies possessing a literary tradition has always been present.

There has occurred, however, a significant development in recent decades in the extent and methods of disseminating traditional Islamic knowledge. The presence of many educated youths and the availability of radios and cassette tape recorders even in remote towns and villages have provided a very large proportion of the rural masses with unprecedented access to popular religious knowledge and entertainment.[20] The new communication technologies have also made possible the emergence of a highly popular *na‘t khawn*, such as Mir Fakhruddin Agha, whose recordings are sold and heard along with the best of the pop singers on the national scene in Afghanistan. The present impact and long-term potential of Islamic broadcasting and dissemination of recorded materials in the area remains, for the most part, unexplored.

In both past and present-day conditions, the extent of an individual's learning and his ability to recall and to retell stories varies considerably. In every locality and community, however, there are always a few illiterate persons who are able to recite and understand substantial parts of the various written texts, particularly poetry, biographies of prophets and saints, and especially the normative sections of the *Panj Ganj* and *Kulliyāt*. Such connoisseurs of local religious knowledge are often able to interpret and comment on these texts with considerable competence. Many children are familiar with portions of these popular Islamic texts long before they are able to read them. Even

169

though there have been no studies of the traditional Afghan and
Turkistani socialization processes, for young people or for adults, it is
clear that popularized Islamic oral and written texts in the vernaculars
play a role in the acquisition and dissemination of language and
cultural knowledge. Indeed, such texts appear to be of vital importance
to the people of Turkistan especially under continued colonial conditions: both the Soviets and the Chinese have been enough concerned
about popular interest in these texts to ban their production, sale, and
dissemination in Turkistan. There are reports that they continue to be
produced and distributed secretly in Soviet Turkistan (Paksoy 1984).

Before the imposition of Soviet and Chinese Communist rule on
Afghanistan and Turkistan, the most important authority structure,
which was also the crucial means of production and transmission of
local Islamic knowledge, was the extended family-household and the
kin-based village community.[21] It is here that decisions, however sub-
jective, are made regarding the uses of particular knowledge available
to the heads of households and other adult members of the family.
Within the broader social, economic, political, and ecological milieu,
the family helps shape the identities and loyalties of individuals in the
social order. The attitude and commitment of individual heads of
households and larger localized kin-based communities towards the
acquisition of Islamic knowledge, from both formal and popular texts,
and the ability of individual members to learn and assimilate them
vary considerably. Such differences in knowledge and commitment
often manifest themselves in the course of the life careers of individuals, families and kinship groups within a community.

That the authority and power structure affect the social production
of knowledge and the perpetuation of values and institutions, while not
easily demonstrable, cannot be denied. From a systematic examination of the Islamic popular texts we may infer the nature and sources of
power and authority. A systematic and comprehensive account of the
contents of popular Islamic texts found in Afghanistan and Turkistan is
beyond the scope of this essay, but we will discuss the organization and
major themes addressed in two of these.

PANJ GANJ AND KULLIYĀT

1. *Panj Ganj* is a relatively short text of about one hundred pages of
poetry and some prose divided into five parts, sometimes referred to as

either the *Chahār Kitāb* (Four Books) or the *Panj Kitāb* (Five Books). The collection has been issued by various publishing institutions, with minor variations and omissions.

The first book of *Panj Ganj* is known as *Karīma* (after the first word in the first verse of the book). It begins with a *hamd* (salutation to God), addressing Allah as *Karīm* ("the Benefactor") in the customary and formalized manner in which all Islamic written texts begin. Authorship of *Karīma* is attributed to Sheikh Muslih al-Din Saʿdi, whose name appears in the last verse. It is entirely in *nazm*, a poetic verse form. Each *nazm* treats a single positive and desirable or negative and abhorrent characteristic of human social conduct, and its consequences for individuals both in this world and the next. Generally, *nazms* dealing with attributes of opposing values are placed in sequence. The specific themes addressed, in their order of appearance, are *hamd* (salutation to God), *thanā* (in praise of the Prophet), *nafs* (human corporal desires), *karam* (magnanimity and munificence), *sakhāwat* (generosity), *bukhl* (stinginess and jealousy), *tawāzuʿ* (humility), *takkabur* (arrogance), *ʿilm* (knowledge), *imtināʿ az suhbat-i jāhilān* (avoiding the company of the ignorant), *ʿadl* (justice), *zulm* (oppression), *qināʿat* (contentment), *hirs* (greed), *tāʿat wa ʿibādat* (obedience and worship of God), *Shaytān* (Satan), *sharāb* (wine), *wafā* (loyalty and fidelity), *shukr* (giving thanks to God), *sabr* (tolerance and patience), *rāstī* (uprightness and truthfulness), *kizb* (lying and falsehood), and *manʿ-i umīd az makhlūqāt* (prohibition of exclusive reliance upon "creatures" – i.e., other human beings, for hope of help).

The second book is known as *Nām-i Haqq*, which is also the initial words of the *hamd* with which the book begins. Following the salutation and praise of the Prophet, the author of *Nām-i Haqq* introduces himself and the purpose of his book. He is a little-known figure in the Persian literary tradition named Sharaf Bukhari; he states that he was born in Bukhara but acquired his knowledge and learning in Khurasan. His goal is to teach all the Islamic rules and regulations concerning ablutions and ritual bathing necessary to ensure purity to perform the daily prayers, the rules and requirements of correctly and accurately performing the prayers themselves, and the rules governing fasting during the month of *Ramazān*. The text is written in the *nazm* form. The author ends with a completion date, the first half of the lunar month of Jimady al-Awal, 693 years after the death of the Prophet or AH 703 (about AD 1303).

171

Book three of the *Panj Ganj*, the "Book of Mahmud" or *Mahmūd Nāmah*, is named after its purported author, Sultan Mahmud Ghaznawi, the ruler of Ghazni, 998–1030. It comprises thirty-one poems, each made up of seven couplets. All the couplets within each poem end with the same letter of the Persian alphabet, and the poems together cover the entire Persian alphabet, except for the letter *lāmalif*. Most of the poems are addressed to someone the poet loves, Ayaz (a masculine name).[22] In popular readings, *Mahmūd Nāmah* is often, but not always, interpreted as Mahmud's love for God, and the yearning for the exalted truth enshrined in the *tarīqa* or Sufi means of worship, and in the renunciation of carnal desires. Most of the poems lend themselves elegantly to such mystical and pious interpretations.

Book four in the *Panj Ganj* is called *Pand Nāmah-i ʿAttār* or "ʿAttār's Book of Advice (or Counsel)." Its author is believed to be Sheikh Fariduddin ʿAttar (d. AD 1230), the famous Sufi poet. In its poetic form and themes it is similar to the book of *Karīma* but is much longer (well over fifty pages of text), and gives broader and more comprehensive coverage.

The fifth book consists of two separate short texts in prose. The first is *Sad Pand-i Sūdmand-i Luqmān-i Hakīm* or "Luqmān Hakīm's One Hundred Useful Pieces of Advice." These enumerated pieces of advice summarize succinctly most of the major themes treated at length in book four; they also contain many points of mundane social etiquette (*ādāb*) not covered in the previous books. The second part is *Risāla-i Qāzī Qutb*, or the "Pamphlet of Qazi Qutb," a catechism raising some fundamental questions concerning Islamic faith and practice. The book concludes with the *Shash Kalīma* (six confessional statements) in Arabic[23] and three quatrains in Persian on the merits of seeking knowledge.

2. *Kulliyāt-i Chahār Kitāb* is made up of four distinct books. Book one is the same as the book of *Nām-i Haqq*. Book four includes *Pand Nāma-i ʿAttār* and many additional poems addressing issues not covered in the *Panj Ganj* text. Books two and three, predominantly in prose, address issues similar to those in *Panj Ganj* but include much additional, detailed information.

Book two of *Kulliyāt* states its aims to introduce "knowledge about faith (*īmān*), commandments (*ahkām*) and pillars (*arkān*) of Islam." These include prayers, fasting, pilgrimage, alms-giving, things which are prescribed or ordained (*farāyiz*), those which are obligatory (*wājibāt*), and those which were practiced or recommended by the Prophet (*sunnat* and *mustahab*), as well as the "pillars of *ta'zīm* (reverence or homage) and *takrīm* (honoring)," which encompass the etiquette (*ādāb*) appropriate in the presence of God as in society. The book is divided into four chapters: on the knowledge of faith, which also contains a slightly abridged text of the recommendations of Luqmān Hakīm; on knowing the effect of the stars on human affairs; on inauspicious days; and on Sunni religious beliefs. Chapter four of book two also contains the genealogy of the Prophet Muhammad, traced back to the prophet Ibrahim (Abraham), and the genealogies of Abu Bakr, 'Usman and 'Ali, as well as an account of how long various earlier prophets lived.

Book three of the *Kulliyāt* is concerned with the explication of different types of religious knowledge and is called the book of *Muhimmāt al-Muslimīn* or "Things of Serious Concern to Muslims." In this book one finds all the elements of the Pamphlet of *Qāzī Qutb* from *Panj Ganj* and more. It includes diverse literary and mnemonic devices, and graphic descriptions of the examination of the dead by the angels Munkar and Nakir, and the punishment they might administer. There are also vivid narratives of the rewards of paradise for the worthy, and the horrible conditions of hell for the fallen. In many instances verses from the Quran and the sayings of the Prophet and his four principal companions are utilized to support and illustrate important points in the narratives. Catechisms and poetry recapitulate the principal themes in books two and three.

The clearest and most unambiguous statements about the source and nature of ultimate power and authority in these texts appear at the beginning of each book and its subunits. The notion that all forms of power and authority emanate from the singular source, the *Qādir-i Mutlaq*, the Absolute Power, God, remains constant throughout the texts. All other foci of power and authority are derivative and contingent upon the ultimate source. This conception of the ultimate authority defines and helps articulate the characteristic nature of the concept of *īmān* (Islamic faith) and knowledge, which together shape the form and content of Islamic ideology and practice.

The knowledge of the details of Islamic belief in the unity of God, rules governing devotional rituals, and the seven articles of Islamic faith, and the specific consequences of their acceptance for the conduct of the Muslim faithful, form the principal corpus of what is considered knowledge. Its coherent presentation is the principal objective of the authors and compilers of the *Kulliyāt* and *Panj Ganj* as well as other popular texts. It is the acquisition of this knowledge and its actualization by the Muslim faithful that is considered "a commandment above [all] commandments" (*Kulliyāt* n.d.:54–5).

Through a series of clearly articulated catechismal questions, these texts paint very vivid and graphic images of the structure of the cosmos and provide the appropriate concepts of the proper temporal power structures in Islamic societies.[24] From these conceptions of order at least three important points emerge concerning the notions of power and authority. First, access to power and authority is entirely contingent upon God and upon those who are granted authority by Him. Second, the historical and social order is integral to a single universe, in which power and authority are structured according to the same spiritual principles. Certain elements within this cosmology assume eternally fixed principles, whereas the activities of ordinary individual human beings, subject to such ordained laws, are never static. Third, the place the ordinary individual occupies in this order, both cosmological and social, depends upon his or her worldly conduct, ritual and secular as well as personal and social. The objective of these texts is to provide detailed instructions for appropriate behaviors and to induce the kinds of moods and motivations that will help the faithful secure a favorable place in the sight of the ultimate authority, God.

The texts put much emphasis on the significance of performing daily prayers, and in many instances suggest that to neglect prayers may lead to loss of faith, which leads to hell.[25] Also offered are short prayers, some in Persian quatrain and others in Arabic verse, which may be recited in order to avoid hell, gain paradise, make one's worldly wishes come true, gain longevity, acquire an ample subsistence, or endow one's work with God's blessing (see *Kulliyāt* n.d.:24–5, 43–6).

The list of approved, disapproved, and recommended behaviors and their consequences, in this life and in the next, is extensive. Often, the reasons for recommending a particular behavior, or pointing out the signs of a particular attribute, are enumerated and succinctly articulated. For example, there are said to be four signs of misfortune: heedlessness, laziness, stinginess, and meanness; the possessors of these traits in this world "shall see nothing but the fire of hell on the

174

Day of Judgement" (*Kulliyāt* n.d.:187–8). Or, the killing of worldly desires may not be possible except by means of the use of "the dagger of silence," "the sword of hunger," or "the spear of solitude and humility." Anyone who does not possess one of these weapons shall never enjoy deliverance (*Kulliyāt* n.d.:188–9, also see *Panj Ganj* n.d.:52–5, 44–6, 64, 65).

These texts also quite specifically address how the personal and public conduct of power-holders influences government authority. It is said, for example, that the corruption and moral decay of kings result from four things: the oppression of subjects by the prince, military leaders, etc.; the treachery of the court minister; disorder in the administration and among clerks; and increase in the power and strength of princes (or commanders) in the provinces. However, if the king stands firm, the corrupt hands of the princes could be stopped. On the other hand, if he is not firm the country could be ruined by useless persons. If the sultan tyrannizes his subjects, there is no hope of his rule continuing (*Kulliyāt* n.d.:192–3). In another instance, the following four things are considered to be harmful to kings: laughing aloud in public; talking to any poor fellow who comes along; spending too much time with women; and acting oppressively and unjustly towards subjects.

An appeal for proper social behavior, which evinces a respect for authority, is strengthened by graphic images concerning the imminence of the Day of Judgment. The texts indicate that although the Day of Judgment has been chosen by God, the actual date is not known to any human being. Some believe, however, that it will occur on a Friday and on the 10th of the month of Mohurram (the day of ʿAshūrā). On the basis of a saying of the Prophet, it is believed that certain patterns in people's behavior will indicate its imminence. Sinful acts will increase and multiply, breach of trust will become common; children will disobey their parents and do injustice to them; debauchery, dance, and music will increase; people will speak ill of their ancestors; ignorant and unwise persons will assume positions of leadership and guidance; miserly people and those with little capital or support will erect tall buildings; and unworthy individuals will hold high office. When all these things begin to appear, one can be certain that *qiyāmat* is drawing nearer (Ahmad n.d.:34).

175

LOCAL KNOWLEDGE OF ISLAM AND
SOCIAL DISCOURSE

On the basis of the above schematic discussion, we can see that a particular conception of power and authority (*qudrat*) found in the discourse of popular Islamic texts in Afghanistan and Turkistan, and closely linked to the notions of faith (*īmān*), religious knowledge and conduct, implies a particular cosmological and social order and eschatology. We have briefly discussed the means and methods through which this body of knowledge is transmitted and communicated throughout the region. How, and to what extent, if at all, does the knowledge contained in these texts influence social discourse in Afghan and Turkistani societies?

In the absence of systematically collected ethnographic data for the specific purposes of addressing such questions, there are at least two ways to explore the constitutive, normative and emotive power of local Islamic beliefs as an influence upon the social discourse of Central Asians. One would be to examine ethnographic records for social practices, behavioral patterns, and social forms which might be correlated to the kinds of popular Islamic knowledge contained in the popular texts. This task, for the purposes of this paper, is not possible. The second approach is to reflect upon my own life experiences both as a native and as a researcher in two rural communities in Afghanistan, trying to understand the impact of the local knowledge of Islam gained through the use of these texts on social discourse in these communities. A detailed treatment of this issue is also impossible here, so I will merely present a few concrete cases in which teachings in the Islamic texts we have considered are reflected in the conduct of people in these communities.

The two communities are in Badakhshan, north-eastern Afghanistan. One is a mixed farming and herding village of about 2,000 people, most of whom are Uzbeks and the rest Tajiks (see Shahrani 1984c). Sunni Muslims, they are divided into five separate mosque-centered communities; the members of each cluster around one or two core agnatic associations. The village as a whole maintains a large common mosque in which Friday prayers are held, and there is also a *madrasa* (school) attached to it. The other community is a pastoral nomadic group of some 2,000 Kirghiz who lived (some still do) in the Pamirs of Afghanistan (Shahrani 1979, 1984b). Because of ecological constraints, the Kirghiz community was scattered over a relatively large area in small camping groups of two or three households. It was not feasible for them to maintain a mosque.

In order to explore the influence of these texts upon the lives of the common Muslims in these two communities, we must depart from the long-held view of Islamic ideology and knowledge as a received, highly rigid, structured, and legalistic phenomenon which exists outside of individual Muslim practitioners, either in a body of inaccessible written texts, or as memorized, but little understood, oral texts in the possession of a privileged class. As has been mentioned in this essay, a substantial part of the corpus of the high tradition of Islamic knowledge has been mediated by the social production and reproduction of vernacular popular Islamic texts, and thereby made available to the masses of non-literate Muslims. Furthermore, illiterate Muslims are not simply the passive subjects or recipients of this popular knowledge; rather the very social and historical existence, reproduction and continuity of this type of local Islamic knowledge, ideology and practice, is contingent upon the activities of its adherents. The kind of Islamic knowledge that common Muslims in specific contexts *have* is constituted partly of what the "textual" Islam is, and partly of the particular social, political, and historical conditions that have acted to change and transform it. When this body of local Islamic knowledge and understanding is acquired and sustained through lifelong exposure to elements of the textual materials and the day-to-day interactions of the members of a community, it *becomes a part* of the individual Muslim practitioner. The possession of the local knowledge of Islam by the Muslim actors provides the critical basis for the influence of Islam upon the social actions of individuals as well as collective discourse.

For practicing Muslims in possession of adequate local knowledge of Islam, Islamic norms and values are not merely cold, oppressive, and formal social-structural principles constantly impinging upon the course of their lives. Rather, the knowledge of Islam serves as a body of "rules and resources" upon which they draw "in the production and reproduction of social action," and by doing so, they act as the means for the reproduction of the system of local Islamic knowledge itself (Giddens 1984:19; Swidler 1982). This knowledge could influence their social discourse in two interrelated ways: one, at the level of the constitution of meanings and interpretations (verbal and non-verbal), participating in a shared Islamic language of discourse; two, applying

177

Islamic normative and evaluative principles in the sanctioning and actualization of social action. It is through the "purposive" and "reflexive"[26] application of this knowledgeability on the part of Muslims that the recursive ordering of their social practices is manifested in the reproduction of Islamic community, social, and political order.

Anthony Giddens suggests that all human beings are essentially "purposive agents," who have reasons for their activities and are able, if asked, "to elaborate discursively upon those reasons (including lying about them)" (1984:3). He, however, points out that

What agents know about what they do, and why they do it – their knowledge-ability *as* agents – is largely carried in practical consciousness. Practical consciousness consists of all the things which actors know tacitly about how to "go on" in the contexts of social life without being able to give them direct discursive expression. (Giddens 1984:xxiii; also see pp. xxx, 4–14 and 26)

A large part of an individual's "practical consciousness" consists of awareness of social rules – i.e., "knowledge of procedures, or mastery of the techniques of 'doing' social activity" – which are by definition methodological and practical rather than theoretical (Giddens 1984:21–2; also see Eickelman 1981:85–104).

We can approach an understanding of the impact of Islamic local knowledge on the social discourse of members of the two Badakhshan communities if we treat them as knowledgeable Muslim actors who, in their day-to-day social actions, purposively and strategically employ their own locally acquired knowledge of Islam, discursively or non-discursively, in a recursive and reflexive manner. Undoubtedly, the extent of knowledge and the competency of particular individuals, members of different families, and larger kinship associations in the two communities, vary considerably depending on the specific political, economic, social, and psychological circumstances in which they find themselves. Yet for all of them the vocabulary of discourse and the symbolic system they acquire from the Islamic texts provides meaning to their experiences and helps regulate their social interactions.

In both communities an important example of how the language of popular Islamic discourse shapes the nature of social relations is in the constitution of individual and group identities. That is, within the village or nomadic community individuals are not merely a member of a family, a lineage, a clan, a nomadic camp, or a mosque. Rather, each individual is also identified in Islamic terms: whether he is knowledgeable or ignorant; generous or miserly; truthful or dishonest; wise or foolish; virtuous or lewd, etc.; and for those in authority, whether he is just or oppressive, etc. Every social unit – individual, family, agnatic association and neighborhood mosque community – is evaluated and labeled by reference to normative and evaluative concepts of virtue and truth of the sort defined in the popular Islamic texts. And such evaluations have consequences. For example, to be labeled as *bēy namāz* (one who does not perform his daily prayers or attend the mosque) in the village could result in being confronted by the entire congregation; they could appear on a cold winter morning and pour a bucket of icy water on the bed of a person caught sleeping at the time of the morning prayers.

One man who had missed the opportunity to attend mosque school during his youth not only sent his own children to *maktab* but required them to teach him how to read the Quran. Also, following a specific injunction in the *Kulliyāt* (most of which he knew by heart and recited verbatim from memory at every opportunity) he actively sought the company and teaching of ʿulamā and Sufi leaders. He often searched for popular religious texts from the surrounding villages, brought them home, invited others with similar interests, and had his sons read the books aloud to them for long hours.

In another instance, in the same village, the attitudes of the heads of two families towards the simple principle of *harām khūry* (eating forbidden things or earning a living at the expense of others) had a profound effect on the future of their sons. The head of one family was a mullah; the other was illiterate, but a very intelligent and influential man who had been the elected village *arbāb* (headman) for several years. The families had sons of about the same age who attended the government school and were eventually sent to Kabul boarding schools for further studies. The eldest son of the mullah went on to study at the government-sponsored religious-studies school and to become a *qāzī* (judge). The son of the *arbāb* wanted to study law to become a district officer (*hākim*), but because of his rural background he was barred from law school by the government. The mullah's son eventually got a degree from the Faculty of Islamic Studies while the *arbāb*'s son graduated from the Faculty of Letters. The mullah's son, aware of the corruption of the *qāzīs* and the system, decided not to apply for a position as judge and instead preferred teaching, a decision which was welcomed by his family and relatives in the village. The *arbāb*'s son managed to get himself a job at the Ministry of the Interior despite his college training to become an English teacher, and was appointed a district officer a short while later. Within a year or two he was one of the richest men in the village. Within the village context, the son of the mullah and his family continued to enjoy greater respect and influence. Nevertheless, such choices for the future education and occupation of children posed a serious dilemma for many individuals and families in the community, particularly in view of the availability of a competing value system, that of "modernity and progress." Since the Communist coup and the Soviet invasion of Afghanistan, the consequences of those bygone decisions are under new and critical scrutiny: the son of the mullah was for a while imprisoned. He later escaped and was active in the resistance. At least two close members of his family were killed and their house in the village bombed and severely damaged. The *arbāb*'s son, who was governor of a province at the time of the Communist coup, merely lost his job and is still living in Kabul.

Another telling example of how popular Islamic conceptions inform individual and collective experiences relates to events following the Marxist coup in Kabul. Villagers were mobilized by a Marxist cabinet minister from a neighboring village and sent to fight against the Islamic resistance fighters who, they were told, were Chinese and Americans. After an initial confrontation the villagers were defeated and realized they were fighting people from the next valley. A number of them returned from the battle explaining that their defeat was inevitable because thousands upon thousands of armed men, all dressed in white, had been fighting in the ranks of their opponents. These, said the villagers, were angels sent by God to help the *mujahedīn* defeat the Communists.[27] In reality there were only a handful of *mujahedīn*.

This example relates to the Kirghiz experiences of repeated flights during this century from Communist revolutions: from the Bolsheviks in 1917, from the Chinese Communists in 1949, and from the Afghan Communists in 1978. In all cases they have produced an elaborate explanation of their misfortunes in terms of the signs of the Islamic notions of *qiyāmat* or the approaching of the Day of Resurrection and Judgment. These explanations consist of a series of omens which they say began to occur a few years before the Chinese, the Afghan Marxist, and the Bolshevik revolutions. They blame their own laxity in practicing Islam properly, but most of all they blame their discontent and thanklessness for what they had. A very detailed account of how the Kirghiz interpreted the Bolshevik Revolution and the fate of the Muslims of Turkistan is depicted in a Kirghiz ode (*er*) written by a Kirghiz resistance fighter named Abdul Satar (Dor and Imart 1982:246–72).

CONCLUSION

While there are illiterate Muslims and ignorant mullahs, it should not be assumed that all rural Muslims of Central Asia who are generally illiterate are cut off from the main currents of Islamic thought, or that all rural mullahs are ignorant of the fundamental teachings of Islam. Most Muslims in Afghanistan and Turkistan, including many mullahs, recite verses from the Quran in their prayers without knowing clearly the meaning of the Arabic verses, but the value of reading and reciting the Quranic text for the Muslim is not predicated upon his knowing or being able to explain its meaning. The fact that natives of Central Asia have and display skills in reading or orally reciting the Quran in Arabic indicates a very different literacy skill and purpose than that assumed by the "autonomous" model of literacy currently in use (Street 1984, chs. 1–2). We must realize that while the source of all ʿ*ilm* is thought to be the Quran, it is not necessary or even possible for all Muslims to acquire such knowledge directly from the Quran or other texts of the high tradition of Islam. Appropriation, and rendering essential knowledge contained in the high tradition into the vernacular languages in the form of the popular Islamic texts, such as *Panj Ganj* and *Kulliyāt-i Chahār Kitāb*, provide much easier access to the masses.

By the same token, neither the existence of practices among the Muslim masses in rural areas that might be regarded as "pre-Islamic" or "non-Islamic" by ʿ*ulamā*, nor the presence of a gap between the knowledge and practices of a segment of the ʿ*ulamā* and the more informed populations of the cities and those of the "illiterate" masses can be denied. However, to assume that the knowledge and practices of the rural masses consist of nothing but pre-Islamic and non-Islamic elements which would be unrecognizable to the sophisticated Muslim scholar is absurd. The seemingly great divide between the "Great and Little Traditions" of Islam is not as great as is sometime assumed, and it is bridged by the popular Islamic texts extensively used by the

181

mullahs and many other people. These popular Islamic texts, socially expressed in the behavior of real people, are the basis of the unofficial Islam that flourishes in Soviet and Chinese Turkistan. The familiar language of Islamic discourse used in these works is employed by the Islamic resistance groups that have won the support of the Afghan people, rural and urban. Indeed, it is through the mediation of the vernacular popular Islamic texts that we may be able to understand the value of the following assertion by Olivier Roy: "For Afghans, their religion is much more than an agglomeration of practices: it is truly a vision of the world, and the source to which they invariably refer whenever they speak of justice, liberty, or ethics – in short, whenever they speak of humanity" (1981:50).

Analytically, we will be at a loss if we continue to ask and respond to the same old questions concerning what Islam *is* and what it *does* to individual Muslims and their societies. The answer to such questions has been to depict Islam in a more or less Durkheimian fashion as a body of abstract and rigid social-structural principles which constantly constrain the Muslims to behave in a particular way. This approach will be of little use to us in understanding the actions of the Afghans, Turkistanis, and Muslims elsewhere today.

Instead we must begin to direct our attention to the individual Muslim actors, the knowledgeable human agents who are the possessors and strategic utilizers of local Islamic knowledge. The same Muslim actors are responsible for the social reproduction of Islamic knowledge and practice, popular or textual. Indeed, sociologically at least, Islam, to use Anthony Gidden's phrase, "has no existence independent of the knowledge that agents [Muslims] have about what they do [as Muslims] in their day-to-day activity" (1984:26). Viewed from this perspective, the questions we must ask are: given the limitations of actual power relations in particular social contexts, how do knowledgeable Muslims apply their knowledge of Islam in their day-to-day social discourse? Or what kinds of Islamic, un-Islamic, or non-Islamic knowledge are implicated in their social actions and why? When we pose our questions in this manner, we transform our conception: rather than a body of abstract social principles which exist outside of the individual Muslim and act to constrain and limit actions, Islam becomes a body of rules and resources that individuals possess and can use as they see fit, within the limits of political power structures. Viewed from this perspective the practices of rural Muslims in Afghanistan and Turkistan cannot be taken as mere forms and externals. Instead, for example, performance of five daily prayers (*namāz*), the most external form of religious conduct in rural as well as urban contexts, could and may be the result of the belief that the non-performance of daily prayers would lead to the "narrowness or stricture of faith (*īmān*)" and that *namāz* is the "offspring of faith" (see *Kulliyāt* n.d.:15, 56–61). Indeed, because Muslims in Afghanistan possess a knowledge of Islam from the popular Islamic texts, we can assume that they have an Islamic vision of the world and can discourse on the Islamic notions of justice (*ʿadl*), liberty (*āzādī*) and ethics (*akhlāq*). It is also by reflexive and recursive use of their knowledge, discursively and non-discursively, that Islamic ways of constructing meaning are sustained; social order created, recreated and maintained; and the "true" Islamic knowledge and practice monitored and authenticated.

Conceived in this manner, Islamic knowledge becomes *one* part of the total supply of resources – ideological and material, normative and regulative, personal and social – an individual may possess. Traditionally, Islam may have served as the only or the dominant ideological resource for many practicing Muslims. However, for increasing numbers, under the changing political and economic realities of the twentieth century, Islam is becoming only one among a number of competing alternative systems of thought to acquire and utilize. It is in this context that we can comprehend the actions of an Uzbek named Saidkorihocaev (Sayyid Qari Khawjaoghlu) and a number of his friends, who were convicted of the crime of having been caught in the Tashkent bazaar selling "an authorless book called 'About the Muslim Religion', which advocated shunning the 'godless' " (Paksoy 1984:123). The accused were labeled by the author of a report, probably another Uzbek, who used a pseudonym "*Adabiyātcī*" (A man of letters), as "The Deceivers." Also it will help us understand those Uighur Muslims who tried to prevent the Red Guards from burning "books outside mosques" during the Cultural Revolution and were arrested and imprisoned for their actions (Mann 1985:10), while, no doubt, many other Uighurs either watched the event in silence or sided with the Chinese revolutionaries, as has happened in Soviet Turkistan and in Afghanistan.

The possibilities of acquiring alternative systems of perceiving and ordering social reality within the consciousness of a single individual have also produced some of the most memorable paradoxes of human social discourse in modern times. For example, in the story of the sons of the mullah and the *arbāb*, there is a twist that needs to be mentioned. The mullah's son who did not want to become a *qāzī* for fear of getting involved in corruption was later so impressed by the monetary success of the *arbāb*'s son that he married the *arbāb*'s son's younger sister. It was a successful marriage strongly approved by the mullah's family, if not by all their relatives in the village.

Finally, to re-emphasize the analytical significance of focusing on the Muslim practitioners' conduct and on their strategic uses of their knowledge of Islam in social discourse, rather than on what Islam *does* to Muslims, let us remember the often quoted Muslim saying, in its Afghan version in the following Persian couplet:

Islām ba zāt khud nadārad aybi.
Har ayb ki hast dar Musulmānī y-e māst.
Islam has no faults in its essence.
Any fault that exists is in our conduct as Muslims.

NOTES

1. This is a greatly abridged version of the original paper presented in the SAR advanced seminar. A full version of it will be published elsewhere. The paper was written during my tenure as an Andrew W. Mellon Fellow at Stanford Humanities Center, Stanford University (1984–5). Following the Advanced Seminar at SAR, the paper was presented at a luncheon meeting of the Fellows at the Stanford Humanities Center, and I have benefited from their discussion: the constructive comments by Jane Collier, Valerie Kivelson, and Paul Robinson at SHC, and Arjun Appadurai, Robert Canfield, Barbara Metcalf, Dale Eickelman, Francis Robinson, Audrey Shalinsky, Kaveh Safa and Mobin Shorish are gratefully acknowledged. My thanks are also due to the staff of the Stanford Humanities Center for their most gracious help.

2. For discussions of Soviet policies towards Islam in Western Turkistan and the persistence of Islamic beliefs and practices see Bennigsen and Lemercier-Quelquejay 1967, 1979; Bennigsen 1980–1; Buciurkiw 1980–1; Buciurkiw and Strong 1975; and Rakowska-Harmstone 1983. For Islam in China see Israeli 1978, 1979, 1981, 1982; Dryer 1976, 1982; Chisti 1981; and Yang 1957.

3. The notion of popular Islam in the literature refers to mystic and Sufi traditions, as opposed to the formal *sharī'a*-orientated Islam. In this paper both *sharī'a* and Sufi traditions are regarded as

formal aspects of Islam. Here, as should be clear from the later discussions, local or popular Islam refers to the knowledge of both *sharī'a* and Sufi traditions of Islam acquired, possessed, and utilized by the masses of Muslim believers in specific places and times. I am grateful to Dale F. Eickelman for his suggestion that "local knowledge" be used instead of "popular knowledge" of Islam in this paper to avoid any misperception that the Islam of the *'ulamā* and the educated lacks "popularity."

4. For an extensive bibliographic review of Sufism in the U.S.S.R., see Bennigsen 1983; also see Lambton 1956, and Lemercier-Quelquejay 1983.

5. For an extensive critique of this dichotomous view of urban and rural Islam, see Martin 1982, especially the article by Dale Eickelman. Also see Eickelman 1985 and Asad 1986.

6. The assumption that Afghanistan's geographical distance from the major centers of Islamic learning resulted in the absence of intellectual and educational ties with such urban centers, thus leading to exotic local cult practices, is not supported or supportable by available documentary sources. For evidence of relations with Islamic centers of learning in Iran and Turkistan see Robinson 1982:32–9 and 100–7; also see Khawand-Mir 1981; with India see Metcalf 1978 and 1982.

7. Although for the purposes of my argument in this paper, a critical examination of relations between notions and practices of "literacy," "illiteracy," and "orality," and the role of "literacy" and "orality" in the social production of the local knowledge of Islam, particularly in light of some significant recent analytical developments in the literature, would be most useful, it is beyond the scope of this project and must await a separate treatment. For an important critical discussion of the theory and practice of literacy and case studies from eastern Iran, see Street 1984; also see Finnegan 1973 and Heath 1980 and 1982. For an earlier critical discussion of the related concepts of "Great" and "Little" traditions in relation to Buddhism in Ceylon, see Obeyesekere 1963.

8. For a detailed and critical discussion of the concept of traditionalism and modernism see Shils 1981; also see Benard and Khalilzad 1984; Asad 1986.

9. Aini, in his *Memoirs*, describes numerous cases of Turkistani *'ulamā*, especially those working for the government of the Amir of Bukhara, who believed in the existence of sharp differences between themselves and the general public (1361 [1983] and 1958).

10. *Panj Ganj* and *Kulliyāt-i Chahār Kitāb* are without any doubt the most widely used popular religious texts in Afghanistan. These are the books which I used as reading texts in *maktab* (mosque

school) during the winter months when the government school
was in recess. Wide use of these same or similar texts is also
reported in Eastern Turkistan (Jarring 1951, IV:117–26), and in
Western Turkistan (Khanikoff 1845:275; Becka 1966; and Aini
1958 and 1361 [1983]). For use of similar texts among the
Muslims of the Indian subcontinent see Metcalf 1984, especially
articles by Metcalf, Lapidus, Digby, Kurin, and Naimi. Also see
Israel and Wagle 1983, especially articles by Metcalf and
Minault. As will be apparent from our discussion below, these
Sunni popular texts contain materials from Shīʿa sources and are
quite similar to those found in Shīʿa Iran (see e.g., Khomeini
1984).

11. For a discussion of *maktabs* (mosque schools) in Eastern
Turkistan, see Jarring 1951, IV:117–26; for Western Turkistan see
Becka 1966; Aini 1958, 1361 (1983); and for eastern Iran see
Street 1984:132–57.

12. It is obvious that the works of some of these poets are held in
highest esteem in the Persian and Turkic literature. What makes
them "popular" Islamic texts for religious learning is the fact that
they are appropriated and transformed by their sheer use by the
less educated and non-literate Muslims in the region (see e.g.,
Jarring 1951, IV:117–26; Aini 1958:5–10 and 1361 [1983]:234–6).

13. In addition to these categories, there are other genres of popular
religious texts widely in use – e.g., prayer books such as *Haft-
haykal* and *Dalāyīl ul-khayrāt*, as well as books on dream interpretations, fortune telling, astrology, palmistry and *tumār* or
taʿwīz (charm) books for writing amulets. Also found are popular
texts on *tib-i Yunānī* or "Galenic-Islamic" medicine (see Good
1977:211).

14. Recently, some of these materials have been recorded and
published (e.g., for proverbs see Dor 1982; Shahrani 1354 [1975];
for tales and stories see Dor 1980; Dor and Imart 1982; Hatto
1969; Heston 1986; Mills 1978a, 1978b; Jarring 1936, 1938,
1946, 1948, 1951; Riordan 1978).

15. *Haftyak* also known as *Panj Sura* (five chapters [of the Quran])
and *Qāʿida-i Baghadādī* (the Baghdad Method) is the beginning
text for learning the Arabic alphabet and how to read Arabic used
in the *maktabs* (see Becka 1966).

16. Sadriddin Aini, the well-known Bukharan Tajik scholar, mentions occasions for such gatherings in his memoirs. He also describes the literary game of *baytbarak* (poetry context) in which an
individual's ability to recite poetry from memory is tested. Both
young and old are said to play the game and take much delight
from it (see 1958:27–8; 1361 [1983]:327). In Afghanistan, it is
called *shīr jangī* (poetry battle) and is an equally popular game.

17. For example, book one of *Kulliyāt* (duplicated as book two in

186

Panj Ganj), concludes the rendition of the *fiqh* in poetry in the following way:

For your sake I told you these
Learn them, I have summarized them
Anyone who reads them honestly
Will know God's commandments of *farz*, *wājib* and *nafl*
May blessings of God be strewn upon the reader
The reteller and the conveyer.

(*Panj Ganj* n.d.:26; also see p. 92; *Kulliyāt* n.d.:13)

Kulliyāt has an additional poem following the one above. The beginning line is:

The soul of the reader, Oh Generous God
You deliver from harsh punishments.

(*Kulliyāt* n.d.:13; also see p. 240)

18. *Kulliyāt* states that "it is *wājib* (a binding duty) for husbands to teach their wife (wives) the knowledge of *sharī'at* and *tarīqat* so that she may learn the requirements of performing *tahārāt* and *namāz* (ablutions and prayers), observance of fasting, performance of *ghusl* (ritual bathing), after sexual acts and during *hayz* (menstruation) and *nifās* (lochia)." One verse from the Quran and a saying of the Prophet are cited to support the view that on the Day of Judgment (*qiyāmat*) the harshest punishment will be meted out to the following *mahārim* or close relatives, should they fail to educate their womenfolk: father, mother, husband, father's brothers, mother's brother and brother (see p. 62).

19. On the role of caravan traders and caravanserais in interregional exchange and communication of oral traditions in Turkistan, see Jarring 1973.

20. For an excellent discussion of the dynamics between written texts, the creative role of narrative-verse singers and the audio cassette recording technology in the North-West Frontiers of Pakistan, see Heston 1986.

21. It is assumed here that the production and dissemination of "authorized" Islamic knowledge, values, and practices, both formal and local, traditional and modern, are the products of particular power structures – central, regional, and familial. For a discussion of this point in the Islamic world, see Watt 1968:121–2; Shahrani 1984a. For the theoretical discussion of the issue see Shils 1982:95–7; Foucault 1980:131; Eickelman 1985; and Asad 1983, 1986).

22. This book is mentioned by Aini under the name of *Mahamud and Ayaz*. For an interesting discussion of the significance of this book in his life see Aini 1958:33; 1361 [1983]:176–8.

23. The *Shash Kalima* are the following: *tayibah*, *shahādat*, *tawhīd*,

tamjīd, rad-i kufr, and *astaghfār.* The text of *tamjīd* is not given in the text I am working with, for the other five see *Panj Ganj* n.d.:103–4.

24. Because of space limitations in this volume, almost all of the illustrative textual materials for this section of the paper have been omitted. Every effort will be made, however, to publish the full-length version of this paper, containing the supportive textual materials for these arguments, in the near future.

25. For a very useful discussion of the expectation of the coexistence of knowledge, belief, and behavior within a faithful Muslim as a precondition for salvation, see Metcalf 1984:1–20, and Lapidus 1984.

26. Anthony Giddens (1984:3) indicates that by "reflexivity," he does not mean merely "self-consciousness" but also "the monitored character of the ongoing flow of social life."

27. For a similar account of angels fighting on the side of the Egyptian soldiers against the Israelis during the 1973 war, see Heper and Israeli 1984:73.

8
Russia's geopolitical and ideological dilemmas in Central Asia

MILAN HAUNER

The last hundred years have witnessed the superimposition of the Russian Eurasian empire over Central Asia, and thereby the creation of a new geopolitical and also a new geocultural reality. The dual Russian presence, not only as administrators but also as settlers, has provided this region with a new cohesion, manifesting itself on the cultural level as well. In this connection, two sets of questions seem to me of particular relevance today in interpreting events in Central and South-West Asia.

1. Why did the Russians want to conquer and then hold on to Central Asia? Compared with previous attempts to set up a larger political entity in Central Asia (by Alexander the Great, Timur, Nadir Shah), what were the determinative factors which made the Russian occupation a lasting one?

2. What was, and what is, the product of the "cultural interaction" between the Russian aliens and the Central Asians? Does it point to the inevitability of a clash or showdown, coexistence of cultural parallelism, or a rather improbable merger?

Providing answers to these questions requires an historical review, as well as an examination of contemporary issues.

GEOPOLITICS

The drive to the warm seas

The nature of Russian expansion in Asia represents a problem to theoreticians of imperialism because it does not seem to fit the model of overseas expansionism practiced by most great European powers throughout the nineteenth century. But then, Russia was not a European power. She was, like her present successor state, a distinct Eurasian empire. Attempts to interpret Russian imperialism by concentrating on economic, political or diplomatic factors will usually miss the most sensible common denominator, which is geography. Throughout their history the Russians have been singularly challenged by the Eurasian space, its climatic vigor and the enormous distances which were involved in controlling it. Furthermore, Russian expansion was usually accompanied by a systematic settlement policy. In that respect Russia resembled the Chinese Empire in possessing, without the interruption of large spaces of water, a compact empire. This dual characteristic of Russian imperialism is particularly relevant for Central Asia where the Russians, unlike the British in India, appear as both intruders and settlers. From a geopolitical standpoint the British geographer, Halford Mackinder (1904:423,436) considered the Russian Eurasian empire unique in that it represented a remarkable "correlation between natural environment and political organization . . . unlikely to be altered by any possible social revolution."

According to R. J. Kerner (1942), the strongest incentive for Russia's territorial expansion over the centuries has been the urge to the sea. In order to overcome the limitations of the Eurasian landmass, circumscribed by land and frozen seas and not offering adequate outlets for safe navigation, Russian foreign policy made its guiding axiom the securing of better access to open, non-freezing, seas (Parker 1969:13–18). To maintain a safe foothold on the Gulf of Finland, and to improve outlets on the Baltic, Black, Mediterranean, and Caspian Seas, and later on the Pacific Ocean, the Russian Tsars since Peter the Great conducted countless wars. Although Peter devoted the best part of his life to the twenty-year-long struggle with Sweden for the domination of the Baltic, he managed nevertheless to secure Russia's first genuine warm sea outlet, the Black Sea (in 1696). However, he lost it fifteen years later and it was not regained until 1739. Commenting on Peter's seizure of Azov almost three hundred years later, Admiral Gorshkov (1974:14), the architect of the recent phenomenal Soviet naval expansion, says approvingly: "Further development of the state and its economy could have proceeded only with the establishment of outlets to the sea."

Peter's name is also associated with the first Russian attempt to gain access through the Indo–Persian Corridor to reach the Indian Ocean, to establish trade links with India and China, either by land or sea (Vernadsky 1927:194). His troops occupied Baku, Gilan, Mazandaran, and Asterabad; but his successor, anxious to avoid confrontation with Nadir Shah, the last Central Asian empire-builder, later ordered their withdrawal. The Russians, however, came back during the Napoleonic wars; and the Peace of Torkamanchay (1828) confirmed the Russian superiority over Persia and granted her prerogatives to interfere in Persia's internal affairs with impunity. Although Russia was to occupy northern Persia on numerous occasions thereafter, she has so far always withdrawn from the Persian glacis if subjected to pressure (1918, 1921, 1946). Although Bolshevik Russia was to relinquish all "imperialistic encroachments" of the overthrown Tsarist regime *vis-à-vis* Persia, she maintained the right to intervene militarily in Iran against a third power threatening the region, as she did in August 1941, by virtue of articles 5 and 6 of the 1921 Treaty signed between Moscow and Tehran (Geyer 1955; Rubinstein 1982:61).

The inspiration for Russian/Soviet expansion toward the warm waters of the Indian Ocean has often been traced back to the apocryphal Testament of Peter the Great. Although for the last one hundred years it has been considered as a definite forgery (Schuyler 1884:512–14), the testament has left a stirring message to the world about Russia's predestined advance to Constantinople and the Persian Gulf. While the fictitious testament helped to incite western Russophobia throughout the ages, the period of Cold War included (Morrison 1952:1,172–9; Resis 1985:692), it does contain, nevertheless, an excellent synopsis of Russia's past and potential territorial targets. Although this southward drive to the warm sea through the Indo-Persian Corridor was duplicated by the rival eastward route to the Pacific Ocean, Peter's original vision could be still seen as the earliest unofficial declaration of Russia's geopolitical doctrine.

So it was interpreted by Admiral A. T. Mahan, the most prominent advocate of navalism, who saw in the rumored testament the self-

191

reflection of Russia's restless tendency to redeem her desperately adverse natural conditions. Thus he visualized her progress toward the Persian Gulf via Khurasan and Seistan, as "strictly analogous movement" with her penetration of Manchuria and the occupation of Port Arthur (Mahan 1900:24–6, 43–5). In order to accomplish that, Mahan realized (1902:232–3), Russia absolutely required, like the railway in the Far East, a railway line connecting her hinterland with the Gulf; otherwise her naval presence there "would be most excentrically placed" (Mahan 1902:232–3).

Mahan was also among the first thinkers who recognized clearly the emerging dilemma of Russia's strategic position in Asia, that she really could not expand further, without securing first adequate supply lines; neither would she pursue two separate aims in Asia simultaneously, i.e., the conquest of the Far East as well as the penetration to the Persian Gulf. Mahan's observations could be complemented by the Heartland Theory, formulated by Halford Mackinder in 1904, who with much greater emphasis and clarity declared Russia to be "the future Empire of the World" because of her pivotal position in Eurasia, where she "inherited the strategical advantage of the central position of the steppe nomads."

Until today all Russian/Soviet designs on the Gulf have been thwarted, partly because of outside pressure, but mainly because of the lack of the infrastructure of penetration, which the Russians did not have time to put in place because of rivalry with the British Empire and adverse geographical conditions. As long as the British controlled the southern rim of Central Asia and the Royal Navy treated the Indian Ocean as its private pool, the object of Russian policy remained primarily confined to the vocabulary of diversionary strategy. True, there was some trade, especially with Persia, but without a direct railway line no grand design could materialize. Only a radical shift in the political and military balance affecting Eurasia could have changed the unfavorable constellation. Such a moment occurred after September 1939, when Great Britain, engaged in a life and death struggle for survival in Western Europe and the Mediterranean with Germany and Italy, had to adopt an appeasement policy *vis-à-vis* Japan in the Far East, and consequently could not pursue any more the effective defence of southern Central Asia. For a while there was a strong possibility that the Soviet Union would join the Axis Powers if she could "center her territorial aspirations . . . in the direction of the

192

Indian Ocean" (Hauner 1981:185–6), instead of pursuing her annexation policy against Finland, the Balkans, and the Turkish Straits.

Under such an alternative the territory of Soviet Eurasia would have been transformed into a landbridge between Germany and Japan, in order to overcome the British naval blockade. There is evidence that several months prior to the secret Molotov–Ribbentrop negotiations of November 1940, the Soviets had been putting considerable pressure on the Iranian Government to gain permission for the stationing of troops and air force in important strategic locations inside Iran, for securing transit rights on the Trans-Iranian Railway and free zones in the Gulf ports (Glaesner 1976:302–12).

But in early December 1940, Hitler had definitely lost patience over Stalin's procrastinations and decided to eliminate the Soviet Union in the following spring. A Soviet contingency plan of 1941 for the occupation of Iran was later captured by the Germans. It envisaged military operations against the Iranian forces and British troops as well, but Gulf ports did not figure as the prime objective (Soviet Command Study of 1941). The subsequent Soviet invasion of northern Iran in August 1941 revealed a different purpose. Moscow set up two puppet republics in north-western Iran after the end of the war, only reluctantly withdrawing its troops when pressed by the West.

Nor have the Soviets shown any signs of preparing the invasion of the Gulf ports in connection with either the recent revolution in Iran or the Soviet occupation of Afghanistan. Since the end of World War II the Gulf region has become even more important to the world economy as a source of more than half of proven world oil reserves; and some experts asked whether the Soviets and their local agents had tried to engineer the Iranian hostage crisis in order to invoke articles 5 and 6 of the Soviet–Iranian Friendship Treaty of 1921 the moment the United States would intervene (Bräker 1983:110–28). As for Afghanistan, although we are still kept guessing about the ultimate reasons which led the Soviets to invade Afghanistan in December 1979, it would be a mistake to conclude that they have abandoned their long-range plans or downgraded their security interests in this region because of failing to win the war in Afghanistan. True, on the one hand, the original Soviet scenario for a slow and systematic penetration of Afghanistan's strategic infrastructure, without antagonizing its inhabitants or outside powers, was completely upset by the 1979 invasion, but on the other hand, Moscow's strategic frontier in Central

193

Asia has become the most volatile and unstable compared with the other sectors of the enormous Soviet Eurasian domain, the perennial difficulties with Poland notwithstanding.

Transportation infrastructure

Introducing a modern communication network into the Indo-Persian Corridor had been the dream of Russia's ambitious statesmen for some time, but was to take a more realistic shape in connection with the spectacular development of railways during the second half of the nineteenth century. There is no space here to go into a detailed review of countless earlier schemes for the Trans-Persian Railway (Curzon 1892, 1:613–39) to provide an alternative land route to India, thus making it possible to travel by rail between London and Bombay in many fewer days than the thirty-three by boat via Suez.

For obvious strategic and commercial reasons Russia seemed to favor strongly a rail extension from her border. The war with Japan (1904–5) momentarily weakened her determination to prevent railway constructions by other powers in Persia if she could not have it her own way. Until 1907 the Anglo-Russian rivalry in Persia was based on suspicion and reciprocal attempts to obstruct each other's railway developments. After signing the Anglo-Russian Convention of 1907, whose primary purpose with regard to Persia was to remove these tensions, the British Government felt that it no longer had the power to oppose railways in the Russian sphere of Persia (Julfa–Tabriz line, 1913–17). Moreover, the fear that Russia could reach an agreement with Germany on the extension of the *Baghdadbahn* via Khanikin to Tehran, very definitely influenced British behavior. The Government of India, on the other hand, was less concerned with the German threat than with the prospect of Russia deciding to build the Trans-Persian Railway via Khurasan and Seistan to Bandar Abbas, overlooking the Strait of Hormuz. British India could not tolerate Russia establishing a second Port Arthur in the Gulf (Sumner 1940:32–43; Sykes 1905:12–19). Precisely for this reason, namely to undercut the anticipated Russian descent to the Indian Ocean via Seistan, the British started to build a 700 km Quetta–Nushki Extension Railway, which ended up in eastern Persia by 1917.

As far as the Afghan border was concerned, Russia established her first railhead at Kushka in 1900, and started to build a second spur to

194

Termez in 1914. Meanwhile the Tashkent–Orenburg line was completed in 1905, providing the uninterrupted link with Russia's European network. At Kushka the Russians assembled the necessary rail material for a lightly constructed military line to Herat, and similar preparations were made at Termez, with the necessary bridging material, in order to reach Mazar-i-Sharif, in case Afghanistan should be invaded. All Russian railways in Central Asia suffered heavily during the civil war; Termez for instance was held by the *basmachi* in 1922–3. Under the Soviets surveyors were sent to investigate the Salang Pass route across the Hindu Kush and negotiations began with Kabul with regard to the construction of the bridge across the Amu Darya at Termez. But the Afghan government resisted for forty years. Only in 1964 did the Soviets finish the Salang Pass Highway – still in time to facilitate the invasion of 1979 – and in 1982 the bridge (Hauner 1985:17).[1]

A rather different scheme was the Trans-Iranian Railway (1927–38), a most ambitious project completed under the reign of Reza Shah by an international syndicate and one in which the great powers had no decisive share. Over 1,400 km long, with many bridges and tunnels, rivaling the best even Switzerland could offer, it remains the only rail connection between the Caspian Sea and the Gulf (Kuniholm 1980:137). It was intentionally designed to avoid direct connection with either the Russian or the British Indian rail systems. During World War II, the railway served as the main artery of the Persian Corridor, which delivered almost eight million tons of vital supplies to the Red Army (Motter 1952:6).

There is still no genuine trunk line west–east across Central Asia. Very probably, if lying outside Soviet control, it could not be tolerated from Moscow's security standpoint. It is, therefore, not surprising that the ambitious plan of the last Shah of Iran, to link up the rail networks of Iran and Pakistan with branch lines to Bander Abbas, Herat, Qandahar, and Kabul, never came to fruition. One must assume that the sheer possibility of establishing a Tehran–Kabul–Islamabad alliance, forged together by this important communication axis, which could easily include China through the Karakoram Highway, opened in 1978, must have been anticipated in Moscow with little pleasure (Rubinstein 1982:149–50).

There are indications that since the Iranian Revolution the former Shah's plans have been resumed on a smaller scale. It remains to be seen whether the present reported Soviet rail spurs, stretching out from Kushka and Termez across the Afghan border, are going to be linked up eventually with the Iranian and Pakistani rail systems which, of course, operate on a different gauge (*Background Brief* September 1984:5). If and when the Soviet intention becomes abundantly clear it will be an event of major geostrategic importance for the future of Central and South-West Asia (Canfield 1981).

The Russian threat to India and the Central Asian question: diversion and subversion

Parallel to the Russian advance to the Persian Gulf was the idea of reaching India across Central Asia. These two ambitions, while often linked together, were two different manifestations of geopolitical thinking, aimed to achieve different results. The Russian conquest of Central Asia, i.e., of Turkistan, believed to be connected with a further advance on India, was a self-contained idea not necessarily linked with the occupation of a warm-water port on the Indian Ocean coast. And the Russian advance into Central Asia, accomplished between the 1860s and 1880s, must be seen in retrospect as an enterprise competing with the Russian conquest of the Far East, which was to gain priority after 1885. As these two distant regions could not be consolidated simultaneously, the Russian southern tier in Central Asia assumed thereafter two important functions: that of diverting British attention from other potential theaters of war and that of buttressing the vulnerable lifeline connecting European Russia with the Far East, soon to materialize in the construction of the Trans-Siberian Railway (1891–1904).

It was the British administration in India that created the notion of the Russian scare in India as a by-product of the "Great Game" played over Central Asia. According to Malcolm Yapp (1981), it was chiefly motivated by fear of an unpredictable internal uprising, such as the Great Mutiny of 1857, which was always simmering below the surface of the diverse social and ethnic structure of the subcontinent. On the other hand, manifestations of external threat to India and British responses to it were even more notorious and numerous. The first British invasion of Afghanistan (1839–42) was preceded by the involvement of both great powers in the siege of Herat in 1837. In 1856 Persia captured Herat but had to give it up when Britain intervened in the Gulf.

The strategem of diversionary actions is an ancient device; the British, enjoying an undisputed naval supremacy, used it as a matter of course. The idea of using it against the British along the Eurasian rimlands of the Russian Empire took shape during the Crimean War (1853–6). Having relinquished their sea power in the Black Sea, the Russians began to contemplate the possibility of restoring their lost power by shifting the center of gravity of their military expansion to Central Asia, and by attempting to threaten India directly (e.g., diversionary schemes by General Duhamel and Admiral Chikhachev). This was the beginning of a new chapter in the Central Asian Question, which not only determined the forthcoming Anglo-Russian rivalry, but helped to shape in a decisive manner the political future of the wider region.

The military conquest of the Caucasus enabled the Russians to dispatch troops into Central Asia. A second Russian spearhead was already pushing from the north across the steppes and deserts into the heart of Turkistan. In rapid succession the great cities of Central Asia, Chimkent, Tashkent, Khojend and Samarqand, were taken. In 1867 the Russians created the Turkistan Province and Military District. In order to justify the policy of further expansion and annexation, Prince Gorchakov, the Russian Foreign Minister, sent out a circular dispatch to his ambassadors, in which he very skillfully defended his country's "civilized mission" against barbarous raiders and pillagers, while promising to settle accounts with the sedentary and agricultural populations of Central Asia peacefully. He gave no hint as to future limitations of Russia's "Forward Policy"; and the process of Russian absorption of Central Asia proceeded relentlessly. After defeating Bukhara and Khiva, Russia turned them into vassals in 1868 and 1873 respectively, and in 1876 annexed the Khanate of Khokand to the Turkistan Province. The absorption of Transcaspia followed suit and a province of the same name was established in 1881.

The next stage of diversionary actions took place during the Russo-Turkish War of 1877–8, when the Congress of Berlin met to thwart Russian designs on the Bosphorus. Facing the gates of Constantinople, the Russians wanted to divert British attention. They decided on a concerted military demonstration in Central Asia and sent 20,000 troops in three columns onto the Afghan and Pamir border.

Simultaneously a diplomatic mission under General Stoletov was sent to Kabul to sign a secret agreement with the Amir. In response to the arrival of a British squadron in the Sea of Marmara, the Russians considered sending a military expedition into Tibet and their cruisers from Vladivostok into the Indian Ocean, in order to test out British reaction (Popov 1934:15–16). The flamboyant General Skobelev put forward in 1877 a plan for a rapid advance against India with 15,000 men. Skobelev's plan consisted of three stages: first, a political agreement with the Amir of Afghanistan combined with an occupation of Kabul by Russian troops then subverting all "disaffected elements in Hindustan"; and finally "hurling masses of Asiatic cavalry upon India as a vanguard under the banner of blood and rapine, thereby reviving the times of Timur" ("Indian Officer" 1894:79–100; Curzon 1889:307, 322–30). This was more than the British could digest. They invaded Afghanistan for the second time (1878–82).

From about 1885 Russia's global strategy was undergoing a conspicuous shift from Central Asia to the Far East, where her major expansion was taking place. Even so, the Central Asian Question remained the main bone of contention in the relationship between the two great powers: in the following years the British regularly learned about new Russian plans to invade India. "The Russians' object," Lord Curzon was convinced, "is not Calcutta, but Constantinople . . . To keep England quiet in Europe by keeping her employed in Asia, that, briefly put, is the sum and substance of Russian policy" (Curzon 1889:313–23).

Fortunately for the British, the increased German penetration along the *Bagdadbahn* in the Balkans and Asia Minor made the Russians readier to sign the St. Petersburg Convention of August 1907, which temporarily suspended any Russian invasion of India. But along her Eurasian rimlands, Russia succeeded quietly, during the very years of the Anglo-Russian Entente, in converting northern Persia and Outer Mongolia into virtual protectorates, and intensified her infiltration of Sinkiang (Sumner 1940:43).

Like diversion, the idea of subversion is an ancient strategem. And although Tsarist Russia was generally more successful in applying subversion *vis-à-vis* the Christian subjects of the Ottoman Empire, especially in the Balkans and in the Caucasus, she found numerous opportunities to make it part of her threat to India as well. When in 1801 Emperor Paul I ordered Ataman Orlov and his Cossacks to march against India, he instructed him to be concerned solely with fighting the British and "to offer peace to all who are against them and assure them of Russia's friendship" (Lobanov-Rostovsky 1933:101). General Skobelev's 1877 scheme of invading India ("Indian Officer" 1894:79–95), is not only very explicit on strategic diversion, but puts a great emphasis on rebellions inside India, which "might even produce a social revolution in England."

However, it was Imperial Germany who became the real promoter of revolution by strategic subversion during World War I. No less than ten schemes were developed in Berlin for the Islamic world, ranging from Lahore to Casablanca (Fischer 1967:126). The Bolsheviks themselves were in the early stages of the Russian Revolution, encouraged by the German General Staff; and they did not hesitate after seizing power to exploit eagerly the double-edged weapon of subversion.

Central Asia at the crossroads

From 1917 to 1922, when Russia was in the grips of a civil war, the whole of Central Asia was undergoing a series of extraordinary upheavals, which created in this region multiple political options. If any of these options, of which at least eight could be counted, had been implemented successfully, the future of Central Asia might have been shaped in a different way from what we know today. This state of continuous flux between 1917 and 1922 created in this region an unpredictable series of challenges and responses among all participants and victims in the division of spoils. Indeed, since the times of Nadir Shah, Central Asia had never experienced such dramatic developments. It is very relevant today, when there is so much speculation on the political future of Central Asia, to provide a summary of these wide options.

One of the ironies, of decisive importance for the reconquest of Central Asia by the Bolsheviks, was the fact that the Austro-Hungarian prisoners-of-war held in Turkistan, and suffering from hunger and boredom, enlisted in the Red Guards. As "internationalists" they became the mainstay of Bolshevik authorities in Tashkent, smashed the provisional Muslim government in Khokand, and survived until the arrival of the main Bolshevik force in the fall of 1919. What the Bolsheviks meant by strengthening "the links between the toiling masses of the Russian and Turkistan peoples" was soon demonstrated by the absorption of the Khanates of Khiva and Bukhara, and by stepping up punitive expeditions against the *basmachi*. During one of these operations in August 1922, the most ambitious protagonist of the Pan-Turan idea in Central Asia, Enver Pasha, was killed in action. With him also died the alternative of establishing a Muslim Central Asian federation of all Turkic peoples.

Among the other options was a Turko-German advance into Central Asia, which of course evaporated after November 1918. The new ruler of Afghanistan, Amir Amanullah, also dreamt of a larger Islamic federation. However, such federation would have rested on the leadership of the Iranian element and, sooner or later, would have clashed with the Pan-Turan aspirations of the Turkic peoples in Central Asia. When Amanullah invaded British India in May 1919, he was convinced that the Bolsheviks would come fast to his side; but Lenin could offer only lofty promises of sending military aid and of recognizing Afghanistan's sovereignty, thereby only conforming to the old German demands as embodied in the Brest-Litevsk Peace Treaty. The primary cause of the abortive coordination was failed communication: The Orenburg–Tashkent Railway remained cut off for the greater part of 1919, and although Tashkent could communicate with Moscow by radio, to and from Kabul only messengers on horseback could be used.

As for the British themselves, in spite of their occupying Baku and Transcaspia between 1918 and 1919, they maintained no political ambitions in expanding their physical control over Central Asia. Although some prominent Muslims, like the Aga Khan, urged the British Empire, already "the greatest Muslim power in the world," to include further Muslim states, "stretching from the Bosphorus to Chinese Turkistan," the temptation was wisely avoided in London, because of fear that the effect of Pan-Islamism "might easily be paralyzing." If the former Russian Empire were to disintegrate, the India Office thought that Turkistan "should look rather to Omsk than to Petrograd or Moscow as its focus." In other words, it was not in the British interest to encourage the reunion of the Russian Eurasian empire. If an Asiatic Russian government centered on Omsk (Admiral Kolchak), and controlling all the railway systems up to Orenburg, could survive the civil war, then Central Asia, the India Office reflected, should be divided into four autonomous units under Siberian (i.e., Omsk) suzerainty: Bukhara and Khiva retaining their nominal independence and the rest of Turkistan being organized into two local administrations, one based in Tashkent, the other in Khokand, with a mixed Muslim and European representation (India Office:December 1918).

Finally, the Bolshevik reconquest of Turkistan coincided with a radical switch in revolutionary strategy from the pursuit of Communist takeovers in Western Europe which experienced a heavy setback because of the defeat in Poland, to the spread of anticolonial uprisings in the East. The rich experience in practicing subversive warfare which the Germans gathered during the war, especially *vis-à-vis* India, was immediately appreciated and applied by the Bolsheviks. The first Bolshevik emissaries to Afghanistan, comrades Bravin and Surits, followed in the footsteps of their German predecessors, von Hentig and von Niedermayer, who had entered Kabul in 1915 with schemes to incite the Frontier tribes against British India. The new "Eastern" strategy was sanctioned by the Second Komintern Congress in July 1920, and scored a great propagandist success at the Congress of Eastern Peoples in Baku the following September. India was to be the probing stone of the new Bolshevik strategy to enhance world revolution by striking at the most vulnerable spot in the edifice of British colonialism. Already in August 1919 Trotsky was thinking about creating a special cavalry corps, which could be launched against India. "The international situation," he wrote, "is evidently shaping in such a way that the road to Paris and London lies via the towns of Afghanistan, the Punjab and Bengal" (Meijer 1964:625).

It was not a coincidence that at the same time the ex-Tsarist General A. E. Snesarev, appointed by Trotsky to head the Academy of the General Staff in Moscow, resumed his lectures on the military geography of Central Asia. Snesarev believed in Russia's historic mission to reach the warm waters of the Indian Ocean, and exhorted his students: "If you want to destroy the capitalist tyranny over the world – beat the British in India!" (Snesarev 1921:243). However, Snesarev's plan of launching a three-pronged invasion of India via Herat, Kabul, and the Pamirs, which must be considered as the best synthesis of the *ancien régime*'s staff planning was never put into operation.

Helping to set the Orient ablaze were Indian revolutionaries, like Maulavi Barakatullah, V. N. Chattopadhyaya, and Raja Mahendra Pratap. During the war they worked for the German Emperor; now they did not mind transferring their allegiance to Lenin. A prominent

Indian Marxist, M. N. Roy, was sent to Tashkent with two trains loaded with weapons and other supplies, including crated aeroplanes. Upon arrival Roy set up a military and propaganda center, where scores of Indian revolutionaries and Muslim *muhajirs* were to be trained and provided with weapons. At a propitious moment they were to be launched via Afghanistan to infiltrate the Indian border.

The whole preliminary phase of this strategy, however, which consisted of spreading unrest among the Frontier tribes and in the Punjab, and which resembled very much the German scenarios of 1915, was not particularly successful. The reason was bad coordination between Kabul, Tashkent, and Moscow, owing to inadequate communications and lack of dedicated agitators. The key link between Turkistan and India, namely Afghanistan, pursued under Amir Amanullah a policy of self-aggrandizement which, although primarily anti-British, also exploited Bolshevik weakness in Central Asia. As far as the problem of timing *vis-à-vis* India was concerned the agitation and subversion from Tashkent came too late to contribute to the unrest, which was still simmering but by and large already contained by the British. The emergence of the new non-violent *satyagraha* movement under Gandhi's leadership also complicated the task of the Tashkent-trained agitators. The Pan-Islamic agitation itself exploited for the time being by the Bolsheviks, constituted also a real menace to them, if carried too far, since they were evidently not willing to lose any part of what was Russian territory under the Tsars.

This combination of expedience and caution might also explain why the Bolsheviks did exploit initially the propaganda and military potential of the "Socialist Pan-Turan," advocated by the "red" Tartar, Sultan Galiev, as a useful springboard for launching agitators into Islamic countries, but turned against the movement and its leaders in 1923 (Bennigsen and Wimbush 1979:66–8). By the time of the Curzon Ultimatum (May 1923), the "Eastern" strategy directed against India, with emphasis on Pan-Islamic agitation, was effectively terminated. The abolition of the Caliphate by Kemal Atatürk caused the *Khilafat* movement in India to die a natural death. Although the Bolshevik forces infiltrated Sinkiang and Outer Mongolia, and continued to fight against the *basmachi* guerrillas well into the 1930s, their main task was to consolidate their hold over the Central Asian territories of Tsarist Russia.

IDEOLOGIES

Merger or ethnic antagonism?

Along with the geopolitical factors, the ideological motivation of the Russians to penetrate and settle in Asia remains important. From the standpoint of a contemporary observer, two chief traits predominate: Great Russian nationalism with its Orthodox-Christian legacy, providing the link of continuity with the Greek and Byzantine heritage; and Communist internationalism. It would be a grave mistake to consider the Orthodox legacy as completely extinct after the Bolshevik Revolution of 1917. The Second World War, called by the Russians themselves "The Great Patriotic War," was a glaring testimony to the surviving strength of Russian patriotism, which demonstrated a much greater vitality than did International Marxism, circumscribed in any case by Stalin's order to dissolve the Komintern in 1943. The emphasis on Communist internationalism predominated in the official Soviet propaganda, because it conveniently allowed the Soviet superpower to appear on the side of the oppressed and exploited, and as the leader of the "irresistible march of History." Appreciating the role of ideology in historical perspective is of fundamental importance for understanding the process of the formation of Russia as a great Eurasian power.

In tracing the ideological roots of Russia's *Drag nach Osten* (*Stremlenie na Vostok*), with special regard for Central Asia, we might dwell for a moment on the published views of the military geographer, Colonel M. I. Venyukov, who became secretary of the Russian Geographical Society in 1873. In 1877, Venyukov published a lengthy and eloquent memorandum entitled *The Progress of Russia in Central Asia*, which represents a remarkably sophisticated argument justifying Russian occupation and colonization of Central Asia on cultural, religious, racial, economic, and political grounds (Venyukov 1877). The colonel's strongest emphasis is on the "ethnological" argument, which today we would plainly call racial. On behalf of the Russian people, Venyukov calls for "the re-establishment or extension of the sway of the Aryan race over countries which for a long period were subject to peoples of Turk and Mongol extraction." But Venyukov was also a Westernized liberal who believed that Russia had a *mission civilisatrice* in the East and should provide Central Asian peoples

203

access to industrial progress. She should proselytize "Christianity, while replacing the elements of Mohammedan fanaticism by humanizing elements . . . and consequently freeing man from the narrow bondage of Islam." In an obvious attempt to placate British apprehension in India, Venyukov speaks of the Russian urge to return to "the cradle of the Aryan or Indo-European race . . . at the sources of the Indus and Oxus," before "our ancestors" had been displaced by the Turko-Mongol invaders.

A strong romantic fascination bordering on mysticism was also present. The Russians no doubt shared the belief with the British and the Germans that somewhere between China and India, in the midst of the highest mountains in the world, there was an ancient center of Aryan cosmography, "a mountain of blazing appearance, the central core of the universe and navel of the Earth" from whose slopes the four mighty rivers of Asia sprang (Allen 1982:11–13, 192–3). Not only British explorers, but Russians too, like Przewalski and Kozlov, were dreaming of reaching the forbidden Tibet; and they mounted numerous expeditions into the Pamirs, the hub of Central Asia.

Venyukov supports his plea for the "return of the Slavs to the neighborhood of their prehistoric home," where they will "meet kindred people, between whom and ourselves, besides commonness of race, there exists similitude of features and even identity of certain historical traditions," by invoking the entire body of Greek civilization culminating in the achievements of Alexander the Great (Venyukov wrote in a century when no less than three Russian emperors carried that name!) and the Byzantine Empire. Venyukov strongly believes in the results of what we would nowadays call social eugenics, in the encouragement of multiracial breeding through mixed marriages, to produce eventually "the same excellent race which we meet with on the banks of the Terek," pointing to the fact that for a long time the Cossacks had been marrying the daughters of the Caucasian mountaineers. Venyukov then concludes with what seems to be his article of faith:

We are not Englishmen, who in India do their utmost to avoid mingling with the natives, and who, moreover, sooner or later may pay for it by the loss of that country, where they have no ties of race; our strength, on the contrary, lies in the fact that up to the present time we have assimilated subject races, mingling affably with them. It is desirable that this historical result should not be forgotten also in the future, especially on our arrival at the sources of the

Oxus, where we must create an entirely Russian border-country as the sole guarantee of the stability of our position in Turkestan.

When summarizing the major factors which led to the Russian conquest of Central Asia, one should pay attention to this fusion of ideological and psychological predispositions.

Venyukov's views on the happy procreation between Russia's Orthodox and Muslim subjects in Central Asia for the benefit of a new vigorous Aryan race may represent a rather isolated offshot from the much more influential trend of aggressive ideologies, exemplified by the Slavophiles. During the 1880s, the most extreme branch of the Slavophiles, called *Vostochniki* ("Easterners"), began to preach a doctrine of Russia's "holy mission" among the peoples of the Orient, thus turning away from the roots of traditional historic Pan-Slavism, which had stressed religious, racial, and cultural affinity between the Russians and the Balkan peoples. None other than Dostoevsky, while comparing the potentialities of a Russian eastward expansion with the drive of European settlers in North America in the aftermath of General Skobelev's senseless massacre at Goek-Tepe, justified the conquest of Asia. "This is necessary because Russia is not only Europe, but also in Asia; because the Russian is not only a European, but also an Asiatic. Not only that: in our coming destiny, it is precisely Asia that represents our main way out" (Dostoevsky 1896[1949] II:1,043–52).

Support for the *Vostochniki* came from leading scholars. Russia's foremost authority in international law, Fyodor F. Martens, wrote two pamphlets, *Russia and China* and *Russia and England in Central Asia*, in which he justified the conquest of Central Asian and Chinese territories by emphasizing the principle that "international rights cannot be taken into account when dealing with semibarbarous peoples" (Malozemoff 1958:42). General N. M. Przewalski, the most noted explorer of Russia's Asiatic frontiers, tried to assure his readership that the inhabitants of Mongolia and Sinkiang were eager to become subjects of the "White Tsar," to whose name they allegedly attributed the same mystic powers as those of the Dalai Lama. The leading sinologist of St. Petersburg's university, V. P. Vasilev, argued in a public lecture that, in contrast to other colonial powers, Russia was advancing in the East to liberate oppressed peoples from the "tyranny of internecine strife and impotency."

This spectrum, of Russia defending Europe against the "Yellow

Peril," was brought to the Russian public by the remarkable religious philosopher and mystic Vladimir S. Solovyov, who developed strong racist views, directly anteceding those of German National Socialists, and argued that inferior races must either submit to the superior ones or disappear. Only the anarchists, like Peter Kropotkin, and later the Bolsheviks, dared to challenge Solovyov's views directly (Malozemoff 1958:43). A pervasive echo of Solovyov's preoccupation with the "Yellow Peril" could be found among the leading poets of the group called the Symbolists, for example Andrey Belyi, and especially in Alexander Blok's famous poem "The Scythians" (Riasanovsky 1967:68; Gollwitzer 1962:94–120). Even the great Russian orientalist, Vasiliy V. Barthold, who never misused his pen in the service of official or sectarian propaganda during either the Tsarist or Bolshevik eras, basically approved of the creation of world empires, either that of Alexander the Great, of the Achaemenids, Sasanids, Arabs, or Mongols; or, for that matter, of the Russian Empire in Central Asia or the British in India. He was convinced that this trend encouraged in the long run the cultural *rapprochement* of various peoples in spite of the ravages which went with the conquests (Bregel 1980a:388; Barthold 1963:13, 164–6, 345–50, 350–433).

The aggressive ideology of the *Vostochniki* was, however, not embraced by the majority of the Russian public, for whom a Europe-centered imperialism in the direction of the traditional outlets in the Balkans and the Turkish Straits remained predominant. The bizarre "Yellow Russia" movement (*Zheltorossiya*), the most extreme variant of the *Vostochniki*, was epitomized in the writings and entrepreneurial activities of Prince Esper E. Ukhtomsky. His megalomaniac vision produced a kind of anthropological theory based on an alleged organic affinity between Russia and China, and even India (Sarkisyanz 1955:218–22). What Malozemoff (1958:43–4) calls the ideological quintessence of the *Vostochniki*, is captured in Ukhtomsky's credo:

Asia – we have always belonged to it. We have lived its life and felt its interests. Through us the Orient has gradually arrived at consciousness of itself, at a superior life . . . We have nothing to conquer. All these peoples of various races feel themselves drawn to us, by blood, by tradition, and by ideas. We simply approach them more closely. The great and mysterious Orient is ready to become ours.

Thus Venyukov's scenario for a racial merger in Central Asia was being now extended across the entire continent. With the coming of the Great Trans-Siberian Railway, of which Ukhtomsky was one of the chief promoters, his collaborator Hermann Brunnhofer (1897:preface) depicted the bright future of Eurasia under the Tsar's scepter, to be linked up from the Yellow Sea to the Baltic and Black Seas by means of this phenomenal railway for the mutual benefit of all races:

Slavic and Turanian blood will soon mix together, new border people, of half European, half Asian stock, will grow up and form a connective bond through which the Slavs will make the higher forms of life of Christian-European culture acceptable to the still enclosed heart of Inner Asia.

From the Eurasian movement to the myth of the "Soviet Man"

It is usually assumed that the First World War and the Bolshevik Revolution, which brought the disintegration of the Tsarist empire, marked also the end of "Eastern" ideologies of the nineteenth-century mold. This is not true. During the 1920s and early 1930s there was a remarkable attempt, by the most original Russian intellectuals in exile, to keep them going. They formed in 1921 the so-called Eurasian Movement, based on the idea of fusion between European Russia and Asia. Thus, Eurasianism as a new *Weltanschauung* emerged in response to the profound crisis which shook Russia during the first quarter of this century. The Eurasians (*Evraziitsy*) believed that Russian civilization, in contrast to any other, was predestined to be truly Eurasian because of its unique features: the dual heritage of the Greco-Byzantine civilization and of the Mongol conquest.

The Eurasians can be divided into two groups: the geopolitical branch, best represented by Peter N. Savitsky; and the ethnocultural, of which the most eloquent spokesmen were the noted linguists, Prince Nikolay S. Trubetskoy, and Roman O. Jakobson. The ethno-culturalists advocated the Eurasian association of languages and cultures, even by overstating the influence of the Turanian element, as can be seen already in the first collective manifesto of the Eurasians, *Exodus to the East (Iskhod k Vostoku)*, published in Sofia in 1921 (Riasanovsky 1967:39–46).

Of particular interest to us should be the attitude of Eurasians to the emancipation of colonial peoples which followed World War I. The rise of colonial peoples is specifically treated in Trubetskoy's *Europe and Mankind (Evropa i chelovechestvo, 1920)* which can be read as a

207

definite indictment of Western imperialism. It broadcasts the message of rebellion against Europe in the name of an authentic native culture and against the traditional Eurocentric approach to extra-European worlds. If Russia, Trubetskoy argues, under the Bolsheviks or some other preferably liberal government, did not prove amenable to a radical change of attitudes toward non-Russian peoples under her political control, she would remain a colonial country like other Western powers. As she was shaken by war and revolution, Russia's humiliation offered a unique opportunity for such a radical transformation of attitudes: "A colonial country herself, Russia could lead other colonial countries, in particular her 'Asiatic sisters', in a decisive struggle against the Romanogermanic colonizers" (Riasanovsky 1967:56; Sarkisyanz 1955:207). It is difficult to ignore in this context the Bolshevik "Eastern Strategy" appealing to the peoples of the Orient to rise in revolt.

However, with regard to the theme of anti-colonial revolutions, one must distinguish between conscious and subconscious motivations of the Eurasians. As Riasanovsky (1967:57) rightly points out, the metaphoric identification on the part of some Eurasians with "our Scythian and Mongol ancestors" had a strongly ambivalent character, combining hate with love, horror with salvation. Some of it was inspired by V. V. Barthold's writings on the impact of Turanian and Mongol cultures, but often led to excesses like the uncritical celebration of Timur's conquest (Savistky 1927a:243–4). Many Eurasians could not overcome this inner contradiction between their deep fear of the "Yellow Peril" on the one hand, and their Great Russian patriotism on the other, which made them believe that they were entitled to absorb Asia as natural heirs and claimants.

As for the distinct geopolitical branch of the Eurasians, this was above all represented by Peter Savitsky (Böss 1961:25–33). From the concept of geographical and climatic unity, which had been pioneered already by the great Russian scientist, D. I. Mendeleev (1906), and in which the Ural barrier ceased to be the traditional divide between Europe and Asia, Savitsky moved further to the concept of Eurasia as an authentic cultural entity (*mestorazvitie*). This is to be understood as a product of the sociohistorical forces in their mutual interplay with the geographical environment, for which Böss (1961:30–3) has used the term *Raumentwicklung*, i.e., location or space in the process of developing. The geopoliticians of the Eurasian movement believed

208

that geography should become the foundation of all other sciences, and that Russia's history and culture were uniquely suited to provide a global geopolitical interpretation of the Eurasian reality (Böss 1961:33). The Eurasian geopoliticians thus sought confirmation, in their selective search of evidence, for their preconceived views that Russian Eurasia was indeed a living proof of a historical, cultural, linguistic, economic, and political unity.

The Eurasians advocated a concept of a planned economy, based on state-owned industry, as the best protection against foreign interests; but they also wanted the private sector to coexist and compete. They emphasized balanced regional development and systematic exploitation of the mineral and energy resources of Eurasia (Böss 1961:104–11). Above all, they believed in the future of Siberia as the main depository of fuel and mineral wealth, which has been fully confirmed by its recent spectacular development, accounting for almost 90 per cent of current Soviet energy and mineral resources today (Kirby 1984). Savitsky's views, too, in a curious way resembled the Bolshevik economic policy pursuing regional autarchy within the Eurasian land fortress. He rejected the colonial and maritime policy of other powers in general, and thought that Russia-Eurasia should gain access to the Persian Gulf in order to maintain her economic independence and to facilitate the economic development of Central Eurasia. In his contribution to the *Exodus to the East*, Savitsky, like Mackinder whom he does not cite, was conscious of the fundamental importance transportation always had and will have for the development of the Eurasian heartland. But with most of the Siberian rivers running in the wrong direction, Savitsky was skeptical whether Central Asia could have a bright economic future within a free world market. He saw, however, along autarchic lines, a way out in the development of an integrated Eurasian continental market independent of the world oceanic trade and diversified in order to satisfy the regional needs. But Russia, Savitsky insisted again, needed a port on the Persian Gulf (Hauner 1985:27).

When Savitsky refers to Russia's expansion into the steppes, he justifies it by the policy of "Forward Frontier." Thus, the entire process of Russian southward and eastward expansion since the sixteenth century is seen by him as a continuous natural process of organic development, almost like an ecological process. There is no hint of political motivation, let alone power politics or imperialist rivalry in connection with the Central Asian question. Consequently, Russian Eurasia is a geopolitical entity in itself (*geopoliticheskoe edinstvo*), brought about by a cultural process of "genetic mutation" (*geneticheskaya mutatsiya*), and not by conquest and destruction (1927a:259–60). This interpretation does not seem substantially different from Friedrich Ratzel's concept of the dynamic *Lebensraum*.

In the writings of Savitsky, and especially of the historian G. V. Vernadsky (1927:230–1), one finds an astonishing similarity between the Eurasianist and Soviet terminology. Vernadsky, for instance, speaks with admiration of the colossal work of cultural merger (*sliyanie*) and mixing (*peremeshivanie*), which culminated in the establishment of the Great Russian culture (*Velikorusskaya kul'tura*). When he states that "under external diversity inner unity is hidden," one is immediately reminded of the current Soviet slogan of "unity in diversity" (*edinstvo v mnogoobrazii*). This inclusion (*vklyuchenie*) of non-Russian groups into the multinational Eurasian empire offers, according to Vernadsky, enormous economic and cultural advantages, for it is a vehicle leading to participation in "universal life." Vernadsky also believed that such a unity must be ecumenical and not achieved by mechanical force and compulsion; and he concludes "the Russian State is a Eurasian state and all separate nationalities of Eurasia must feel and recognize that it is *their* state" (emphasis by Vernadsky). However, even if it is "the Russian people who constitute the main force of the Eurasian state, and the Russian language the fundamental layer of Eurasian culture," it must not be enforced upon the others. The strength of this Eurasian entity lies in its "free cultural creativity." Despite these lofty assurances, proclaimed by the Eurasians in exile, who therefore carried no political responsibility and little influence inside the new Soviet Eurasian empire, they were not trusted by other Slavic nationalities, above all the Ukrainians, who turned against them (Riasanovsky 1967:70). It would be of great interest to find out what the non-Europeans, especially Central Asians, thought of Eurasianism: probably, that it was, like the earlier liberal opinions of men like Venyukov, just another, though more sophisticated, form of Russian imperialism. This preliminary conclusion is supported by the melancholic fate encountered by the seminal proposal for a Russo-Muslim cultural coexistence and cooperation, suggested by the leading educationalist of the Turko-Tatar peoples, Ismail Bey Gasprinsky. His

Russian Islam (1881) remained completely ignored by both Tsarist authorities and Russian intelligentsia (Togan 1947:556).

Homo Sovieticus versus *Homo Islamicus*

The remarkable contribution of the Eurasian Movement, often ignored when the origins of the utopian "Soviet Man" are being discussed, is cited here not only for reasons of historical curiosity. It demonstrates the dominant trend among those authors, whether opposing or serving the Soviet system, whose major concern is with the survivability of the multinational Eurasian land fortress under the leadership of the Russian "elder brother." What must be borne in mind at this juncture is that the Eurasianist generation had been brought up in the optimistic spirit that Russia's demographic projections were to maintain the highest increment among the great powers, which on the basis of the last comprehensive census of the Russian Empire (1897–1905) led scientists like Mendeleev to predict that by the year 2000 the Russian Eurasian empire would have almost 600 million souls (*Toward the Understanding of Russia*, 1906).

In surveying the attitude of the Bolsheviks to Muslim Central Asia we can clearly observe the continuing clash between the geostrategic dicta, inherited by the new Soviet state from the Tsarist empire, and the convulsive attempts to justify the refusal of self-determination to its border nationalities. The present Soviet "trinity" model of flowering –rapprochement–fusion (i.e., *rastsvet–sblizhenie–sliyanie*), so reminiscent of the Eurasian arguments of the 1920s, did not become fully developed until the eras of Khrushchev and Brezhnev in the 1960s and 1970s (Rwykin 1982:138–48). As Hélène Carrère d'Encausse has shown (1981:13–46), the whole Soviet concept of formulating and legalizing the relationship between the Russians and non-Russians had undergone many peripeties. In contrast to Lenin's Utopian vision of states and nations withering away and being replaced by a new universal community of proletarian class solidarity, the more realistic Stalin gradually transformed the idea of cultural federation into one of more centralist control over the nominally autonomous member nations of the Soviet Union.

Five union republics were finally constituted in Soviet Central Asia in three stages (1926, 1929, 1936). New ethnic boundaries were drawn up to respect national principles but not to conflict with economic and

211

strategic requirements of central authorities. The two radical language reforms, the first changing from Arabic and other scripts to Latin, the other from Latin to Cyrillic scripts for each language, intensified artificially local idiosyncrasies and hampered any large pan-movements, like Pan-Islamism or Pan-Turanism (Caroe 1967:144–5). Carrère d'Encausse (1981:30) considers the 1936 Constitution as an implicit declaration on the part of the Soviet state to follow the legacy, historical as well as territorial, of the old Tsarist empire. Like other areas of the Soviet Union, Central Asia was not spared the Stalinist purges that had taken a heavy toll among the local national elites who collaborated with the Soviet power throughout the 1920s. These were replaced by a new class of collaborators, who would carry out Moscow's directives without any consideration for the cultural traditions and diversities of Central Asia and behave like a true universal "Soviet Man." Russian history, too, was to be vindicated. The entire school of the Marxist historian M. N. Pokrovsky (1868–1932), which regarded Tsarist colonialism as an "absolute evil," was denounced and replaced by the reference to "lesser evil." Oppressive though the Tsarist system may have been, the Stalinist apologists argued, it was less evil and oppressive than the alternative then open to non-Russian nationalities, such as annexations by Turkey, Persia, Afghanistan, or even the British Empire.

The painful test for Stalin's unequal multinational federation came during the Nazi-Soviet War (1941–5), which demonstrated how precarious was the foundation of the Central Asian society ravaged by subsequent waves of collectivization and political purges. The majority of Central Asian soldiers taken prisoner opted for the enemy – a fact still hidden from the Soviet public today – although systematic starvation and cruel treatment in German hands, which resulted in appalling losses, must have been one of the major inducements to change sides. As Turkistanis they joined the so-called "Eastern Legions," which were part of the *Wehrmacht* and later the *Waffen SS*, to fight the Red Army (Hauner 1981:339–57). The estimates of their numbers vary between 250,000 and 400,000, which include the Kalmyks, the Tatars and members of the Caucasian ethnic groups (Alexiev 1982:33). Although the Germans were flirting with the idea of Pan-Turanism – unsuccessfully, because of Hitler's veto – the Central Asian Turks, under the leadership of Mustafa Chokaiev and Kayum Khan, preferred to follow a middle course, confined to Turkistan alone. Their attempt, however, to create a common "Turkistani" nationality and political allegiance, underlined by a common middle language, *Ortatili*, which was to become a lingua franca, was not successful. Their fate was a tragic one. The Germans used them only to serve a German purpose (Caroe 1967:252). Stalin's punishment was swift and ferocious. At least one million Soviet citizens, composed of several selected nationalities – the Volga Germans, Kalmyks, Crimean Tatars, and several Caucasians nationalities (Chechens, Ingush, Karachays, Balkars) – and mostly old men, women and children, were deported with a stigma of traitors to Central Asia.

After Stalin's death in 1953 the pursuit of the Utopian *Homo sovieticus* was resumed. In the meantime, however, his main challenger has emerged in Central Asia: the real *Homo islamicus*, who has now become a great focus of attention for Western scholars. Having survived decades of suffering and tribulations under the godless Russian regime, he is now emerging like Phoenix from the ashes. The revolution in Iran and the war in Afghanistan have provided additional strong arguments to focus on Central Asia.

The vision of *Homo islamicus* was greatly enhanced by French political scientists and historians working on Soviet Central Asia and Islam in the U. S. S. R., such as Hélène Carrère d'Encausse and Alexandre Bennigsen. The belief in the inevitable break up of the multinational Soviet State is clearly expressed in the former's provocative book *L'Emire éclaté* (1981), in which she argues that the new sociological and demographic factors, caused basically by the birth rate among Soviet Muslims (at least three times higher than among the Russians), employment shortages in Central Asia, and the growing Muslim self-assertiveness on tradition and religion, cannot but lead to increased imbalances between various national groups. This, she argues (1981:90), is the most serious challenge to Soviet power in the near future.

Bennigsen, the recognized authority on Islam in the Soviet Union, stated several times his case centered on the belief of the enormous vitality of Islamic traditions and beliefs, especially as manifested through the remarkable survival of Sufi brotherhoods, to the effect that his application of the term *Dar ul-Islam* seems appropriate. However, since most of his data came from the Caucasus, they are not applicable to Central Asia. He summed up his experience from "over thirty years of observation," into the most pessimistic vision of an inevitable

213

"showdown" between the Muslims of the Soviet Union on the one hand, and the non-Muslims on the other (1983:86–7, 149–50). His forecast was that Soviet Central Asia (presumably meaning all five union republics?) was to become independent under whatever ideology or political form, e.g., ranging from the revival of Sultan Galiev's National Communism to conservative Islamic radicalism. While Bennigsen denied that Pan-Islamism or Pan-Turanism had a future in Central Asia, and cautiously avoided speculation on the would-be political form of the future Central Asian political entity, and the nature of relationship between Muslims and non-Muslims, he recently hinted (1985:90), though hyperbolically, at the remote possibility of a *jihād* against Russian settlers in Kazakhstan.

Such a proposition, even if suggested as a rather boastful metaphor, ought to be avoided. A juxtaposition between the Muslims on the one hand, and the infidels (*kufār*) on the other, implies cultural discrimination and an almost inevitable degeneration of this dichotomy, for whatever reasons, into one of religious and racial antagonism. The non-Muslim population of Central Asia is composed not only of the descendants of Russian and Ukrainian colonists, but of a wide variety of other nationalities, including for instance about one million forcibly deported Germans in Kazakhstan since World War II. If the non-Russian Christian population of the Caucasus is included, the non-Muslims will amount to at least 25 million according to the last Soviet census of 1979.

The more balanced summary of diverse views on and interpretations of Soviet Central Asia remains perhaps Michael Rywkin's *Soviet Central Asia* (1963), recently re-edited and expanded under the new title, *Moscow's Muslim Challenge* (1982). Although Rywkin hints at "the existence of growing racial antagonism between two non-integrated communities" in Soviet Central Asia, he also acknowledges the contributions of those who do not necessarily agree with the vision of the *Homo islamicus*. Michael Zand and Gregory Massell, for instance, both believe that there is cultural pluralism in Soviet Central Asia and that Soviet rule has resulted in the establishment of various subtypes of "Russified Soviet subculture"; and above all, that the Communists succeeded in coopting the native elites, who consequently became members of the new class thereby alienated from their original ethnocultural milieu. One might add to this dissenting group of scholars Nancy Lubin who, in her recent book (1984:236, 242),

214

rejects the simplistic dichotomy between *Homo sovieticus* and *Homo islamicus*. On the basis of a detailed analysis of the labor situation in Uzbekistan she demonstrated convincingly that it would be premature to assume that the rapid growth of Central Asian manpower, in combination with militant Islam from across the southern border, might soon lead inexorably to a clash with Soviet power. Lubin's main contribution lies in the demonstration that underneath superficial appearances there is a peculiar mechanism of containment, not necessarily of Moscow's creation, which has helped so far to keep balance and diffuse tension. She concludes that:

So far, Soviet policy seems to have been successful in keeping the Soviet Muslim community fragmented, in part appeased, and without a clear cut issue which could possibly divide all Muslims from non-Muslims, or on which Soviet Muslims might unite against Moscow . . . Even if nationalist sentiments were strong in Uzbekistan, and aims clearly defined, factors such as lack of leadership and arms, lack of control of communications . . . imposed by the Soviet system, would make effective advancement of these aims almost impossible. (Lubin 1984:236–7)

In summing up the lessons of acculturation in Soviet Central Asia, Rywkin predicts a rather gloomy solution. By overstating such factors as demographic pressure and labor resources imbalance, Soviet leaders, he feels, might turn back to Stalin's policy of either integration or repression. Although Mikhail Gorbachev has yet to formulate his nationality policy, it seems already highly unlikely that he would adopt the Stalinist solution. Rather than trying the policy of total integration and/or repression, Gorbachev would try to "muddle through," like the Austro-Hungarian bureaucracy prior to 1914, without taking up immediately any of the complex and pressing issues burdening Central Asia. This is the impression one gets from the attention Central Asian topics received during the recent Twenty-Seventh Party Congress (February 1986). To modernize the aging infrastructure of the Soviet economy and to continue with the exploitation of energy and mineral resources in western Siberia will be absolute priorities in the next five to ten years. Moreover, there are other factors which specialists on the Central Asian area tend to underestimate, but which the masters of the Kremlin must always bear in mind in their widest geostrategic correlation of forces, such as military and internal security, growing discrepancy in the regional resource balance (i.e., not only in manpower, but also in raw materials, fuels, energy, water, and transportation infrastructure). Meanwhile the Muslim elements in civilian manpower and in armed forces will be steadily growing, reaching the level of one-third of the Soviet total before the end of this century – provided that the present favorable birthrate in Central Asia is maintained. By then, Gorbachev, if he is still alive and in power, will have to have formulated a definitive nationality and population policy which will bear witness to the major spatial shift eastward within the Soviet Eurasian empire. The center of gravity is inexorably moving beyond the Urals toward the Pacific Ocean; and if Soviet Central Asia can, at the present birth rate, double its population within the next twenty-five to thirty years, the masters of the Kremlin will have to think seriously about restructuring their empire.

NOTE

1. The discussion between the India Office and the Government of India concerning the Trans-Persian Railway scheme, with particular emphasis on the Russian plans and British countermeasures, is contained in the India Office Records (IOR), Secret Memoranda, files: L/P & S/18/C 124, 128, 129, 130, 131, 133, 134, 135, 152, 153, 154, 179 and A200. Contemporary British opinion on the subject is well covered in public lectures delivered before the Royal Central Asian Society and subsequently published in the Society's *Proceedings*: see: Picot (1904), Sykes (1905), Yate (1911). For the parallel Russian opinion, see: P. A. T. (1910?), Rittich (1900 and 1901), Romanov (1891). Further information in this section has been compiled from: Curzon (1892), Hennig (1909), Hughes (1981), Kazemzadeh (1957), Popov (1925, 1934), Pratt (1916), Sumner (1940), Spring (1976), Treue (1939), Williams (1966), Wilson (1985). For data on Russian strength and communication in Central Asia, gathered by British military intelligence, see: Napier (1904) and General Staff (1907). For a map of the existing and projected railways prior to 1918 see Hauner (1985).

Chronology of major events and developments in the history of the Turko-Persian ecumene

Mesopotamia/Arabia Asia Minor/Anatolia West Iran/Caucasus Iran Plateau Khurasan/Sistan Transoxiana/North Steppes Balkh-Afghan Turkistan Afghanistan/Baluchistan Indus Valley North India/Gangetic Plain/China

c. **1500–1200** B.C.: Aryan invasions of Indian subcontinent; earliest hymns of *Rig Veda*.

1200–600 B.C.: Vedic Period.

c. **1000** B.C.: Iranians descend out of Central Asia into the Iranian plateau, calling themselves "Aryan" like those that moved into the subcontinent earlier.

800 B.C.: Rise of the Medes.

745–626 B.C.: Assyrians. Their empire at its height (c. 640 B.C.) stretched from the Persian Gulf to Egypt and Asia Minor.

626–539 B.C.: Neo-Babylonians (Chaldeans) dominated Palestine and Fertile Crescent.

500–330 B.C.: The Achaemenid Empire; at its height stretched from Asia Minor to the Indus.

356–323 B.C.: Alexander, conqueror of the territory from Macedonia to the Indus Valley.

c. **322–183** B.C.: Mauryas arise in upper Ganges, spread to dominate most of South Asia.

Meso-
potam-
ia/
Ara-
bia

Asia
Minor/
Anato-
lia

West
Iran/
Cau-
casus

Iran
Plat-
eau

Khurasan/
Sistan

Trans-
oxiana/
North
Steppes

Balkh-
Afghan
Turkistan

Afghan-
istan/
Baluch-
istan

Indus
Valley

North
India/
Gangetic
Plain/
China

c. **312–64** B.C.: Seleucids dominate the region from the Euphrates to the Indus during most of this period.

c. **150** B.C.: Seleucids collapsing, give way to Parthians coming out of Central Asia and Khurasan.

c. **78–250**: Kushans rule north-west India from Peshawar.

A.D. **224–651**: Sasanians arise, overthrow Parthians, dominate the region between the Euphrates and the Indus.

Late 400s: Mazdak institutes a movement against the Sasanids, accused of founding a "joyous pleasure religion" (Khurramiyya).

c. **mid 400s**: Chionites and Hephthalites invade out of Central Asia. Hephthalites form an empire (c. 450–565) that dominates the region between Sinkiang and Iran and between Sogdiana and the Punjab.

c. **500s**: In the steppes of northern Central Asia Iranian populations are being replaced by Turkic populations.

c. **565**: Hephthalite empire gives way to the Turkic qaghanate on the north and Sasanids on the west and south. Turks by this time dominate the region as far south as the Oxus.

622: Muhammad's flight from Mecca to Medina, beginning of the Islamic calendar. Muhammad dies 10 years later.

632–661: The "rightly guided" caliphs; expansion of Arabs and Islam to Syria and the Oxus, and in the west to the Gulf of Sidra.

660–750: Umayyad caliphate dominates the region from the Atlantic to the Indus.

699: Language of bureaucracy in eastern Islamic lands is changed from Pahlavi to Arabic.

711–712: Conquest of Transoxiana by Muslims.

711–713: Conquest of Sind by Muslims.

736: Khidash, missionary of Abbasids who instituted a movement focused on himself, dies.

748 or 749: Bihafarid dies after leading an uprising in Nishapur and Badghis.

750: Abbasid uprising begins in Khurasan.

744–749: ʿAbd Allah b. Muʿawiya is focus of an uprising in Kufa, accused of supporting "pleasure religion."

750–1258: Abbasid caliphate, capital at Baghdad after 762; their political power begins to decline in ninth century until they are merely symbolic rulers.

755: Death of Abu Muslim, former missionary of Abbasids who became focus of a large popular movement.

758: Sunbadh leads a revolt in the name of Abu Muslim.

750s: Rizamiyyas arise, believe that spirit of God was in Abu Muslim and would pass to a series of legitimate successors.

750s: Abu Muslimiyya movement under the belief that Abu Muslim was still alive, accused of being a pleasure religion.

219

Meso-
potam-
ia/
Ara-
bia

Asia
Minor/
Anato-
lia

West
Iran/
Cau-
casus

Iran
Plat-
eau

Khurasan/
Sistan

Trans-
oxiana/
North
Steppes

Balkh-
Afghan
Turkistan

Afghan-
istan/
Baluch-
istan

Indus
Valley

North
India/
Gangetic
Plain/
China

757: Ishaq ("Turk") leads an uprising claiming Abu Muslim was not dead.

757–8: Ustadhsis leads an uprising of peasants in Badghis and Herat.

759: Al-Muqanna' leads uprising in Transoxiana, eventually claimed to be a god.

778–9: Muhammira arise claiming that Abu Muslim is alive.

816–837: Revolt of Babak against large landlords and Arabs, centered in Azerbaijan.

819–873: Tahirids, hereditary governors, become autonomous in Khurasan.

819–1004: Samanids arise, dominate Central Asia and Khurasan mainly between 875–998.

833+: Turkish mercenaries introduced into Abbasid court, become basis of caliphal power.

861: Abbasid caliph murdered by his Turkish mercenaries, caliphate falls under the control of Turkish soldiery.

861–910: Saffarids rule independently in Khurasan and Sistan.

864–928: Zaydi Shi'ites rule independently in sub-Caspian area.

869: Death of Ibn-Karram, Muslim preacher in Khurasan.

869–892: Caliphal authority reestablished in the region between Syria and Khurasan.

935: Kodak-i Dana leads a movement, is considered omniscient, heir to spirit of Abu Muslim.

945–1055: Buyids arise in Shiraz, govern Kirman and Iraq.

c. 956: Seljuq Turks move into Bukhara, adopt Islam.

998–1186: Ghaznavids, at their height dominate the region from western Iran to Delhi.

999–1140: Qarakhanids replace Samanids and dominate Central Asia.

c. 1000–1218: Seljuqs invade Transoxiana from east, push south and west.

1040–1118: Seljuqs dominate the region from Oxus to Arabia.

1040s: Turkmen push westward into Azerbaijan and Jazirah; their successes attract more Turkmen from the east; Seljuq rulers try to divert them further north and west.

1118: Seljuq domains break up into independent principalities. Seljuq dynasties preside in Rum (i.e., Anatolia, 1077–1307), and Khurasan (1097–1157); Iraq and Syria are under local rulers, some of them Seljuqs.

1141–c. 1200: Qara-Khitays defeat Seljuqs, dominate Transoxiana.

1140–1231: Khorezmshahs prominent, rise to greatest influence in 1199–1220 to dominate most of Iran as well as Transoxiana.

1148: Ghorids arise to control Sistan, Khurasan, push eastward against Ghaznavids.

1153: Oghuz defeat Seljuqs in Khurasan, Turkic pastoralists become important influence in Iran.

1161–1186: Ghaznavids are centered in the Punjab.

1186–1206: Ghorids defeat Ghaznavids, take Delhi in 1193; last Ghorid assassinated in 1206.

1206–1526: Former Turkish slaves become sultans of Delhi, dominate most of the subcontinent.

Meso-potamia/Arabia

Asia Minor/Anatolia

West Iran/Caucasus

Iran Plateau

Khurasan/Sistan

Trans-oxiana/North Steppes

Balkh-Afghan Turkistan

Afghan-istan/Baluch-istan

Indus Valley

North India/Gangetic Plain/China

1218–1334: Mongols invade, eventually rule the region from the Levant to China; empire soon collapses into local dynasties.

1240: Bektashiyya revolt under leadership of Baba Ishaq, believe 'Ali is incarnation of God. Ishaq's poetry, in Turkish, influenced succeeding Turkish generations.

1256–1335: Il-Khanid Mongols rule Iran and Iraq, become Muslim. Chagatai Mongols rule Transoxiana until 1336.

1258: Fall of Baghdad to the Mongols. The end of the Abbasid caliphate.

1288–1326: 'Uthman founds the Ottoman dynasty.

1337–1381: Sarbadars at Sabzawar (Western Khurasan), Shi'ite dynasty; 12 successive chiefs, 9 of whom die violently.

1370–1502: Timur (Tamerlane) invades from Transoxiana, dominates the region from the Euphrates to the Indus.

1394: Fadl Allah, leader of Huruffiyya movement, dies.

1398: Sack of Delhi by Timur (Tamerlane).

1400s: Ahl-i Haqq movement begins, popular among the Turkic tribes; persisted for centuries, appeared in organized form in eighteenth century.

1453: Ottomans seize Constantinople, end the Byzantium empire.

15th century: Al-Musha'sha declares himself the Mahdi, uses magic to attract Arab tribal followers in southern Iraq.

1491–1722: Safavids arise, invade Iran from Anatolia in 1501, dominate Iran, establish Shi'ism as state religion and separate Central Asian Sunnis from Arab world.

222

1496: First Muslim sultanate in the East Indies (now Indonesia), soon to be followed by many others.

1500–1599: Shaybani Uzbek Turks dominate Transoxiana.

Early 1500s: Zikris arise in Baluchistan following Jaunpur who claimed to be the "pure light," to be the Mahdi.

1500–1922: Ottoman empire, which at its peak (in 1600s) stretches from Europe to North Africa and Mesopotamia.

1517: Ottomans take Syria from the Mamluks.

1520–1566: Sulaiman the Magnificent advances Ottoman influence into Europe.

1525–1585: Bayazid leader of the Rowshania movement, claimed to be incarnation of God.

1526–1757: Babur, claiming descent from both Genghis and Timur, invades India from Afghanistan, founds Mughal empire; Mughals dominate north India; at their height (c. 1686) control most of South Asia.

1588–1629: Safavids defeat Ottomans and Uzbeks, threatening on their borders, establish strong central government in Iran.

Meso-potamia/Arabia	
Asia Minor/Anatolia	1700s: Ottoman empire weakening.
West Iran/Caucasus	
Iran Plateau	1590–91: Nuqtavis, led by blind poet who claimed to have reached union with God, rise, are crushed by Safavids.
Khurasan/Sistan	1722: Afghans from Qandahar attack Isfahan and destroy Safavid empire. 1736–1748: Nadir Shah conquers Khurasan, Afghanistan, India; tribal rule in Iran after his death.
Trans-oxiana/North Steppes	
Balkh-Afghan Turkistan	
Afghan-istan/Baluch-istan	1747: Abdali (later called Durrani) Afghans ascend to prominence under Ahmad Shah.
Indus Valley	
North India/Gangetic Plain/China	1658–1707: Under Awrangzeb Mughal empire reaches its greatest extent. 1761: Delhi sacked by Ahmad Shah Abdali of Afghanistan. 1700s: Mughal successor states emerge: Hyderabad, Arcot, Mysore, Murshidabad (Shiʿa), Awadh (Shiʿa), Marathas (Hindu), Punjab (Sikhs), Bengal (East India Company).

1750–1795: Zand dynasty rules from Shiraz.

1785–1791: Naqshbandi revolt in the Caucasus against the Russians.

1796–1925: Qajar dynasty rules Iran from Tehran.

1798: Napoleon invades Egypt.

1800s: Central Asia gradually falls under Roman control despite Naqshbandi Sufi holy war of resistance; is mostly under Russian control by 1876.

1802–1805: Wahhabi revolt in Iraq, Syria and Arabia.

1813: Treaty of Golestan, end of Russo-Persian War; Iran renounces claims to Caucasian territories.

1820–63: Khoja Naqshbandis rise up against Manchu rule in Kashgar.

1826: Sayyid Ahmad Barelwi leads a movement to establish an Islamic state in Northwest Frontier of India.

1828: Treaty of Turkmanchai, end of Second Russo-Persian War; Iran pays war indemnity, cedes territory and grants Russia commercial rights.

1834–59: Second Naqshbandi revolt against the Russians in the Caucasus.

1838–1842: First Anglo-Afghan War.

1845–1849: Anglo-Sikh Wars; British occupy Lahore.

1852: Group of Babis attempts to assassinate the Shah; wave of anti-Babi persecutions.

Meso-potam-ia/Ara-bia	Asia Minor/Anato-lia	West Iran/Cau-casus	Iran Plat-eau	Khurasan/Sistan	Trans-oxiana/North Steppes	Balkh-Afghan Turkistan	Afghan-istan/Baluch-istan	Indus Valley	North India/Gangetic Plain/China
									1857: India Mutiny Uprising; rebels rally round the last Mughal emperor; rebellion is crushed.
									1867: Deobandi reformist Islamic theological school founded.
									1867–1877: Yaqub Beg establishes strict Islamic state in Kashgar.
							1872: Russia assures Britain that Afghanistan is outside Russia's sphere of influence.		
									1877: Aligarh College founded offering Muslims Western education.
							1878–1879: Second Anglo-Afghan War.		
							1880–1901: 'Abdul Rahman subjects most of the population of Afghanistan to Kabul rule, establishes army and bureaucracy.		
							1885: Russians seize Panjdeh.		

1891–1892: Iranian popular revolt against Tobacco Concessions.

1893: Durand line between British India and Afghanistan is fixed.

1901: Habibullah ascends to the throne after his father's death.

1905: First National Assembly convenes in Tehran.

1906–1911: Constitutional movement.

1906: All-India Muslim League founded.

1907: Russian and British agreement, divides Iran into spheres of influence, leaves Afghanistan and Tibet outside their spheres of influence.

1909: Anglo-Persian Oil Co. founded; Britain secures majority share by 1914.

1915–1916: Military expedition of Central Powers (Germany, Austria, Turkey) to reach Kabul across Persia.

1917: Russian Revolution, Bolsheviks are resisted by Central Asian Muslims into the 1930s.

1919: Habibullah assassinated, replaced by his third son, Amanullah.

1919: Peak of political upheavals in Central Asia; Bolshevik troops secure connection between Russia and Turkestan and begin to overpower their opponents in the region.

1919: As British troops withdraw from Trans-caspia, Amir Amanullah attacks British India (Third Anglo-Afghan War).

Meso-potam-ia/Ara-bia	Asia Minor/Anato-lia	West Iran/Cau-casus	Iran Plat-eau	Khurasan/Sistan	Trans-oxiana/North Steppes	Balkh-Afghan Turkistan	Afghan-istan/Baluch-istan	Indus Valley	North India/Gangetic Plain/China

1921: Reza Khan takes power in bloodless coup, takes throne (1925–1941).

1929: Amanullah overthrown, replaced by Habibullah ("Bache-Saqaw"); overthrown by General Nadir Khan, who made himself King.

1933: Nadir Shah assassinated, succeeded by his son, Zaher.

1937: Saadabad Pact: Iran, Iraq, Turkey and Afghanistan agree to respect common borders and refrain from interfering in each other's affairs.

1938: Trans-Iranian Railway between the Gulf and Caspian Sea completed.

1941: Anglo-Soviet occupation of Iran.

1941: German and Italian nationals expelled from Afghanistan.

1947: Pakistan formed; India becomes independent.

1950–1953: Iranian Oil crisis with Britain.

1951: Musadeq becomes prime minister.

1953: Musadeq overthrown by royalist coup with aid of CIA, who establish Muhammad Reza Pahlavi as Shah.

1963: Khomeini attacks Shah and his program; rioting in Tehran bazaar. Khomeini is exiled in 1964.

1973: Muhammad Daood overthrows his cousin, Zaher Shah, establishes Afghanistan Republic.

1978: Riots and demonstrations in Qum, Tabriz, Tehran.

1978: "Saur Revolution," Afghan Marxists overthrow Muhammad Daood, establish new government.

1979: Muhammad Reza Shah leaves Iran; Khomeini returns from exile; monarchy is overthrown.

1979: Soviets invade Afghanistan.

References

Ahmad, Aziz. 1964. *Studies in Islamic Culture in the Indian Environment*. Oxford: Oxford University Press
1967. *Islamic Modernism in India and Pakistan 1857–1964*. London: Oxford University Press
1969. *An Intellectual History of Islam in India*. Edinburgh: Edinburgh University Press
Ahmad, Imtiaz. 1966. The Ashraf-Ajlaf dichotomy in Muslim social structure in India. *Indian Economic and Social History Review* 3(3):268–78
1973. ed. *Caste and Social Stratification among the Muslims*. Delhi: Manohar Book Service
Ahmad, Qari Sharif, ed. n.d. *Muʿalim Addin*. Karachi: Maktaba Rashidiya
Ahmed, Ishtiaq. 1987. *The Concept of the Islamic State: An Analysis of the Ideological Controversy in Pakistan*. New York: St. Martin's Press
Ahmed, Rafiuddin. 1981. *The Bengal Muslims 1871–1906: A Quest for Identity*. Delhi: Oxford University Press
Aini, Sadriddin. 1958. *Pages from My Own Story: Memoirs*. Trans. George H. Hanna. Moscow: Foreign Languages Publishing House
1361 (1983). *Yādāsht-hā (Memoirs)*, the complete 5 volumes in one, ed. Saʿid Sīrjāni. Tehran: Intisharat Agah (in Persian)
Akishev, K. A. 1978. *Kurgan Issyk*. Moscow: Iskusstvo Publishers
Alexiev, Alex. 1982. *Soviet Nationalities in German Wartime Strategy, 1941–1945*. Special Rand report, R-2772-NA, August 1982. Santa Monica, CA: Rand

230

References

Algar, Hamid. 1969. *Religion and State in Iran, 1785–1906: The Role of the Ulama in the Qajar Period*. Berkeley: University of California Press

  1976. The Naqshbandi order: a preliminary survey of its history and significance. *Studia Islamica* 42:123–52

  1979. The oppositional role of the ulama in twentieth century Iran. In *Scholars, Saints, and Sufis: Muslim Religious Institutions since 1500*, ed. N. R. Keddie. Berkeley: University of California Press

Allen, Charles. 1982. *A Mountain in Tibet: The Search for Mount Kailas and the Sources of the Great Rivers of India*. London: Futura, Macdonald & Co.

Allworth, Edward. 1964. *Uzbek Literary Politics*. The Hague: Mouton

  1967. *Central Asia: A Century of Russian Rule*. New York: Columbia University Press

Anesaki, M. 1922. Transmigration (Buddhist). *Hastings Encyclopaedia of Religion and Ethics* XII:p. 430

Ansari, Ghaus. 1960. *Muslim Caste in Uttar Pradesh*. Lucknow: Ethnographic and Folk Culture Society

Ansari, Khizr H. 1984. The emergence of Muslim socialists and their ideas in India 1917–1947. Ph.D. dissertation, University of London

Ansari, Muhammad Raza. 1973. *Banī-yi Dars-i Nizāmī*. Lucknow: Nami Press

Arjomand, Said Amir. 1981. Religious extremism (Ghuluww), sufism and Sunnism in Safavid Iran: 1501–1722. *Journal of Asian History* 15:1–35

Arnold, Ruth, and Anthony Arnold. 1985. Afghanistan. In *Yearbook on International Communist Affairs 1985: Parties and Revolutionary Movements*, ed. Richard Staar and Margit Grigory, pp. 143–55. Stanford: Hoover Institution Press

Asad, Talal. 1983. Anthropological conceptions of religion: reflections on Geertz. *Man* (N.S.) 18:237–59

  1986. *The Idea of an Anthropology of Islam*. Occasional Papers Series. Washington, DC: Center for Contemporary Arab Studies, Georgetown University

Atkin, Muriel. 1985. To the editor. *Problems of Communism* 34:87–8

  1989. *The Subtlest Battle: Islam in Soviet Tajikistan*. Philadelphia: Foreign Policy Research Institute

Ayalon, D. 1976. Aspects of the Mamluk phenomenon. *Der Islam* 53(2):196–225

Background Brief. 1984. Afghan economy. Foreign and Commonwealth Office. September 1984:1–5

Bailey, H. W. 1971. *Zoroastrian Problems in the Ninth Century*. 2nd ed. Oxford: Oxford University Press

Banani, Amin. 1988. Ferdowsi and the art of tragic epic. In *Persian Literature*, ed. Ehsan Yarshater, pp. 109–19. (Columbia Lectures on Iranian Studies, no. 3.) Albany: Bibliotheca Persica and State University of New York

References

Barthold, Vasiliy Vladimirovich. 1963. *Akademik Bartol'd-Sochinseniya*, vol. II.1, ed. B. G. Gafurov *et al.* Moscow: Izd. Vostochnoi literatury

Barthold, W. 1913. Arslān-Khān. *Encyclopaedia of Islam* (first edition) I:p. 462

  1927. Khwārizm. *Encyclopaedia of Islam* (first edition) II:pp. 908–12

  1968 [1900]. *Turkestan down to the Mongol Invasion*. Third edition. Trans. Mrs. T. Minorsky and ed. C. E. Bosworth. E. J. W. Gibb Memorial Series. New Series V. London: Luzac

  1934. Turkistan. *Encyclopaedia of Islam* (first edition) IV:pp. 895–6

Bartol'd, V. V. 1963a. *Sochineniia*, I (Moscow: Nauka)

  1963b. *Sochineniia*, II.1 (Moscow: Nauka)

  1964. *Sochineniia*, II.2 (Moscow: Nauka)

  1966. *Sochineniia*, VI (Moscow: Nauka)

  1968. *Sochineniia*, V (Moscow: Nauka)

Bausani, A. 1956a. Al-Ahsā'ī, Sahykh Ahmad b. Zayn al-Dīn b. Ibrāhīm. *Encyclopaedia of Islam* (second edition) I:p. 304

  1956b. Hurufiyya. *Encyclopaedia of Islam* (second edition) III:pp. 600–1

Bayly, C. A. 1980. The small town and Islamic gentry in north India: the case of Kara. In *The City in South Asia*, ed. Kenneth Ballhatchet and John Harrison, pp. 20–48. London: Curzon Press, Centre of South Asian Studies, School of Oriental Studies, University of London, Collected Papers on South Asia No. 3

  1982. *Rulers, Townsmen and Bazaars: North Indian Society in the Age of British Expansion, 1770–1870*. Cambridge: Cambridge University Press

Becka, Jiri. 1966. Islamic schools in Central Asia [maktabs] *New Orient* 5:186–90

Beckwith, C. I. 1984. Aspects of the early history of the Central Asian guard corps in Islam. *Archivum Eurasiae Medii Aevi* 4:29–43

Benard, Cheryl, and Zalmay Khalilzad. 1984. *"The Government of God": Iran's Islamic Republic*. New York: Columbia University Press

Bennigsen, Alexandre. 1969. The Turks under Tsarist and Soviet rule. In *Central Asia*, ed. Gavin Hambly, pp. 187–207. London: Weidenfeld and Nicolson

  1980–1. Religious belief in Soviet Islam: the current status. *Journal of the Institute of Muslim Minority Affairs* 2 and 3(1):37–41

  1983. Sufism in the U.S.S.R.: a bibliography of Soviet sources. *Central Asian Survey* 2(4):81–107

  1984. Mullahs, Mujahidin and Soviet Muslims. *Problems of Communism* 33:28–44

  1985. Response to Martha Brill Olcott and Muriel Atkin. *Problems of Communism* 34:90

Bennigsen, Alexandre, and Marie Broxup. 1983. *The Islamic Threat to the Soviet State*. London: Croom Helm, and New York: St. Martin's

Bennigsen, Alexandre, and Chantal Quelquejay. 1961. *The Evolution of the Muslim Nationalities of the U.S.S.R. and their Linguistic Problems*.

References

Oxford: Central Asian Research Centre and St. Anthony's College Soviet Affairs Study Group

Bennigsen, Alexandre, and Chantal Lemercier-Quelquejay. 1967. *Islam in the Soviet Union.* London: Praeger

1979. "Official" Islam in the Soviet Union. *Religion in Communist Lands* 7(3):148–59

Bennigsen, Alexandre A., and Enders S. Wimbush. 1979. *Muslim National Communism in the Soviet Union: A Revolutionary Strategy for the Colonial World.* Chicago: University of Chicago Press

1986. *Muslims of the Soviet Empire: A Guide.* Bloomington: Indiana University

Blichfeldt, Jan-Olaf. 1985. *Early Mahdism.* Leiden: Brill

Böss, Otto. 1961. *Die Lehre der Eurasier. Ein Beitrag zur russischen Geschichte des 20sten Jahrhunderts.* Wiesbaden: Harrassowitz

Bosworth, C. E. 1963. *The Ghaznavids: Their Empire in Afghanistan and Eastern Iran, 994–1,040.* Edinburgh: Edinburgh University Press

1973. Barbarian incursions: the coming of the Turks into the Islamic world. In *Islamic Civilization*, ed. D. S. Richards, pp. 950–1,150. Oxford: Cassirer. (Reprinted in C. E. Bosworth. 1977. *The Medieval History of Iran, Afghanistan and Central Asia.* London: Variorum Reprints)

1975. The political and dynastic history of the Iranian world (A.D. 1000–1217). In *The Cambridge History of Iran* V:pp. 1–202. Cambridge: Cambridge University Press

Bosworth, C. E., Peter Hardy, Halil Inalcik, and D. Sourdel. 1965. Ghulām. *Encyclopaedia of Islam* (second edition) II:pp. 1,070–91. Leiden: E. J. Brill

Bräker, Hans. 1983. The implications of the Islamic question for Soviet domestic and foreign policy. *Central Asian Survey* 2(1):110–28

Bregel, Yuri. 1978. The Sarts in the Khanate of Khiva. *Journal of Asian History* 12(2):120–51

1980a. Barthold and modern oriental studies. *International Journal of Middle Eastern Studies* 12:385–403

1980b. *The Role of Central Asia in the History of the Muslim East.* The Asia Society: Afghanistan Council, Occasional Paper No. 20 (New York)

1981. Nomadic and sedentary elements among the Turkmens. *Central Asiatic Journal* 25(1–2):5–37

1982. Tribal tradition and dynastic history: the early rulers of the Qongrats according to Munis. *Asian and African Studies* (Journal of the Israel Oriental Society) 16:357–98

Browne, E. G. 1910. *The Persian Constitutional Revolution.* Cambridge: Cambridge University Press

Bruk, S. I. 1981. *Naselenie mira: ʿetno-demograficheskii spravochnik.* Moscow: Nauka

Brunnhofer, Hermann. 1897. *Russlands hand über asien. Historisch-*

geographische essays zur Entwicklung des russischen reichsgedankens. St. Petersburg

Brydges, Harford Jones. 1833. *Dynasty of the Kajars.* London: J. Bohn. (Reprinted 1973 by Arno Press, New York)

Buciurkiw, Bohdan R., and J. W. Strong, eds. 1975. *Religion and Atheism in* scene. *Journal of the Institute of Muslim Minority Affairs* 2 and 3(1):9–25

Buciurkiw, Bohdan R., and J. W. Strong, eds. 1975. *Religion and Atheism in the USSR and Eastern Europe.* London: Macmillan

Cagnat, René, and Michel Jan. 1981. *Le Milieu des empires ou le destin de l'Asie centrale.* Paris: Editions Robert Laffont

Cahen, Claude. 1968. *Pre-Ottoman Turkey: A General Survey of the Material and Spiritual Culture and History c. 1071–1330.* London: Sidgwick and Jackson

   1975. Tribes, cities and social organization. In *The Cambridge History of Iran* IV:pp. 305–28. Cambridge: Cambridge University Press

Canfield, Robert L. 1973. *Faction and Conversion: Religious Alignment in the Hindu Kush.* Ann Arbor: Museum of Anthropology, The University of Michigan, Anthropological Papers, No. 50

   1978. Religious myth as ethnic boundary. In *Ethnic Processes and Inter-group Relations in Contemporary Afghanistan,* ed. J. Anderson and R. Strand. New York: Asia Society, Afghanistan Council

   1981. Soviet gambit in Central Asia. *Journal of South Asian and Middle Eastern Studies* 5(1):10–30

   1985a. Islamic sources of resistance. *Orbis: A Journal of World Affairs.* Spring 1985:57–71

   1985b. Western stakes in the Afghanistan war. *Central Asian Survey* 4(1):121–35

Caroe, O. 1965 [1958]. *The Pathans.* London: Macmillan

   1967. *Soviet Empire. The Turks of Central Asia and Stalinism.* New York: St. Martin's Press

Carrère d'Encausse, Hélène. 1967a. The stirring of national feeling. In *Central Asia: A Century of Russian Rule,* ed. Edward Allworth, pp. 172–88. New York: Columbia University Press

   1967b. Social and political reform. In *Central Asia: A Century of Russian Rule,* ed. Edward Allworth, pp. 189–206. New York: Columbia University Press

   1981. *Decline of an Empire. The Soviet Socialist Republics in Revolt.* New York: Harper

Chisti, Syed Kahlil. 1981. Muslim population in mainland China. *Journal of Muslim Minority Affairs* 2(2):66–9

Clinton, Jerome W. 1988. Court poetry at the beginning of the classical period. In *Persian Literature,* ed. Ehsan Yarshater, pp. 75–95. (Columbia Lectures on Iranian Studies, No. 3.) Albany: Bibliotheca Persica and State University of New York

CNRS Jeune Equipe, La Transmission du savoir dans le monde musulman

References

périphérique. 1984. Table ronde sur les Naqshbandis. *Lettre d'information* 2. Paris
Cohn, Bernard S. 1983. Representing authority in Victorian India. In *The Invention of Tradition*, ed. Eric Hobsbawm and Terence Ranger. Cambridge: Cambridge University Press
Cole, Juan Ricardo Irfan. 1984. Imami Shi'ism from Iran to north India, 1722–1856: state, society and clerical ideology in Awadh. Ph.D. dissertation, University of California, Los Angeles
Curzon, George N., Lord. 1889. *Russia in Central Asia in 1889 and the Anglo-Russian Question.* London: Longmans Green
1892. *Persia and the Persian Question.* 2 vols. London: Longmans Green
Daniel, Elton. 1979. *The Political and Social History of Khurasan under Abbasid Rule. 747–820.* Minneapolis and Chicago: Bibliotheca Islamica
1988. Khurasan. *Encyclopedia of Asian History* II, pp. 305–6. New York: Scribner's
Demko, George J. 1969. *The Russian Colonization of Kazakhstan, 1896–1916.* Bloomington: Indiana University Press
Dor, Rémy. 1980. "Si tu me dis: chante! chante! . . ." Documents pour servir à la connaissance de la tradition orale des Kirghiz du Pamir Afghan. Ph.D. dissertation, Université de Lille, Paris
1982. Mete ou l'apprentissage du comportement: le proverbe chez les Kirghiz du Pamir Afghan. *Journal Asiatique* 270(1–2):67–146
Dor, Rémy, and Guy Imart. 1982. *Etre Kirghiz au XXme siècle.* Université de Provence, Marseilles: Jeanne Laffitte
Dörfer, G. 1966. Die Turken: Mittler kulturellen und sprachlicher Stromungen in Eurasien. *Bustan* 7(2–3):24–32
Dostoevsky, F. M. 1949 [orig. 1896]. *The Diary of a Writer.* Trans. and ed. Boris Brasol. New York: Charles Scribner
Dryer, June. 1976. *China's Forty Millions.* Cambridge: Harvard University Press
1982. The Islamic community of China. *Central Asian Survey* 1(2–3):31–60
Dumont, Louis. 1972. *Homo Hierarchicus.* London: Granada Publishing Ltd.
Dumont, Paul. 1986. Disciples of the Light – the Nurju movement in Turkey. *Central Asian Survey* 5(2):33–60
Dupree, Louis. 1961. Religion, technology and evolution: a case study of a Muslim community. In *Aspects of Religion in Indian Society*, ed. L. P. Vidyarthi. Meerat, India: Kedar Nath Ram Nath
1966. Islam in politics: Afghanistan. *The Muslim World* 56(4):269–76
1967. The political uses of religion: Afghanistan. In *Churches and States*, ed. K. H. Silver. New York: American University Field Staff
1980. *Afghanistan.* Princeton: Princeton University Press
Eaton, Richard Maxwell. 1978. *Sufis of Bijapur 1300–1700: Social Roles in Medieval India.* Princeton: Princeton University Press

Eickelman, Dale. 1981. *The Middle East: An Anthropological Approach.* Englewood Cliffs: Prentice-Hall

1985. *Knowledge and Power: The Education of a Twentieth-Century Notable.* Princeton: Princeton University Press

Elphinstone, Mountstuart. 1815 (1972). *An Account of the Kingdom of Caubul.* 2 vols. London and New York: Oxford University Press

Emmerson, D. K. 1984. "Southeast Asia:" what's in a name? *Journal of Southeast Asian Studies* 15:1–21

Fahd, T. 1967. Hurūf. *Encyclopaedia of Islam* (second edition) III:pp. 595–6

Finnegan, Ruth. 1973. Literary versus non-literary: the great divide? In *Modern Thought: Essays on Thinking in Western and Non-Western Societies,* ed. Robin Horton and Ruth Finnegan. London: Faber and Faber

Fischer, David Hackett. 1970. *Historians' Fallacies: Toward a Logic of Historical Thought.* New York: Harper and Row

Fischer, Fritz. 1967. *Germany's Aims in the First World War.* New York: W. W. Norton

Fischer, Michael. 1980a. Becoming Mollah: Reflections on Iranian clerics in a revolutionary age. *Iranian Studies* 13(1–4):83–117

1980b. *Iran: From Religious Dispute to Revolution.* Cambridge: Harvard University Press

1983. Imam Khomeini: four levels of understanding. In *Voices of Resurgent Islam,* ed. John L. Esposito. New York: Oxford University Press

Foucault, Michel. 1980. *Power/Knowledge: Selected Interviews and Other Writings 1972–1977.* New York: Pantheon Press

Frye, R. N. 1954. *The History of Bukhara.* Cambridge, MA: The Medieval Academy of America

1965. *Bukhara, the Medieval Achievement.* Norman: University of Oklahoma Press

1975a. *The Golden Age of Persia: The Arabs in the East.* London: Weidenfeld and Nicolson, and New York: Barnes and Noble

1975b. The Sāmānids. In *The Cambridge History of Iran* IV. Cambridge: Cambridge University Press

1985. Two Iranian notes (the Pahlavi Alexander romance). In *Mary Boyce Festschrift,* Acta Iranica. Leiden: E. J. Brill

Frye, R. N., and A. M. Sayili. 1943. Turks in the Middle East before the Saljuqs. *Journal of the American Oriental Society* 63:194–207

Fusfeld, Warren. 1981. The shaping of Sufi leadership in Dehli: the Naqshbandiyya Mujaddidiyya, 1750 to 1920. Ph.D. dissertation, University of Pennsylvania

Gabain, A. von. 1973. *Das Leben im uigurischen Königreich von Qoço (850–1250).* Textband, Wiesbaden: Otto Harrassowitz

Gasprinskiy, Ismail Bey. 1881. *Russkoe Musul 'manstvo: Mysli, Zametki i Nablyudeniya. Simferopol: Spiro Typography.* Reprint No. 6 by the Society for Central Asian Studies, Oxford (1985)

References

Gaury, Gerald de, and H. V. F. Winstone, eds. 1982. *The Road to Kabul: An Anthology.* New York: Macmillan

General Staff. 1907. *The Military Resources of the Russian Empire.* WO 33/419 Public Record Office (London): WO 33/419

Geyer, Dietrich. 1955. *Die Sowjetunion und Iran. Eine Untersuchung zur Aussenpolitik der UdSSr im Nahen Osten.* Tübingen: Arbeitsgemeinschaft für Osteuropaforschung XVI

Ghirshman, R. 1962. *Iran, Parthians and Sassanians.* London: Thames and Hudson

Gibb, H. A. R. 1961. *Muhammedanism.* New York: Oxford University Press 1970. The heritage of Islam in the modern world, II. *International Journal of Middle East Studies* 1(3):221–37

Gibb, H. A. R., and Harold Bowen. 1950, 1957. *Islamic Society and the West: Islamic Society in the Eighteenth Century.* Vol. I (in 2 parts). London: Oxford University Press

Gibb, H. A. R., and J. H. Kramers. 1953. *Shorter Encyclopaedia of Islam.* Leiden: E. J. Brill

Giddens, Anthony. 1984. *The Constitution of Society: Outline of the Theory of Structuration.* Berkeley and Los Angeles: University of California Press

Gilsenan, Michael. 1982. *Recognizing Islam: Religion and Society in the Modern Arab World.* New York: Pantheon Books

Glaesner, Heinz. 1976. Das Dritte Reich und der Mittlere Osten. Politische und wirtschaftliche Beziehungen Deutschlands zur Türkei 1933–1939, zu Iran 1933–1941 und zu Afganistan 1933–1941. Ph.D. dissertation, University of Würzburg

Göbl, R. 1967. *Dokumente zur Geschichte der iranischen Hunnen in Baktrien und Indien,* I. Wiesbaden, Otto Harrassowitz

Goetz, H. 1938. *The Crisis of Indian Civilisation in the Eighteenth and Early Nineteenth Centuries.* Calcutta: University of Calcutta Press

Gollwitzer, Heinz. 1962. *Die gelbe Gefahr. Geschichte eines Schlagworts. Studien zum imperialistischen Denken.* Göttingen: Vandenhoeck and Ruprecht

Good, Byron, J. 1977. The heart of what is the matter: the structure of medical discourse in a provincial Iranian town. Ph.D. dissertation, University of Chicago

Gorshkov, Sergei. 1974. Russia's road to the sea. Peter I to Napoleon. In *Red Star Rising at Sea,* ed. H. Preston. Annapolis: U. S. Naval Institute

Grabar, Oleg. 1964. Islamic architecture and its decoration. In *Islamic Architecture and Its Decoration, A. D. 800–1500; A Photographic Survey,* by Derek Hill. London: Faber and Faber

Gran, Peter. 1979. *Islamic Roots of Capitalism: Egypt, 1760–1840.* Austin: University of Texas Press, Modern Middle East Series

Halm, Heinz. 1978. *Kosmologie und Heilslehre in der Fruher Ismailiyya.* Wiesbaden: Franz Steiner

Hambly, Gavin, ed. 1969. *Central Asia.* London:Weidenfeld and Nicolson

Hanaway, William L. 1988. Epic Poetry. In *Persian Literature,* ed. Ehsan

Yarshater, pp. 96–108. (Columbia Lectures on Iranian Studies, No. 3). Albany: Bibliotheca Persica and State University of New York

Hasan, Mohibbul. 1971. *History of Tipu Sultan* (second revised and enlarged edition). Calcutta: The World Press

Hatto, A. T. 1969. Almambet, Er Kokco and Ak Erkec (an episode from the Kirghiz Heroic Cycle of Manas, A.D. 1862). *Central Asiatic Journal* 13(3):161–98

Hauner, Milan. 1981. *India in Axis Strategy. Germany, Japan, and Indian Nationalists in the Second World War.* London, Stuttgart: Clett/Cotta

 1985. Seizing the third parallel: geopolitics and the Soviet advance into Central Asia. *Orbis: A Journal of World Affairs* 29(1):5–31

"Hazin." 1830. *The life of Sheikh Mohammed Ali Hazin*, trans. F. C. Belfour. London: Oriental Translation Fund of Great Britain and Ireland

Heath, Shirley Brice. 1980. The function and uses of literacy. *Journal of Communication* 30(1):123–33

 1982. What no bedtime story means: narrative skills at home and school. *Language and Society* 2:49–76

Hefner, Robert W. 1985. *Hindu Javanese: Tengger Tradition and Islam.* Princeton: Princeton University Press

Hennig, Richard. 1909. *Bahnen des Weltverkehrs.* Leipzig: J. A. Barth Verlag

Heper, Metin, and Raphael Israeli, eds. 1984. *Islam and Politics in the Modern Middle East.* London: Croom Helm

Herodotus. 1920. *Histories*, ed. A. D. Godley. Cambridge, Mass., Harvard University Press

Heston, W. L. 1986. Verse narrative from the bazaar of the storytellers. *Asian Folklore Studies* 45:79–99

Hoag, John D. 1975. *Islamic Architecture.* New York: Rizzoli

Hodgson, Marshall G. S. 1954. 'Abd Allah b. Saba'. *Encyclopaedia of Islam* (second edition) I:p. 51

 1965. Ghulāt. *Encyclopaedia of Islam* (second edition) II:p. 1,093

 1974. *The Venture of Islam.* 3 vols. Chicago: University of Chicago Press

Holt, P. M., Ann K. S. Lambton, and Bernard Lewis, eds. 1970. *Cambridge History of Islam.* Cambridge: Cambridge University Press

Hughes, Hugh C. 1981. *Middle East Railways.* Harrow: Continental Railway Circle

al-Hujwīrī, 'Ali b. 'Uthman al-Jullabi. 1910 [c. 1050]. *The Kashf al-mahjub: The oldest Persian treatise on sufiism.* Trans. Reynold A. Nicholson. Leiden: E. J. Brill, and London: Luzac

Husain, Shah Muhammad. n.d. *Bil Tanzim-i Nizam al-Ta'allum wal Ta'lim.* Allahabad: Jalal al-Din Ahmad

Ikram, S. M. 1964. *Muslim Civilization in India.* New York: Columbia University Press

India Office. 1918. *The Future of Russian Central Asia. A Memorandum*, India Office Records: L/P & S/18/C.186, December 3, 1918

References

"Indian Officer." 1894. *Russia's March towards India, by "an Indian Officer"* II. London: Sampson Low

Israel, Milton, and N. K. Wagle. 1983. *Islamic Society and Culture: Essays in Honour of Professor Aziz Ahmad*. New Dehli: Manohar Publications

Israeli, Raphael. 1978. *Muslims in China: A Study in Cultural Confrontation*. London: Curzon Press

1979. Islamization and sincization in Chinese Islam. In *Conversion to Islam*, ed. Nehemia Levtzion, New York and London: Holmes and Meir

1981. The Muslim minority in the People's Republic of China. *Asian Survey*, August, 201–19

1982. Islam in the Chinese environment. In *Islam in Local Contexts*, ed. R. Martin, pp. 159–96. Contributions to Asian Studies No. 17. Leiden: E. J. Brill

Jarring, Gunnar. 1936. *The Contest of the Fruits: An Eastern Turki Allegory*. Lunds Universitets Arsskrift. New series 1, vol. 32, no. 4. Lund: C. W. K. Gleerup

1938. *Uzbek Texts from Afghan Turkestan*. Lunds Universitets Arsskrift. New series, 1, vol. 34, no. 2. Lund: C. W. K. Gleerup

1946. *Materials to the Knowledge of Eastern Turki*, part 1. Lunds Universitets Arsskrift. New series, 1, vol. 43, no. 4

1948. *Materials to the Knowledge of Eastern Turki*, part 2. Lunds Universitets Arsskrift. New series, 1, vol. 44, no. 7

1951. *Materials to the Knowledge of Eastern Turki: tales, poetry, proverbs, riddles, ethnological and historical texts from the southern parts of eastern Turkistan with translation and notes*. Parts 3 and 4. Lunds Universitets Arsskrift. New series, 1, vol. 47, nos. 3 and 4

1973. A tall tale from Central Asia. *Script Minora* 1972–73:3

Jaza'iri, Ni'mat Allāh. 1961. *al-Anwār an-Nu'maniyah* IV, pp. 302–26. Tabriz

Kamali, A. H. 1971. The heritage of Islamic thought. In *Iqbal: Poet-Philosopher of Pakistan*, ed. Hafeez Malik. New York: Columbia University Press

Karmysheva, B. Kh. 1974. *Ocherki 'etnicheskoi istorii iuzhnykh raionov Tadzhikistana i Uzbekistana (po 'etnograficheskim dannym)*. Moscow: Nauka

Kasymov, S. S. 1956. Liberatira (Uzbekistan). *Bol'shaia Sovetskaia Entsiklopediia* XLIV:pp. 31–4

Kaushik, Devendra. 1970. *Central Asia in Modern Times: A History from the Early Nineteenth Century*. Moscow: Progress

Kazemzadeh, Firuz. 1957. Russian imperialism and Persian railways. In *Russian Thought and Politics*. Harvard Slavic studies IV, pp. 355–73. Cambridge, MA: Harvard University Press

Keddie Nikki R. 1983. *An Islamic Response to Imperialism*. Berkeley: University of California Press

Kent, R. 1953. *Old Persian*. New Haven: American Oriental Society

Kerner, R. J. 1942. *The Urge to the Sea: The Course of Russian History*. Berkeley: University of California Press

239

Khanikoff. 1845. *Bokhara: Its Amir and Its People*. London: James Madden
Khawand-Mir, Ghiyatth-ud-din. 1981. *Makarīm-ul-Akhlāq (exalted standards of virtues): a short treatise on the character of Amir Ali-Sher Navayi (1441–1501 A.D.)*. A summarized English translation by A. G. Ravan Farhadi. Kabul: Afghanistan Academy of Sciences
Khomeini, Ayatollah Rohullah. 1984. *A Clarification of Questions: An Unabridged Translation of Resaleh Towzih Al-Masael*, trans. J. Borujerdi. Boulder, Colorado: Westview Press
Kirby, Stuart. 1984. *Siberia and the Soviet Far East: Resources for the Future*. The Economist Intelligence Unit, Special Report No. 117. London
Koshelenko, G. A. 1966. The beginning of Buddhism in Margiane. *Acta Antiqua Hungarica* 14:175–83
Kulliyāt. n.d. *Kulliyāt-i Chahār Kitāb*. Peshawar: Nurani Kutub Khana (in Persian)
Kuniholm, Bruce R. 1980. *The Origins of the Cold War in the Near East. Great Power Conflict and Diplomacy in Iran, Turkey, and Greece*. Princeton: Princeton University Press
Lambton, A. K. S. 1956. *Islam and Russia: A Detailed Analysis of an Outline of the Islamic Studies in the U.S.S.R. by N. A. Smirnov*. London: Central Asian Research Centre
    1973. Aspects of Saljuq-Ghuzz settlement in Persia. In *Islamic Civilization: 950–1150*, ed. D. S. Richards. Oxford: Cassirer
    1975. The internal structure of the Saljuq Empire. In *The Cambridge History of Iran* v, pp. 203–82. Cambridge: Cambridge University Press
Lapidus, Ira M. 1984. Knowledge, virtue, and action: the classical Muslim conception of Adab and the nature of religious fulfillment in Islam. In *Moral Conduct and Authority*, ed. Barbara D. Metcalf, pp. 38–61. Berkeley and Los Angeles: University of California Press
Lelyveld, David S. 1978. *Aligarh's First Generation: Muslim Solidarity in British India*. Princeton, NJ: Princeton University Press
Lemercier-Quelquejay, Chantal. 1983. Sufi brotherhoods in the U.S.S.R.: a historical survey. *Central Asian Survey* 2(4):1–35
LeVine, Robert. 1984. Properties of culture: an ethnographic view. In *Culture Theory: Essays on Mind, Self and Emotion*, ed. R. A. Shweder and R. A. LeVine. Cambridge: Cambridge University Press
Levtzion, Nehemia. 1979. Toward a comparative study of Islamization. In *Conversion to Islam*, ed. N. Levtzion. New York: Holmes and Meier
Lewis, B. 1960. 'Ayn Djālūt. *Encyclopaedia of Islam* (second edition). I:pp. 786–7
    1973. The Mongols, the Turks and the Muslim polity. In *Islam in History*, ed. B. Lewis. London: Alcove Press
Lings, Martin. 1969. Sufism. In *Religion in the Middle East*, ed. A. J. Arberry, pp. 253–69. New York: Cambridge University Press
Lobanov-Rostovsky, Prince A. 1933. *Russia and Asia*. New York: Macmillan
Lubin, Nancy. 1984. *Labour and Nationality in Soviet Central Asia. An Uneasy Compromise*. Princeton, NJ: Princeton University Press

240

References

McChesney, R. D. 1980. The reforms of Baqi Muhammad Khan. *Central Asiatic Journal* 24(1–2):69–84

n.d. Unpublished manuscript, Muhammad Badi' Samarqandi's Muzakkir al-Ashab, p. 25

Mackinder, Halford J. 1904. The geographical pivot of history. *The Geographical Journal* 23:421–44

Madelung, Wilfred. 1971. Imāma. *Encyclopaedia of Islam* (second edition) III:pp. 1,163–9

1973. Ismā'īliyya. *Encyclopaedia of Islam* (second edition) III:pp. 198–206

1976. Kaysaniayya. *Encyclopaedia of Islam* (second edition) IV:pp. 836–8

1979. Khurramiyya. *Encyclopaedia of Islam* (second edition) IV:pp. 63–5

Mahan, Alfred T. 1900. *The Problem of Asia.* Boston: Little and Brown

1902. The Persian Gulf and international relations. *National Review* 40(140):37

Malozemoff, Andrew. 1958. *Russian Far Eastern Policy 1881–1904. With Special Emphasis on the Causes of the Russo-Japanese War.* Berkeley: University of California Press

Mann, Jim. 1985. China's Uighurs – a minority seeks equality. *Los Angeles Times,* July 13, I:1, 10–11

Martin, Richard, ed. 1982. *Islam in Local Contexts.* Contributions to Asian studies XVII. Leiden: E. J. Brill

Mazzaoui, Michel M. 1972. *The Origins of the Safawids: Šīʿism, Ṣūfism, and the Gulāt.* Freiburger Islamstudien, III. Wiesbaden: Franz Steiner Verlag GMBH

1983. East and West: Moslem intellectual history during the eighteenth century. *Graeco-Arabica* 2:87–97

Meijer, Jan H. 1964. *The Trotsky Papers, 1917–1919,* I. London and Paris. The Hague: Mouton

Mendeleev, D. I. 1906. *K poznaniyu Rossii.* St. Petersburg: A. S. Suvorin

Metcalf, Barbara Daly. 1982. *Islamic Revival in British India: Deoband, 1860–1900.* Princeton: Princeton University Press

1978. ed. The Madrasa at Deoband: a model for religious education in modern India. *Modern Asian Studies* 12(1):111–34

1984. ed. *Moral Conduct and Authority: The Place of Adab in South Asian Islam.* Berkeley: University of California Press

Mills, Margaret. 1978a. Oral narrative in Afghanistan: the individual in tradition. Unpublished Ph.D. dissertation, Harvard University

1978b. *Cupid and Psyche in Afghanistan: An International Tale in Cultural Context.* New York: Afghanistan Council of Asia Society, Occasional Paper No. 14

Millward, W. G. 1976. Iran. In *Introduction to Islamic Civilization,* ed. R. M. Savory, pp. 169–77. Cambridge: Cambridge University Press

Minault, Gail. 1974. Urdu political poetry during the Khilafat movement. *Modern Asian Studies* 8(4):459–71

Moosa, Matti. 1988. *Extremist Shiites: The Ghulat Sects.* Syracuse: Syracuse University Press

Morgan, D. O. 1979. The Mongol armies in Persia. *Der Islam* 56(1):81–96

Morrison, John A. 1952. Russia and warm water. A fallacious generalization and its consequences. *U. S. Naval Institute Proceedings* 78:1,169–79

Mottahedeh, Roy. 1980. *Loyalty and Leadership in an Early Islamic Society.* Princeton: Princeton University Press

1985. *The Mantle of the Prophet.* New York: Simon and Schuster

Motter, Thomas H. Vail. 1952. The Persian corridor and aid to Russia. The Middle East theater. *U. S. Army in World War II*, vol. VII, part 1. Washington, DC: Office of the Chief of Military History, Department of the Army

Moynihan, Elizabeth B. 1980. *Paradise as a Garden in Persia and Mughal India.* London: Scholar Press

Mukminova, R. G. 1954. K voprosu o pereselenii kochevykh uzbekov v nachale xvi v. *Izvestiia Akademii nauk UzSSR* 1:70–81

Munkuev, N. Ts. 1977. Zametki o drevnikh mongolakh. In *Tataro-mongoly v Azii i Evrope* (second edition). Moscow: Nauka

Naff, Thomas, and Roger Owen, eds. 1977. *Studies in Eighteenth Century Islamic History.* Carbondale, IL: Southern Illinois University Press

Nalle, David. 1983. *Conference on the Study of Central Asia.* Washington, DC: Kennan Institute for Advanced Russian Studies of the Woodrow Wilson International Center for Scholars

Napier, H. D., Lt. Col. Military Attaché. Nov. 9, 1904. *Diary of the Military Attaché's Visit to Central Asia*, India Office Records: L/P & S/10/54

Nasr, S. H. 1974. Ithnāʿashariyya. *Encyclopaedia of Islam* (second edition) III:pp. 276–9

Nath, R. 1979. Scrutiny of the Persian data related to the builders of the Taj Mahal. *Indo-Iranica* 32:1–18

Newel, Richard. 1980. Islam and the struggle for Afghan national liberation. In *Islam in the Contemporary World*, ed. Cyriak Pullapilly. Notre Dame, IN: Cross Road Books

Newell, Richard and Nancy Newell. 1981. *The Struggle for Afghanistan.* Ithaca and London: Cornell University Press

Nicholson, Reynold Alleyne, ed. and trans. 1898. *Selected Odes from the Divan-i Shams-i Tabrīz.* Cambridge: Cambridge University Press

Nizam al-Mulk. 1960. *The Book of Government, or, Rules for Kings*, trans. H. Darke. New Haven: Yale University Press

Nizami, Farhan Ahmad. 1983. Madrasahs, scholars and saints: Muslim response to the British presence in Delhi and the Upper Doab 1803–1857. Ph.D. dissertation, Oxford University

Obeyesekere, Gananath. 1963. The great tradition and the little in the perspective of Sinhalese Buddhism. *The Journal of Asian Studies* 22(2):139–53

Olcott, Martha Brill. 1985. To the editor. *Problems of Communism* 34:87

Paksoy, H. B. 1984. The Deceivers. *Central Asian Survey* 3(1):123–31

1986. Chora Batir: A Tartar admonition to future generations. *Studies in Comparative Communism* 19(3–4):253–65

References

1987a. Central Asia's new Dastans. *Central Asian Survey* 6(1):75–92
1987b. "Sun and Fire": by Alisher Ibadinov. Paper read to the Meetings of
   the Council on Islamic Societies and Cultures in Philadelphia, April
Pandit, R. S. 1968. *Kalhana's Rājataranginī*. New Delhi, Sahitya Akademi
Panj Ganj. n.d. *Panj Ganj*. Peshawar: Taj Mahal Company (in Persian)
Parker, W. H. 1969. *An Historical Geography of Russia*. Chicago: Aldine
Pastner, Stephen L. 1978. Power and pirs among the Pakistani Baluch.
   Journal of Asian and African Studies 13(3–4):231–43
P.A.T. (anon.) (1910?) "Zheleznodorozhnyi vopros v Persii i Velikiy
   Indijiskiy put" Velikaya Rossiya 2. Moscow: V. P. Riabushiuskiy
Perry, John. 1978. Justice for the underprivileged: the ombudsman tradition
   in Iran. *Journal of Near Eastern Studies* 37(3):203–15
Picot, H. 1904. *Railways in Western Asia*. London: Proceedings of the
   Central Asian Society
Pipes, Richard. 1954. *The Formation of the Soviet Union: Communism and
   Socialism, 1917–1923*. Cambridge, MA: Harvard University Press
Popov, A. L. 1925. Angliiskaya politika v Indii i Russko-Indiiskie otnosheniya
   v 1897–1905 gg. *Krasnyi Arkhiv* 19:53–63
   1934. Ot Bosfora k Tikhomu Okeanu. *Istorik-Marksist* 37(1):3–28
Pratt, E. A. 1916. *Rise of Rail Power in War and Conquest 1833–1914*.
   Philadelphia: J. B. Lippincott
Pritsak, O. 1951. Von den Karluk zu den Karakhaniden. *Zeitschrift der
   Deutschen Morgenländischen Gesellschaft* 101:270–300
   1975. Lecture on nomadic empires, at Harvard University
Qidwai, Altaf Al-Rahman. 1924. *Qiyam-i Nizam-i Taʿlim*. Lucknow: Nami
   Press
Rahman, Fazlur. 1966. *Islam* (second edition). Chicago: University of Chi-
   cago Press
   1970. Islamic modernism: its scope, method and alternatives. In *Interna-
   tional Journal of Middle East Studies* 1:317–33
   1982. *Islam and Modernity: Transformation of an Intellectual Tradition*.
   Chicago: University of Chicago Press
Rakowska-Harmstone, Teresa. 1983. Islam and nationalism: Central Asia
   and Kazakhstan under Soviet rule. *Central Asian Survey* 2(2):7–87
Rekaya, Mohamed. 1984. Le Hurran-din et les mouvements hurramites sous
   les "Abbasides." *Studia Islamica* 60:5–59
Resis, Albert. 1985. Russophobia and the "Testament" of Peter the Great,
   1812–1980. *Slavic Review* 44(4):681–93
Riasanovsky, Nicholas V. 1967. The emergence of Eurasianism. *California
   Slavic Studies* 4:39–72
Riordan, James. 1978. *Tales from Tartary, Russian Tales* II. New York: The
   Viking Press
Rittich, Petr A. 1900. *Zheleznodorozhnyi put' cherez Persiyu*. St. Petersburg:
   Porokhovshchikov
   1901. *Otchet o poezdke v Persiyu i persidskiy Beludzhistan v 1900 g.* St.
   Petersburg: General Staff

Rizvi, Saiyid Athar Abbas. 1975. *Religious and Intellectual History of the Muslims in Akbar's Reign with Special Reference to Abu'l Fazl (1556–1605)*. New Delhi: Munshiram Manoharlal

1980. *Shah Wali-Allah and his Times: A Study of Eighteenth Century Islam, Politics and Society in India*. Canberra: Ma'rifat Publishing House

Robinson, Francis. 1974. *Separatism among Indian Muslims: The Politics of the United Provinces' Muslims 1860–1923*. Cambridge: Cambridge University Press

1982. *Atlas of the Islamic World since 1500*. Oxford: Phaidon Press

1983. Problems in the history of the Farangi Mahall family of learned and holy men. Paper presented to the South Asia Seminar, University of Oxford

Romanov, P. M. 1891. *Zheleznodorozhnyi Vopros v Persii i Mery k Razvitiyu russko-persidskoi torgovli*. St. Petersburg: Yu. N. Erlikh

Rorlich, Azade-Ayse. 1986. *The Volga Tartars: A Profile in National Resilience*. Stanford: Hoover Institution

Roy, Olivier. 1981. What is Afghanistan really like? *Dissent* (Winter):47–54

1983. Sufism and the Afghan Resistance. *Central Asian Survey* 2(4):61–79

1984. The origins of the Islamist movement in Afghanistan. *Central Asian Survey* 3(2):117–27

1986. *Islam and Resistance in Afghanistan*. New York: Cambridge University Press

Rubinstein, Alvin Z. 1982. *Soviet Policy toward Turkey, Iran, and Afghanistan. The Dynamics of Influence*. New York: Praeger

Rudenko, S. I. 1960. *Kul'tura Naseleniya Gornogo Altaya v Skifskoe Vremya*. Leningrad: Akademii Nauk SSSR

Russell, Ralph, and Khurshidul Islam. 1969. *Ghalib 1797–1869* I: *Life and Letters*. London: George Allen and Unwin, Unesco Series of Representative Works

Rypka, Jan. 1968. *History of Iranian Literature*. Dordrecht: D. Reidel

Rywkin, Michael. 1982 [1963]. *Moscow's Muslim Challenge: Soviet Central Asia*. Armonk, NY: M. E. Sharpe

Sachau, C. E. 1876. *Chronologie Orientalischer Völker von Albīrūnī*. Leipzig: Brockhaus Verlag

Sachedina, Abdulaziz Abdulhussein. 1981. *Twelver Shi'ism*. Albany: State University of New York Press

Sadiq, Muhammad. 1964. *A History of Urdu Literature*. London: Oxford University Press

Sarianidi, V. I. 1984. *Baktriya Skvoz' mglu Vekov*. Moscow: Mysl' Press

Sarkisyanz, Samuel. 1955. *Russland und der Messianismus des Orients. Sendungsbewusstsesin und politischer Chiliasmus des Ostens*. Tübingen: J. C. B. Mohr

Saunders, J. J. 1977. The Mongol defeat at Ain Jalut and the restoration of the Greek Empire. In *Muslims and Mongols: Essays on Medieval Asia*, ed. J. J. Saunders. Christchurch: University of Canterbury

References

Savitsky, P. N. 1927a. Geopoliticheskie zametki po russkoi istorii. In *Nachertanie russkoi istorii*, ed. G. V. Vernadsky. pp. 234–60. Prague: Evraziisko knigoizd

Schacht, Joseph. 1959 (1950). *The Origins of Muslim Jurisprudence*. Oxford: Clarendon

Schimmel, Annemarie. 1980. *Islam in the Indian Subcontinent*. Leiden-Cologne: E. J. Brill

Schuyler, Eugene. 1884. *Peter the Great: Emperor of Russia* ii. Reprinted in 1967. New York: Russell and Russell

Shahrani, Enayatullah A. H. 1354 (1975). *Amsāl wa Hakam: Majmuʿā-i zarbulmasal-hā-i muhalī*. *(Proverbs and wise sayings: a collection of folk sayings)*. Kabul: Bayhāq-i Kitāb Khaparawulu Muʾasisa (in Persian)

Shahrani, M. Nazif. 1979. *The Kirghiz and Wakhi of Afghanistan: Adaptation to Closed Frontiers*. Seattle: University of Washington Press

  1984a. "From tribe to Umma:" comments on the dynamics of identity in Muslim Soviet Central Asia. *Central Asian Survey* 3(3):27–38

  1984b. Afghanistan's Kirghiz in Turkey. *Cultural Survival Quarterly* 8:31–4

  1984c. Causes and context of response to the Saur revolution in Badakhshan. In *Revolutions and Rebellions in Afghanistan: Anthropological Perspectives*, ed. M. Nazif Shahrani and Robert L. Canfield. Berkeley: Institute of International Studies, University of California, Berkeley

Shahrani, M. Nazif and Robert L. Canfield, eds. 1984. *Revolutions and Rebellions in Afghanistan: Anthropological Perspectives*. Berkeley: Institute of International Studies, University of California, Berkeley

Shaniiazov, K. Sh. 1974. *K ʿetnicheskoi Istorii Uzbekskogo Naroda (istoriko-ʾ etnograficheskoe issledovanie na materialakh kipchakskogo komponenta)*. Tashkent: Fan

Sharar, Abdul Halim. 1974. *Lucknow: The Last Phase of an Oriental Culture*, trans. and ed. E. S. Harcourt and Fakhir Hussain. London: Paul Elek, Unesco, Indian Series

Sharon, Moshe. 1983. *Black Banners from the East*. Jerusalem: Magnes Press, Hebrew University, and Leiden: E. J. Brill

Shibli Numani, Mawlana. 1955. *Maqālat-i Shiblī* i. Azamgarh: Dar Mutbah Muʿaraf

Shils, Edward. 1981. *Tradition*. Chicago: University of Chicago Press

  1982. *The Constitution of Society*. Chicago and London: University of Chicago Press

Siddiqi, Moʿazzam. 1979. The influence of Bedil on the Indo–Persian poetic tradition. In *The Rose and the Rock: Mystical and Rational Elements in the Intellectual History of South Asian Islam*, ed. Bruce B. Lawrence. Durham, NC: Duke University Programs in Comparative Studies on Southern Asia, No. 15

Sinor, Denis. 1969. *Inner Asia: A Syllabus*. Bloomington: Indiana University Publications, Ural Altaic Series, volume 96

245

1970. Central Eurasia. In *Orientalism and History* (second edition). Bloomington and London: Indiana University Press

Slobin, Mark. 1976. *Music in the Culture of Northern Afghanistan.* Tucson: University of Arizona

Smith, J. M. 1975. Mongol manpower and Persian population. *Journal of the Economic and Social History of the Orient* 43(3):271–99

Snesarev, A. N. 1921. *Afghanistan.* Moscow: Gosizdat

Soviet Command Study of Iran (Moscow 1941). 1941. Produced by the Soviet General Staff, translated into German by the Military Intelligence at the German High Command (OKW/Abwehr), English version by Gerold Guensberg. Arlington, VA: SRI International, 1980

Spring, Derek W. 1976. The Trans-Persian railway project and Anglo-Russian relations. *Slavonic and East European Review* 54(1):60–82

Spuler, Bertold. 1970. The disintegration of the caliphate in the east. In *The Cambridge History of Islam,* 2 vols., ed. P. M. Holt, Ann S. K. Lambton, and Bernard Lewis. I, pp. 143–74. Cambridge: Cambridge University Press

Steensgaard, Niels. 1974. *The Asian Trade Revolution of the Seventeenth Century: The East India Companies and the Decline of the Caravan Trade.* Chicago: University of Chicago Press

Street, Brian. 1984. *Literacy in Theory and Practice.* Cambridge: Cambridge University Press

Subatay, Arslan. 1930–31. Dichter und Dichtung in Turkestan. *Osteuropa* 6:393–5

Sufi, G. M. D. 1977. *Al-Minhaj being the Evolution of the Curriculum in the Muslim Institutions of India.* Delhi: Idarah-i Adabiyat-i Delli

Sukhareva, O. A. 1966. *Bukhara: XIX – nachalo XX v. (Pozdnefeodal'nyi gorod i ego naselenie).* Moscow: Nauka

1982. *Istoriia sredneaziatskogo kostiuma: Samarkand (2ia polovina XIX – nachalo XX v.).* Moscow: Nauka

Sumner, B. H. 1940. Tsardom and imperialism in the Far East and Middle East, 1880–1914. Raleigh lecture in History, *Proceedings of the British Academy* 27:3–45

Suwaydi ʿAbd Allāh 1323/1905. *al-Hujaj al-Qatʾiyah.* Cairo: al-Matbaʾah al-Halabiyah

Swidler, Ann. 1982. Culture in action: symbols and strategies. Paper presented to the American Sociological Association. San Francisco, September 6–10

Sykes, H. R. 1905. Our recent progress in Southern Persia and its possibilities. *Proceedings of the Central Asian Society (London),* Lecture delivered on March 1, pp. 1–20

Taheri, Amir. 1985. *The Spirit of Allah: Khomeini and the Islamic Revolution.* Bethesda, MD: Adler and Adler

Tanakabuni, Mirza Muhammad. n.d. *Kitab Qisas al-ʿUlamaʾ.* Tehran: Ilmiyah

Tirmizi, S. A. I., ed. 1969. *Persian Letters of Ghalib.* New Delhi: Ghalib Academy

References

Titley, Norah M. 1983. *Persian Miniature Painting and its Influence on the Art of Turkey and India*. Austin: University of Texas

Togan, Zeki Validi. 1947. *Bügünkü Türkili (Turkistan) ve Yakin Tarihi (Turkistan Today and its Recent History)* Istanbul: Arkadas, İ.

Tolstov, S. P. 1947. Goroda guzov. *Sovetskaia etnografiia* 3:55–102

Toynbee, A. J. 1953. *Civilization on Trial*. London: Oxford University Press

Treue, Wilhelm. 1939. Russland und die persischen Eisenbahnbauten vor den Weltkrieg. *Archivfür Eisenbahnwesen* 2:471–94

Trubetskoy, N. S., Prince. 1920. *Evropa i chelovechestvo*. Sofia: without publisher

Ullah, Najib. 1963. *Islamic Literature*. New York: Washington Square

Vaglieri, L. Veccia. 1956. "ʿAlī b. Abī Tālib." *Encyclopaedia of Islam* (second edition) I:pp. 381–6

Van Bruinessen, M. M. 1978. Agha, Shaikh and state: on the social and political organization of Kurdistan. Ph.D. dissertation, University of Utrecht

Venyukov, M. J. 1877. *The Progress of Russia in Central Asia* (translation from Sbornik gosudarstvennykh znaniy). St. Petersburg, 22 pp., India Office Records: L/P&S/18/C 17 (Political and Secret Memoranda)

Vernadsky, G. V. 1927. *Nachertanie Russkoi Istorii*. Prague: Evraziiskoe knigoizdatel'stvo

Voll, John Obert. 1982. *Islam: Continuity and Change in the Modern World*. Boulder, CO: Westview Press

Wasserstrom, Steve. 1985. The moving finger writes: Mughīra b. Saʿīd's Islamic gnosis and the myths of its rejection. *History of Religions* 25:1–29

Watt, Montgomery. 1968. *Islamic Political Thought: The Basic Concepts*. Edinburgh: Edinburgh University Press

Williams, Beryl J. 1966. The strategic background to the Anglo-Russian entente of August 1907. *The Historical Journal* 9:360–73

Wilson, Keith M. 1985. *The Policy of the Entente: Essays on the Determinants of British Foreign Policy 1904–1914*. Cambridge: Cambridge University Press

Wint, Guy. 1969. Introduction. In Joseph Wolff, *A Mission to Bokhara* (reprint of 1845 edition). New York: Praeger

Wolff, Joseph. 1969 [orig. 1845]. *A Mission to Bokhara* (new abridged edition), introduction by Guy Wint. New York: Praeger

Wolters, O. W. 1982. *Culture and Region in Southeast Asian Perspectives*. Singapore: Institute of Southeast Asian Studies

Yang, Iyang. 1957. *Islam in China*. Hong Kong: The Union Press

Yapp, Malcome E. 1981. *Strategies of British India. Britain, Iran and Afghanistan, 1798–1850*. Oxford: Clarendon Press

Yarshater, Ehsan. 1988. The development of Iranian literatures. In *Persian Literature*, ed. Ehsan Yarshater, pp. 3–37. (Columbia Lectures on Iranian Studies, no. 3.) Albany: Bibliotheca Persica and State University of New York

247

Yate, A. C. 1911. The proposed trans-Persian railway. *Proceedings of the Royal Central Asian Society,* February 8, 1911

Zettersteen, K. V. 1954. ʿAbd Allah b. Muʿāwiya. *Encyclopaedia of Islam* (second edition) I:pp. 48–9

Zürcher, E. 1967. The Yüeh-chi and Kaniska in Chinese sources. In *Papers on the Date of Kaniska,* ed. A. L. Basham. Leiden: E. J. Brill

Index

'Abbas I, Shah, 150
Abbasids, 5–6, 137–8, 139–41
Abu Hashem, 138, 140
Abu Muslim, 141–2
Achaemenid Empire, 4, 37, 40–6
Afghani (Sayyid Jamal ad-Din Asadabadi), 93
Afghanistan
  foreign control, 23–4, 161–2
  and Great Britain, 23, 196–7, 198
  and India, 200
  and Islam, 163–4, 166–7, 176–83
  and Russia, 23, 198, 201, 202
  and Soviet Union, 193–4
  transport routes, 194–5
Ahsai, Sheikh Ahmad-i, 89
Akhbaris, in India, 117
'Ali, 133, 144–5
Amanulla, Amir, 200
Amri, 151
Ansari, Bayazid, 152
Aq-qoyunlu, 81
al-'Arabi, Ibn, 108–9, 110
Arabic, 4–5, 7
Aramaic, 45
architecture, 18, 100

armies *and see* military power, name of
  country
  manpower, 57–8
  organization, 66–8
  training, 40–1, 43–4, 90–1
  and Turks, 56–8, 66–70
art, Persian influence in India, 18, 111
Aryans, 38
Ashraf, 105–6, 118, 121, 127, 129
Asia, and Russia, 207–11
Astrakhan, 91
Awadh, 114, 116, 117–18
al-Aziz, Shah 'Abd, 119, 120

Babi-Bahai faith, 89
Bactria, 50
Baghdad, 5
Baluchi, influence of Persian, 107
Barelwi, Saiyid Ahmad, 120
Bedil, Mirza 'Abd al-Qadir, 107
Bengal, 116
Bengali, 107, 118
Bihār al-Anwār, 88
Bihari, Muhibb Allah, 114
Bolsheviks, 199–202, 211
Buddhism, 50

249

Index

Bukhara, 9, 52, 197, 199–200
Bukhari, Sharaf, 171
bureaucracy, 42–3
Buyids, 6, 9

Caliphate, 140–1
canon, and balance of power, 19
Central Asia *and see* name of country
    and colonial powers, 91
    definition of area, 28, 35–7, 53–4, 78–9
    ethnic boundaries, 211-12
    and Great Britain, 200–1
    languages, 212
    migrations, 38–9
    and Mongols, 54, 56, 60–1, 64–73
    and nationalism, 96–7
    and Russia, 90, 91–2, 97–8, 197–202,
        205–6
    and socialism, 101
    and Turks, 54–73
Chaghatai, 15, 63, 87, *and see* Turki
Chaghatais, 61
Chahār Kitāb see Panj Ganj
charisma, 41–2
Chionites, 49
Chishti Sufis, 18, 109, 110, 111, 116
Christianity, and Islam, 92–3
cities, towns, and regions in the Turko-
    Persian ecumene, *see* Astrakhan,
    Awadh, Baghdad, Bengal, Bukhara,
    Ghazni, Herat, Hughli, Jaunpur,
    Kazan, Kirghizia, Khiva, Khokand,
    Khorasan, Khwarazm, Lahore,
    Lucknow, Merv, Murshidabad, Sialkot,
    Samarqand; *and see* Central Asia, India,
    Iran, Iranian Plateau, Iraq, Turkey
clans, 40, 41–2
colonialism
    in Iran, 89–91
    Russian, 89–90, 97–8, 190–4, 203–10
Communism, and Islam, 161–3, 170, 183
cultural tolerance, 42

Damad, Mir Baqir, 107
Dar al-'Ulum, Deoband, 126–7, 128
Darius, 40–1, 43
dating, problems and solutions, 80–1, 84
Dawani, Jalal al-Din, 107, 110
Day of Judgment, 175, 180–1
Delhi sultanate, 15, 18
Deoband, Dar al-'Ulum, 126–7, 128

al-Din, Shah Rafi, 119
ud-Din, Sheikh Safi, 148–9
dynasties and empires, *see* Abbasids,
    Achaemenids, Buyids, Delhi sultanate,
    Ghaznavids, Ghorids, Kushans,
    Mamluks, Marathas, Mauryas,
    Mongols, Mughals, Ottomans,
    Parthians, Safavids, Saffarids,
    Samanids, Seleucids, Seljuqs, Tahirids,
    Timurids, Umayyads

education, 88
    Anglo-Oriental College, 122
    Dars-i Nizami syllabus, 108, 115, 126
    Farangi Mahal, 114–15, 126, 127
    importance in India, 113
    use of Islamic texts, 167–70
    Khayrabad school of logic and philosophy,
        114–15
    madrasas, 14, 108, 115, 126–7
    teaching methods, 108, 109, 115, 126
esoteric extremism, 132–4, *and see* mystical
    knowledge
    and culture, 155–8
    and Imamism, 143–4
    and Isma'ilis, 145–6
    and Safavids, 148–50
    and Shi'ites, 143–4, 151
    and Sufism, 146–50, 152
    in the twentieth century, 152–5
ethnic relations *and see* racial policies,
    Russia, 211–12
ethnolinguistic groups, *see* Ashraf, Mongols,
    Pushtuns, Russians, Tajiks; *and see*
    Iranian peoples, Turkish peoples
Eurasian Movement, 207–11
Europeans, and Turko-Persia, 21–4, 31
Evraziitsy, 207–11
exaggeration, theological, 132–5
extremism, esoteric, 132–5

Fadl Allah ('Abd al-Rahman), 150–1
Falah, Muhammad ibn (al-Musha'sha),
    151
families, and clans, 40
Farangi Mahal, 114–15, 126, 127
finance in Perso-Islamic society, 118, 123
Firdowsi, 7
Fitrat, 'Abd ar-Rauf, poetry of, 97

Gasprali, Isma'il (Gasprinski), 99

250

Index

Ghauth, Muhammad, 110
al-Ghazali, and Sunni thought, 14
Ghaznavids, 8, 13–14, 15, 57
Ghazni, 8
Ghorids, 15, 18
ghulāms see Mamluks
ghulāt, ghulūw, 132–5
Gilani, Muhammad ʿAli "Hazin", 88, 114, 117
government
  in India, 113
  Perso-Turkic, 85
Great Britain,
  and Afghanistan, 23, 196–7, 198
  and Central Asia, 200–1
  colonial expansion, 89–90
  Forward Frontier Policy, 209–10
  and India, 112–13, 115, 196–7
  and Russia, 196–8
  and Sufism, 123–4
  and Turko-Persia, 23–4
gunpowder empires, 19–22

Hadiths scholarship, 108, 119–20
Hafiz, poetry of, 82–3
Hanafi jurisprudence, 9, 18
al-Hanafiyya, Muhammad ibn, 136, 140
al-Haqq, Sheikh ʿAbd, 108
al-Harb, ʿAbd Allah b. (Ibn Harb), 138
Hasan, Jalal al-Din, 146, 157
Hasan, Mullah, 114, 115
Haydar, Mullah, 115
Haydari Sufis, 111
"Hazin", Muhammad ʿAli Gailani, 88, 114, 117
Heartland Theory, 192
Hephthalites, 49
Herat, 51, 196–7
al-Hilli, Ahmad ibn Fahd, 151
Hindus
  and art, 111
  and languages, 114, 124
  religious tolerance, 108–9
  and Sufism, 111, 123–4
Hughli, 116
Hujwiri, on *walīs*, 147–8
Huns, 49
Hurufiyya, 151

Ibn Harb (ʿAbd Allah b. al-Harb), 138
Imams
  concept of, 156

and esoteric extremism, 143–4
importance of, 135–6
and Shiʿites, 135, 137, 144–5
and Sunnis, 135
use of title, 154–5
Imdad Allah, Hajji, 116
India
  and Afghanistan, 200
  art, 18, 111
  and Ghaznavids, 13
  and Great Britain, 112–13, 115, 196–7
  languages, 113–14, 118, 123
  religions, 38, 50–1, 123–4
  and Russia, 196–9, 201–2
  and Turko-Persian culture, 15
Iqbal, Muhammad, 125, 128–9
Iran
  armies of, 90–1
  and colonial powers, 89–91
  constitution, 96
  definition of area, 78–9
  development of, 24
  government, 101
  and Iraq, 116–17
  Islamic Revolution, 153–5
  and nationalism, 96
  and Russia, 90, 91, 96
  and Soviet Union, 193
  transport routes, 195–6
Iranian peoples
  see Aryans, Huns, Khwarazmians,
    Parthians, Sakas/Scythians, Sarts,
    Sogdians; *and see* Iranians, Persia
Iranian Plateau, definition of area, 35–6
Iranians
  and Abbasids, 5–6
  culture of, 5–13, 21
  in India, 117
  in Khurasan, 5, 137
  and language *and see* Persian, 4, 55
  and Persians, 4, 40
  and Samanids, 6
  sphere of influence, 37–8
Iraq, and Iran, 116–17
irrigation, 45–6
Islam
  in Afghanistan, 163–4, 166–7, 176–83
  and Bolsheviks, 211
  case studies, 176–81, 183–4
  and Christianity, 92–3
  and Communism, 161–3, 170, 183

251

Index

Lahore, 13
language *and see* languages
  in Bactria, 50
  bilingualism, 62–3
  and employment in India, 113–14, 123
  official, 123, 124–5
  and printing, 124
  and society, 7, 12, 18
  translation, 90–1
languages, *see* Arabic, Aramaic, Baluchi,
  Bengali, Chaghatai, Kashmiri, Marathi,
  Ortatili, Pahlavi, Persian, Punjabi,
  Pushtu, Sindhi, Tajik, Urdu, Uzbek,
  and see Turkic peoples
law *see* judicial systems, Islamic
  jurisprudence
leadership, 41–2, *and see* Islamic leaders,
  rulers
literature *and see* language, poetry
  development of, 18, 22, 82
  dissemination of, 90–1
  importance of, 7, 30, 109–10
  Islamic, 79–80, 82, 166–75, 181–3
  and the Mughal Empire, 106–7
  and religion, 87–9
Lucknow, 115, 117

Madari Sufis, 111
madrasas, 14, 108, 115, 126–7
Maharwardin, Bihafarid b., 139
Mahdis, 136, 137, 143–4, 154–6
Mahdum, Ahmad (Makhdum), 99
Mahmūd Nāmah, 172
Majlisi, Muhammad Baqir, 88
Maliki jurisprudence, 18
Mamluks, 56–7, 66–8, 80–1, 85, 94–5
Marathas, 112–13
Marathi, influence of Persian, 107
Mathnawī-ya Ma'nawī, 83
Mauryas, 44–5
Mawlawiya Sufis, 18
Mazdak, 'Ali b., 142
Merv, 51
military power, and sedentarization, 68, 69–
  70
Mongols
  armies of, 68
  and Central Asia, 54, 56, 60–1, 64–73
  and culture, 15, 69–70, 72–3
  in Turko-Persia, 14–15
Muawiya, 'Abd Allah b., 138

Mubin, Mullah, 114
Mughal Empire, 20–1, 81, 85, 94–5,
  112–13
  and literature, 106–7
Muhammira, 142
Muhimmāt al-Muslimīn, 173
mullahs, and sacred leadership, 156–7
Al-Muganna', 142
Murshidabad, 116–17
al-Musha'sha (Muhammad ibn Falah), 151
music, Persian influence in India, 111
Muslims *see* Islam
mystical knowledge, 108–9, 115–16, 120,
  and see esoteric extremism, Sufism

Nadir Shah Afshar, 88
Nām-i Haqq, 171
Naqshbandi Sufis, 18, 72, 109, 110, 120–1,
  153
Nasirabadi, Sailyid Dildar 'Ali, 117
nationalism, and Islam, 95–6, 97–8
Nazi–Soviet War, 212–13
nazms, 171
Niyazi, Hamzah Hakim-zadah, poetry of, 97
Nizam al-Din, Mullah, 114
Nizami Sufis, 109, 116, 126
nomads
  and culture, 69–70
  empires, 44, 47–8
  and settled populations, 19, 21–2, 31,
    41–4, 65–6
Nur Pak, 152
Nurbakhsh, Muhammad, 151–2
Nurbakhshiyya Sufis, 151–2
Nurjus, 153

oases, 31, 36
oasis states, 47
Ortatili language, 213
Ottoman Empire, 19, 20–1, 23, 80, 85,
  94–5

Pahlavi, 4–7
Pakistan, development of, 24
Pan-Islamism, 93
Pand Namāh-i, 'Attār, see Panj Ganj
Panj Ganj, 166, 167–9, 170–2
Panj Kitāb see Panj Ganj
Parthians, 47
Peace of Torkamanchay, 191

Index

and Sufism, 148–50, 157
and Turks, 149–50
Saffarids, 5–6, 7
Saidkorihocaev (Sayyid Qari Khawjaoghlu), 183
Sailkot, 107
St Petersburg Convention, 198
Sakas, 38, 43
Salang Pass Highway, 195
Samanids
  army of, 44, 56–7
  culture, 8, 10
  and Iranians, 6
  and Islam, 9
  language, 7
  and slave trade, 56–7
  and Turks, 8–9
Samarqand, 52
Sandilwi, 'Alim, 114–15
Sarts, 63
Sasanians, 4–5, 51
sciences
  rational, 107–8, 114–15, 125–6
  revealed, 108
Scythians see Sakas
sedentarization
  and military power, 68, 69–70
  and nomads, 19, 21–2, 31, 41–4, 65–6
Sehalwi, Mullah Nizam al-Din, 114
Sehalwi, Mullah Qutb al-Din, 114, 115
Seleucids, 45, 46
Seljuqs, 13–14, 57, 58, 67–8
Shafi'i jurisprudence, 18
Shāhnāma, 7
Sharar, 'Abd al-Halim, on Persian language, 114
shari'a, 120
Shi'a culture, 116–17
Shi'ism, 21, 86, 89
Shi'ites, 116, 135, 136, 137, 143–5, 151
Shirazi, Fadl Allah, 107
Siberia, wealth of, 209
silk route, 46
Sindhi, 107, 118
Sirhindi, Sheikh Ahmad, 109
slave trade, 56–7
Slavophiles, 205–6
socialism
  in Central Asia, 101
  and Islam, 95–6, 97–8, 99–100
Sogdians, 37, 43–4, 50, 66

Soviet Union *and see* Russia
  and Afghanistan, 193–4
  and Iran, 193
  and Islam, 25, 28, 213–14
Sufi groups, *see* Chishtis, Haydaris, Jalalis, Kubrawiyas, Madaris, Mawlawiyas, Naqshbandis, Nizamis, Nurbakhshiyyas, Qadiris, Sabiris, Yasaviya; *and see* Sufism
Sufism
  and the British, 123–4
  development of, 18, 72–3, 83, 108–9, 127, 146–7
  and esoteric extremism, 146–50, 152
  and Hindus, 111, 123–4
  influence of, 115–16
  and Islam, 162–3
  and Safavids, 148–50, 157
  in Turkistan, 162–3
  and Urdu, 124
Sunbadh, 141
Sunni Islam, 14, 71–2
  and Imams, 135
  and Isma'ilis, 146
  and mahdis, 136
  and Samanids, 9
  and Shi'ism, 21

Tahirids, 5, 7, 137
Tahmasb, Shah, 149–50
Taj Mahal, 112
Tajik, and Turkish, 62–3
Tajikistan, 25, 28
Tajiks, 63–4
Tamerlane *see* Timur
Tārīk-i 'ālam-ārā-yi Amīnī, 87
teaching methods *and see* education, 108, 109, 115, 126
Thanwi, Ashraf 'Ali, 127
Tibet, 203
Timur, 80
Timurids, 14–15, 81, 85
Torkamanchay, Peace of, 191
trade routes *and see* railway routes, 21, 22–3, 70–1, 84–5
  Russian, 22–3, 190–1, 209
  silk route, 46
Transcaspia, 197
Transoxiana, 4–5
al-Turk, Ishaq, 142

255